But What If I'm the Ninety-Ninth?

The House of Prisca and Aquila

Our mission at the House of Prisca and Aquila is to produce quality books that expound accurately the word of God to empower women and men to minister together in a multicultural church. Our writers have a positive view of the Bible as God's revelation that affects both thoughts and words, so it is plenary, historically accurate, and consistent in itself, fully reliable, and authoritative as God's revelation. Because God is true, God's revelation is true, inclusive to men and women, and speaking to a multicultural church, wherein all the diversity of the church is represented within the parameters of egalitarianism and inerrancy.

The word of God is what we are expounding, thereby empowering women and men to minister together in all levels of the church and home. The reason we say women and men together is because that is the model of Prisca and Aquila, ministering together to another member of the church—Apollos: "Having heard Apollos, Priscilla and Aquila took him aside and more accurately expounded to him the Way of God" (Acts 18:26). True exposition, like true religion, is by no means boring—it is fascinating. Books that reveal and expound God's true nature "burn within us" as they elucidate the Scripture and apply it to our lives.

This was the experience of the disciples who heard Jesus on the road to Emmaus: "Were not our hearts burning while Jesus was talking to us on the road, while he was opening the scriptures to us?" (Luke 24:32). We are hoping to create the classics of tomorrow, significant and accessible trade and academic books that "burn within us."

Our "house" is like the home to which Prisca and Aquila no doubt brought Apollos as they took him aside. It is like the home in Emmaus where Jesus stopped to break bread and reveal his presence. It is like the house built on the rock of obedience to Jesus (Matt 7:24). Our "house," as a euphemism for our publishing team, is a home where truth is shared and Jesus' Spirit breaks bread with us, nourishing all of us with his bounty of truth.

We are delighted to work together with Wipf and Stock in this series and welcome submissions on a wide variety of topics from an egalitarian, inerrantist global perspective.

For more information, see our Web site:
https://sites.google.com/site/houseofpriscaandaquila/.

But What If I'm the Ninety-Ninth?

(And Other Questions I Wasn't Supposed to Ask)

J.M.D. MYERS

WIPF & STOCK • Eugene, Oregon

BUT WHAT IF I'M THE NINETY-NINTH?
(And Other Questions I Wasn't Supposed to Ask)

House of Prisca and Aquila Series

Wipf & Stock
An Imprint of Wipf and Stock Publishers
199 W. 8th Ave., Suite 3
Eugene, OR 97401

www.wipfandstock.com

PAPERBACK ISBN: 979-8-3852-5358-6
HARDCOVER ISBN: 979-8-3852-5359-3
EBOOK ISBN: 979-8-3852-5360-9

VERSION NUMBER 02/06/26

To my dear sisters Amelia and Maya
who have walked the stony road beside me

Contents

Illustrations

Acknowledgements

MAMA AND DADDY: you not only introduced me to Jesus and put up with me my whole life, but encouraged me in my endeavors and made it possible to pursue them. Thank you! It's not possible to thank individually all of the people who have shaped my thinking and my relationship with Jesus over the years, but I do want specifically mention Cathie McCoy, Jonathan Friz, Bill Hodgeman, and Suzanne Carter, whose insights appear in this book, and Amelia Smith, who is my biggest encourager as a fellow writer. Many thanks also to my chief cheerleader, my amazing husband Peter, and to my sister Laurel, niece Rachel, and friends Becca Rybaltowski, Rachel Condry, and Jaime Adili who prayed me through the difficult home stretch of this process.

Friends who did an early-draft read-through, your feedback was invaluable! Thank you tons to Jim Clouser, Maya Simpson, Jean Risley, Paul Sorrentino, Cathie McCoy, and David Huntley. Many thanks also to Bill and Aída Spencer, Grace May, and the whole HPA crew, who encouraged me along the publication journey and made it possible. I need to mention Maud Sandbo separately, because her eye as both a copy editor and a theologian with a pastoral heart blessed me beyond measure. Thank you so much for your time, hard work, and insight, dear sister!

My Patreon supporters have helped lighten the financial load that comes from taking time out to write; thank you to all of you for your encouragement and your gifts, and special thanks to my top-tier fluffy-wigged benefactors Doug and Harriet MacDougal, Cathie McCoy (you just bless in every sector, don't you?), Jim and Maura Clouser, and Sam Hicks. Many thanks also to those who run The Internet Archive and BibleGateway: your work made crucial reference books available to me even when I was halfway around the world.

Many thanks to the Father, Son, and Holy Spirit for being with me through so many questions, and giving me the opportunity to help others think through them too.

Abbreviations

Books of the Bible are abbreviated as follows:

Gen: Genesis

Exod: Exodus

Lev: Leviticus

Deut: Deuteronomy

1 Sam: 1 Samuel

2 Sam: 2 Samuel

2 Kgs: 2 Kings

2 Chr: 2 Chronicles

Neh: Nehemiah

Ps: Psalms

Eccl: Ecclesiastes

Isa: Isaiah

Jer: Jeremiah

Ezek: Ezekiel

Dan: Daniel

Zeph: Zephaniah

Zech: Zechariah

Matt: Matthew

Rom: Romans

1 Cor: 1 Corinthians

2 Cor: 2 Corinthians

Gal: Galatians

Eph: Ephesians

Phil: Philippians

Col: Colossians

1 Thess: 1 Thessalonians

1 Tim: 1 Timothy

2 Tim: 2 Timothy

Heb: Hebrews

Jas: James

1 Pet: 1 Peter

2 Pet: 2 Peter

Rev: Revelation

(Other books of the Bible are either not abbreviated or not quoted, but all are loved.)

Introduction

No one said I shouldn't ask. I was blessed to grow up in a home that was open to questions and in a church that was open to struggles—something I know many can't say. But it was hard to ask anyway. Oh, I did. I wrestled endlessly inside: but the wrestling left me bruised, and when I would ask aloud, people didn't even seem to understand the question, let alone how to answer.

I wrote this book because I knew I wasn't the only one.

The problem is that when a Christian struggles with something like guilt, we often also struggle to talk about those feelings constructively. We know we're "not supposed to" feel like this—Jesus came to free us from guilt, after all, (and besides, who wants to reinforce negative stereotypes about Christians being "rigid" and "condemning"?)—but still . . . the struggle is there. And it's frankly hard to know whom to blame. After all, the Bible is supposed to be God's Word (so it feels a little awkward to criticize *it*) and Jesus clearly wasn't about guilt, (so the faith he started shouldn't be to blame either . . . right?). So mostly we pretend that our troubling questions aren't there. Instead, we assume something is wrong with *us* and hope we can "get over it" before anyone notices—and if we *do* talk about it, many of the responses we get are so ill-considered and unhelpful that they leave us feeling worse.

But as embarrassed as we are about some of our questions, they don't seem to go away. What does it really mean to be judgmental? What does it really mean to be "a Pharisee"? If I'm supposed to not be self-righteous but also not supposed to feel guilty, how am I supposed to see myself? And if the Shepherd rejoices more over one sheep that was lost than over ninety-nine who never strayed . . . then what if I'm one of the ninety-nine?

This book is not the result of a seminary degree nor of any impressive credentials, but of many years of slogging through these questions. It was originally meant to be a standalone short story, with a few brief thoughts after it. Soon I realized the story brought up far more questions than I'd planned.

So now this book consists of three sections: Part 1 is the original short story, *Henry,* a retelling of the Prodigal Son for those who don't seem to fit into either of the iconic son roles. Part 2 focuses on the questions raised by the story's themes, with discussions of guilt, self-righteousness, repentance, identity, and more. Each chapter addresses a specific question or fear, which is listed after the chapter title, and each one is followed by "food for thought" questions for those who want to dig deeper. Because some questions are more personal than others, and different groups have different levels of trust, I have divided these prompts into two sections: reflection/journaling questions designed to be addressed in solitude with God or with very close friends, and discussion questions that are designed to be appropriate for larger groups. Each chapter can more or less stand alone, so have no qualms about skipping around and reading them out of order. Part 3 contains my own story.

This book is for my sisters and brothers who struggle with these questions. You are not alone, and God does not judge you for your struggle. It is also for those who aren't quite in that category: if you identify more with "the prodigal," know that the loving Father discussed here is the same, no matter what the struggles of the individual child are; I pray that the lens of this book helps you see even more of God's face. Welcome. For those who don't feel they particularly struggle with the questions in this book at all . . . well, *wow,* thank God for that!—and welcome to you, too. Someone you know does struggle with these things, deeply. I pray that this book equips you to understand and encourage them well.

If you are not a Christian and some crackpot handed you this book, first of all I'm sorry, and second, I'm so glad you're here! This book might make a little sense of some of the Christians around you; more importantly, I pray that the Jesus discussed in this book might be intriguing enough for you to take a closer look on your own. We Christians don't always see or portray him clearly, but he is well worth the seeing.

Part 1: Henry

Henry

The First Bit

THERE WAS A MAN who had two sons. Well, three sons. It's a bit confusing. Henry's part isn't very dramatic, so people usually just leave him out. It's even more confusing because this story is very like one that Jesus told, although I can't tell mine nearly so well as he did.[1] They might even be about the same man: I've heard he shows up in quite a lot of people's stories. In any case, there once was a man who had three sons. He also had quite a few cats, but they unfortunately don't come into the story at *all*.

One day, the younger son—sorry, the youngest son, I should say—went to his father and said, "Give me my share of the inheritance." So he divided his property between them. Not long after this, the youngest son gathered all he had and went off to a foreign country, where he squandered his wealth in wild living. His eldest brother put the money wisely aside, and continued to work in the field he now technically owned as if nothing had happened. But Henry, the middle son, padded into his father's study, sat on the arm of the chair and waited until his father looked up.

"I'm sorry, Abba," he said. "I know how much you miss him." Looking at the lines in his father's face, he felt like his heart might break too.

"I wanted to give you this," he went on, pressing the sack of gold and the deed to his own plot of land back into Abba's hands. "I don't want it—that is, I'm grateful, of course, you know—but I'd rather you have it. Why should *you* be the only one who doesn't have an inheritance? Besides, you're better at keeping track of things than I am; you know what to do with it, and it's yours, and—and, well, I'd rather be with you anyway."

1. And if you want to read that one, it's in Luke 15. This story is lovingly ripped off from that one, along with a number of its iconic phrases, with the big difference being that my story is not in fact the word of God.

His father cupped Henry's cheek in one of his big hands, and Henry realized the tears welling in his father's eyes were the first ones that hadn't been sad since his brother left.

"It's *yours*, son," he replied, kissing Henry on the head and squeezing him so tightly that Henry almost forgot how to breathe. "But I'll keep it safe for you as long as you like."

Anyway, after some time, there was a famine in the foreign country, and the youngest son began to be in need. So he hired himself out to a fellow from that country, who sent him to the field to feed pigs. He longed to fill his stomach with the pods that the pigs were eating, but no one gave him anything. When he finally came to his senses, he said, "How many of my father's hands have food to spare, and here I am starving to death! I will go back to my father and say to him, 'Father, I have sinned against heaven and against you. I am no longer worthy to be called your son. Make me like one of your hired servants.'"[2] So he set off for his father's house. But while he was still a long way off, his Abba saw him, and ran to him and kissed him. The boy tried to say, "Father, I have sinned against heaven and against you," but his father could barely let him get a word in edgewise.

"Quick!" he called to the servant who had trailed him uncertainly through his wake of kicked-up dust, wondering if that was indeed the lost son in the distance, and if perhaps his master had lost some marbles into the bargain. "Bring a ring for his finger and sandals for his feet!" the father continued. "Bring my best robe and put it on him, and take the fatted calf and kill it! Let's have a feast and celebrate, for this son of mine was dead and is alive again; he was lost and is found!"

The servant was not the sort to argue, so he doubled his pace back the way he had come, still rather uneasy about the whole marbles issue. On his way past the field, Henry stopped him.

"What's wrong?" Henry asked.

"Oh, um, nothing," said the servant. "That is, your brother came back—"

"*What?!*" cried Henry. "For serious?!" And, unable to find any other way to release his excitement, he began to jump up and down.

"Yes, um, well," said the servant, his eyes following Henry up and down with each bounce. "Your father wants me to kill the fatted calf for him, so, um—I guess I'll just be off then."

"Ooh!" said Henry, landing abruptly. "Can I cook it? I know just how he likes it done, and obviously I haven't had time to buy a present, so I'd love it if I could do *something*."

2. This paragraph is largely taken from Luke 15:14–19, TNIV.

"Knock yourself out," muttered the servant, trying to remember the list of the things he was supposed to bring back to the weeping and embracing lunatics on the road.

Henry ran to the bucket to wash his hands, and then dashed into the house to start mixing spices to put on the meat. He was slowed considerably in the process by glancing out the window every few moments to see if he could see his father and brother on the road yet. He knew he oughtn't to interrupt their reunion, but he dearly wanted to.

The house began filling up with workers called suddenly in from the fields, wiping their hands quizzically on their tunics, neighbors hastily invited as kitchen staff ran down the street for last-minute ingredients, and even a few curious passersby wondering what the fuss was all about and whether they were about to get a free meal out of it. Henry realized too late that he had cumin smeared across his forehead, and then promptly forgot about it again when Abba walked in with his arm around his youngest son.

There was silence for just a moment: some were shocked at seeing the most respected man in the community such a mess—eyes red with crying, nose still questionably runny, grinning like a fool. Others felt suddenly awkward at seeing a boy who should have been disowned—and probably spat upon, if not sacrificed in an honor killing—clearly not in trouble at all. Most were embarrassed by *both* of these things and trying to figure out which was worse; a few were too short to see and still trying to figure out what had caused the sudden pause in the hubbub.

But Henry ran forward, spices on his face and flour in his hair, threw his arms around his brother and began jumping again (which of course made his brother have to jump up and down with him, his pained shy expression melting quickly to laughter). At a gesture from Abba, the wide-eyed musicians began playing, and the tension in the crowd began to ease, little conversations starting up here and there. Henry released his brother and grabbed his hands instead.

"Perfect timing!" he crowed, before realizing how stupid that phrase sounded, considering the circumstances and the endless days and months that Abba and his brother had suffered. He tugged his brother's hand and grinned anyway. "It should be just about done; grab a plate! You're never going to guess what I made."

And of course, once food was passed around, people forgot to judge whether or not they approved of Abba's actions. Henry and his brother had just returned from dancing to get a third helping when Henry saw the troubled look on his brother's face. Henry plucked him by the elbow and jerked his head towards a little alcove.

"What's wrong?" he murmured, low enough so that the others couldn't hear.

"I'm just—it's just—I mean it's kind of embarrassing," answered his brother, eyes on the ground and face growing red. "It's not like I did something great to warrant all this fuss. All these people are here because I'm such a screw-up."

"Hey," said Henry, planting a hand firmly on his brother's shoulder and ducking his head so his brother had to look at him. "I've screwed up before too. We've all screwed up. That's what makes it so awesome: Abba loves you just because you're you. Or just because he's him, I don't know—I just know you can't screw up enough for him not to love you. Just—come and enjoy being his, OK?"

And when his brother still looked doubtful, Henry went on,

"Look, you weren't here to see it, but he didn't stop thinking about you the whole time you were gone. Seriously, he has been looking forward to this day since the moment you walked away—I thought *I* was going to bust, just from *watching* him look at you tonight—I mean, really—"

Henry gestured vaguely out to the dance floor, where he assumed his father was. His brother followed the gesture, looking rather blank, and Henry followed his gaze. Now it was his turn to be embarrassed.

He caught the arm of a servant going by.

"Hey," he whispered, "where's Abba?"

"I don't know, sir."

By the third servant, he gathered that his father was outside, and by the fifth servant, he'd heard most of the story, because there were quite a lot of them and news traveled extraordinarily quickly between them. Henry hadn't even noticed his older brother wasn't there, and with a little stab of guilt realized he must have been missing the whole time. He realized, too, that Abba had probably noticed right away, had probably held that concern for his eldest even as he was feasting with his youngest. How like Abba, thought Henry, to leave his own feast for a son who's causing him trouble.

"It's alright," he said to his little brother. "Abba's taking care of something outside. But *you*—you hold your head up high. Abba's not like any other father. Tonight, you're the most honored person here. Now come slip out into the kitchen with me—I saved the best piece for you."

Henry

The Second Bit

THE STORY SPREAD QUICKLY through the surrounding towns—how the wealthiest landowner in the region had been dishonored by his own son, how he'd pined for the boy until he came home, how he'd welcomed the scoundrel with a feast and dancing . . . and then how the older son had dishonored him even more, questioning his father's decision and railing against him on what should have been the most joyous night in years.

"He really missed the point entirely," said a woman at the market stall, hefting a handful of grapes. "Ironic, since he was the one who *lived* with him every day and saw firsthand how merciful that man is."

"Ah, but consider what pride will do," answered the seller at the cart sagely. "That young man preferred to live like a slave than to join in the feast, just so long as he could say he earned everything he had. Many's the man who's passed up a fortune, just to spite the fact that it's a gift."

"Well, I say it's just pure stubbornness," returned the first woman. "Really, he's worse than the younger one. The younger one at least came back; I hear that older one is still out in the field, won't even speak to his father anymore."

"Well *I've* never heard of such a gracious father," said a third villager, not even pretending to look at the wares on the cart but hopping into the conversation anyway. "To go out in the middle of the feast and answer that boy's questions, even when he was so disrespectful—I've never heard of a father like that."

Henry, piling his basket with garlic from a nearby cart, overheard that last comment and looked up with a grin.

"You're right," he said. "He's the best father in the world—I should know, he's my Abba."

"Oh so *you're* the runaway son!" the first woman said with interest. "Well, young man, I know you made some terrible choices, but your story has inspired countless—"

"Oh, no no, sorry," said Henry, laughing. "I'm not that one; you're thinking of my little brother."

"*Oh,*" said one of the others significantly. Henry thought he detected a slight curl of the lip with the word. "You're the *older* brother."

"I—well I suppose I am, to him anyway."

"Huh!" There were definitely raised eyebrows with that one. "Listen to him comparing himself—he thinks he's so much better."

"I don't!" protested Henry.

"Ah, but you said you hadn't run away," pointed out the vegetable seller.

"Well—I hadn't," said Henry, confused.

"See!" said the vegetable seller, as if that settled it.

"Won't even admit he's run away—what *hubris*," muttered someone.

"It's not as though I think I'm perfect," put in Henry uneasily. "I just haven't run away."

"Someday you'll learn," said the first woman, shaking her head, "it's all about the relationship. Think how much you missed, refusing to go in and join your Father's feast."

"Oh!" said Henry, smiling again. "I see where the confusion is. You're thinking of my older brother."

"So you *are* the younger brother?"

"What?" asked Henry helplessly. His eyebrows were feeling tangled enough to give him a headache.

"We're *all* the younger brother," intoned a scholarly-looking man, laying a fatherly hand on Henry's shoulder. "We've *all* run away, and we need only admit it to be welcomed in. Now then," he turned toward Henry and gave his shoulder a kindly squeeze, "don't be afraid to say it—why don't you tell these nice people just how far you ran away?"

"I—I don't think I did," said Henry shrinking a little under the worry that perhaps he *was* being self-righteous, "at least, not that I remember. I mean, I've known my father for a very long time and he's very nice, so I've always preferred being with him rather than—than . . . being *not* with him."

He heard the restless whisper in what was now a crowd, a whisper that sounded like "Cheeky."

"I don't mean I've never messed up," Henry added hastily, "just nothing like *running away*."

The disapproval in the crowd was palpable.

"I can't believe he'd come out and *say* it."

"No wonder it took his brother so long to come back, with judgment like *that* at home."

"You've got to pity him, really, not realizing it's by grace not by works."

Murmurs of agreement rippled around.

"He doesn't *want* grace. Doesn't want to be his brother's *equal*."

"And all that time at home he was just as far off—didn't know his father any better than the youngster did."

"Less—at least his brother was honest about running off; this one's nothing but a hypocrite."

"Really! Resenting his father, all the while living under his roof, eating from his table—"

Henry raised his hand timidly.

"I didn't resent him, I don't think. I actually really enjoy my father."

"Hmph!" said one woman, arching an eyebrow. "Enjoys *himself*, I expect. Probably gets a good deal of pleasure out of imagining he's earned his father's love."

Henry was stricken. Had that been all it was?

The man next to him jabbed him in the ribs playfully with an elbow.

"We all like a little ego boost now and then, huh?"

"I—I guess, when you put it that way," said Henry uncertainly. "I suppose—I suppose maybe I *am* a little arrogant."

"A *little!*" crowed someone incredulously. "When he still won't admit to running away!"

"I—I didn't mean—well I'm sure whatever I did was just as bad as what my brother did, I suppose," floundered Henry, "I just can't remember anything particularly—"

"I'll bet he was pleased at feeling like the 'good one'—I'll bet he *enjoyed* being the one who was at home 'making Daddy proud' while his brother was away."

"I suppose I did, some," whispered Henry, feeling more miserable by the second.

"You're not fooling anyone," said another voice—a harsher one, and he didn't see where it came from, but it somehow felt familiar, like some shadow he'd met in a dream. "You *still* think, deep down, that what you did isn't as bad—you still *feel* better than him."

"Do you even love your brother at all?" someone else scoffed. "Or has it only been about you and your daddy?"

"I—I don't know," Henry whispered, squirming at how trapped he felt. "Abba *is* my favorite . . ."

A few tears spilled out at the thought of how selfish he must be as he explained, "He's easy to love." *That* barely counted as love; his father was so good it was only natural to love him.

He'd been happier about how happy Abba was than he'd been for his brother.

And his brother—he *had* noticed that his brother had left and that he himself hadn't: it had been impossible not to; he *had* felt good about staying home and keeping Abba company.

They must be right. He must never have loved his brother at all, only his imaginings of what Abba thought of him.

What a disgrace to his father he was.

How embarrassing that he'd always felt so close to his father, when really he must have been missing everything important.

How arrogant must he be, not to remember when he'd run away?

He screwed his face up in concentration. There must have been a time; they'd said so. Had it been when he was young? Or if it was something since then, was he simply so blind to his faults he hadn't even noticed it as running away? He thought back through the last few days. Everything wrong he could think of he'd already talked through with his father and been forgiven for. He seized onto one of them at random, trying to deepen it, to expand it into feeling just as bad as running away for months and months on end. He tried harder, with just a little twinge of worry that it was disrespectful to Abba, seeing as he'd already told him he was forgiven.

Perhaps that worry was breaking his concentration. He tried harder.

It was no good.

It must be that this arrogance itself was his form of running away, then. And judging by this recent experiment, he'd never be able to conjure up enough humility to make it home.

Henry

The Third Bit

Henry sat in the dust, morosely picking at weeds. He used to love working in his father's field. Now he felt almost guilty for it. He felt cut off from the growing plants, cut off from even the servants around him, as if he shouldn't be there—and yet he couldn't *not* be there.

"You don't *have* to work through lunch, you know," said a servant girl, passing by with a water jug.

"It's all I'm good for," Henry muttered, knowing as he did that it was rather melodramatic. The girl didn't hear him, but held out a hand to help him up so he could join the workers opening their bundles of bread and cheese at the edge of the field.

"It's alright," Henry said more loudly, not taking her hand. "It's the only thing I really like doing."

She eyed him kindly.

"Your father doesn't love you just for what you can get done, you kn—"

"I *know*," interrupted Henry, jaw clenched. He did his best to mask it with a friendly smile. "Thanks."

The girl walked away. Henry pounded a fist into the dirt. He wished with all his might to rip some of the growing stalks right out of the earth, but couldn't bring himself to do it. As much as he avoided saying he loved his father, for fear of being proven a hypocrite—after all, it was common knowledge that it was his own ego, and not his father, that he loved—he cared too much for how his father would feel about it, knew too well Abba's care for each green shoot, couldn't *really* consider doing such a thing to him.

"I just have to say," came another voice. Henry's head snapped up. Would they never leave him alone? "I think it's so beautiful how you're out here every day."

Henry twisted around to glare at the speaker, hoping the fact that the sun was in his eyes made it look like he was merely squinting.

"You take such good care of these plants," the old woman went on. "You don't see that in young people much these days. And you've got a gift for it—I know *my* rows never looked so neat."

Henry tried to smile at her, but it was really more of tucking his lips inward. He wondered if someday he'd do it one too many times and his face would turn inside out. The old woman beamed back at him.

"It's beautiful to see," she said again. "Your love for your father shines through in everything you do, and it's beautiful."

Henry couldn't decide if the words felt like they were stabbing him or just covering him in something slimy. *It's not true!* he wanted to shout. Instead, he fixed his eyes on the ground.

"Well, um, well thanks. Your plants are nice too."

"Oh, they're not mine," said the woman cheerfully, "they're all your father's, of course."

"Of course, yeah," mumbled Henry as she moved on. Had he forgotten that again? Was he again looking at the plants as though they were his, as though they existed just to stoke his pride? He twisted an uprooted weed around and around his fingers, watching the skin turn unnaturally pale before the little stem snapped. Why was he even here? He'd never do these plants any good, and his father probably didn't like his work anyway; it all felt stolen and unauthorized.

"Henry?" called a voice from a few rows over.

Grumbling inwardly, Henry got to his feet.

"What's up?" he asked the stringy youth. The boy looked up at him and grinned, seeming to be all oversized teeth—what wasn't long gangling limbs, that is. He looked like a weed himself, Henry thought, and a half-smile thought about reaching his lips without quite getting there.

"Hey, thanks," said the young man, tugging at an absurdly inefficient angle. "Can you help me with this one? It's stubborn."

Henry glanced at the thick stalk that had somehow been missed in all of the previous weedings and gently peeled the young man's hands from around it.

"Well first of all, stop pulling if you're not getting anywhere. No sense tiring yourself out if it's not budging." He got down on his knees in the dirt. "This one we'll have to dig out."

Together they dug around the roots. Henry couldn't help it—he loved this. He loved working the fields, loved mentoring the other workers. Together they pulled, and with a ripping noise the weed came free and sent them both tumbling onto their backsides.

"Victory!" Henry declared, making the youth laugh.

"Thanks, man," said the boy again. "I always feel better when you're around."

An almost-forgotten glow sparked up for a moment from somewhere deep and hidden. Henry cuffed the boy on the shoulder.

"Keep up the good work."

He returned to his row, the glow fading and the heaviness returning almost as soon as he'd stepped away from the young man's side. He kept on weeding for he didn't know how long, but found himself stopping and sitting with his hands in his lap rather often, the weight on his heart making it just too difficult to lift his hands.

"You're sad."

Henry jumped to his feet, wiping as much dirt onto his face as sweat off of it, not bothering to look up to see who was interrupting him this time.

"I know," he said, with a resigned and not-at-all-amused ghost of a laugh. "I'm so spoiled. Here I am, a son of the best father in the world, everything I could ask for around me—not to mention a *very* well-stocked kitchen—and here I sit, slacking off, as though I've got a right to be sad about anything."

He continued pulling weeds, feeling a new energy in his limbs as he demonstrated just how silly it was for him to be unhappy.

"Really I'm fine," he went on, starting to believe his own cheerfulness. "I sometimes get gloomy for no good reason, but I'm really fine. I've got a wonderful Abba, and I love being out here in the fields, and—"

"You're sad."

Henry was rather annoyed at the accusation.

"I'm *not,*" he insisted. "In fact, I try very hard to maintain a good attitude. I'm just frustrated that I fall short so often."

"You're sad."

"Now look here!" Henry whirled, furious, and found he was looking at his Abba. "Oh," he said. "Oh, I'm sorry, I didn't—"

"Say it," Abba encouraged.

"Sorry, I thought you were . . . I don't know."

"But I'm the one you're angry at. So go ahead. Tell me why you're angry."

"I'm not!" cried Henry, horrified. "At least, I don't think—I mean it's *silly* to be angry at you, when you're so good. I'm angry at *me*, I think—or—I don't know, I don't think I'm really angry at anyone; I'm just *angry!*"

Tears started in his eyes.

"Very well, then," said Abba. "No matter who: be angry."

Henry picked up a rock and threw it against the dusty ground as hard as he could. He picked it up again and threw it down again, but it did nothing to ease the pinch in his chest.

"Speak," Abba coaxed softly.

"Why don't you like me?!" Henry burst out, the tears chasing one another out of his blazing eyes. "All I ever wanted was to love you! What's so wrong about that?! You love him even more because you almost lost him—why don't you love the ones who don't run away?! And yet . . ." The old familiar guilt washed over him. "I know it's horrible to say I've never run away. I'm sorry. I hate being the hypocritical older brother. But that's what I am."

"Who said you were the older brother?"

"Everyone. I must be. I've got a younger brother, don't I? But it isn't fair—it isn't fair that I'm bad and disappointing, just for wanting to please you!"

He bent to pick the rock up again, but in his tearful half-blindness grabbed a fistful of uprooted thorn branches instead. He dropped them immediately as the pain pierced his skin, but when he looked up it was Abba's hand that was bleeding, not his.

"Oh," he said, a little embarrassed and more than a little confused. "Sorry . . ." Not being quite sure what had happened, he wasn't really sure if he should be apologizing.

"Go on," said Abba simply. Henry dropped his head again and kicked at the dirt.

"And I know it's my fault, so really I'm angry at *myself*."

"I know," said Abba, with a catch in his voice. "You've hated yourself for a long time."

Henry was startled, but didn't look up. If he did, he might not be able to be fine anymore.

"Have I?" he asked vaguely. It seemed almost an odd idea, considering how long he'd been ashamed of his sick and intractable self-love. "Well, if I have, I deserve it. I ought to love you, but I know my love is actually quite insincere and self-centered."

"Who says that?"

"Oh, it's just . . ." Henry waved his hand around to indicate the world generally. "I mean, you know, it's how the older brother *is*."

"Is it?"

"Well, they say 'he who's been forgiven little loves little,' and so—and so—" Henry stopped, his thoughts swirling. It was arrogant, terribly arrogant, to suppose he'd been forgiven little. It was even more arrogant, surely, that he couldn't remember much of what he'd been forgiven *for*—probably a sign that he'd never really admitted his guilt in the first place, had never really—

"And so?" prompted Abba gently.

"I *tried*, Abba, I *tried!*" Henry wailed. "I wanted to love you as deeply as possible, so I supposed . . . I supposed I'd need to be as bad as possible, or—or, I don't know, *feel* as bad as possible. But I couldn't remember running away—I mean you've been my father quite a long time, really, and you've been quite a good one, so I've never had a reason to *want* to run away, or to hurt your feelings, or . . . or . . . but if that's what it would take to *really* and truly love you as much as possible, it almost seemed I *ought* to run away. It's just that I couldn't really bring myself to do it."

"Ah," said Abba's deep voice, and he put his finger out as if to pin that last statement down before it could skitter away. "Why?"

"Because . . ." started Henry, confused. "Wait, what?"

"You couldn't *really* bear to hurt your father: why?"

"Because . . . because . . . I don't know."

Abba waited.

"Because . . ." Henry said tentatively, feeling as though he was about to get a sum stupidly wrong, ". . . because I love you?"

Abba smiled.

"But wait!" cried Henry. "Does that *count?* I mean—I mean if it's just sort of regular love, and not from being forgiven? I mean, I know you've forgiven me for things—"

"You wanted to love me," said Abba. "And you do. You loved me so much you weren't willing to hurt me, even when people told you it would make me love you more. Tell me, Henry: did you get your wish or not?"

"I . . . I suppose . . ."

"You've loved me ever since you were a little child. You used to sit in my study for hours, just to keep me company. You were out in my fields almost before you could walk, trying to water the plants, just because you knew they meant something to me."

"I barely remember that" said Henry in a colorless voice, closing his eyes so he wouldn't have to look at his father. He felt like he had cried out all the contents of his heart a long time ago, leaving just a dull emptiness, but a tear leaked out from between his eyelids anyway. "I kicked that memory like a dog and now it's hiding."

"But I remember," came Abba's soft voice. "I've kept it close to my heart all this time. And I've been told I'm very good at keeping track of things."

Henry stared at the dirt. His Abba's kind voice, the welcoming words—Henry was reminded of how the rain would roll right off this ground when the drought broke. The dull emptiness was so familiar he was sure none of these things would ever soak in.

"You're sad."

Henry did look up this time, and saw with surprise that his father's hands were still bleeding, quite a lot more than before. In confusion, he raised his eyes to his Abba's face, and found that tears were flowing down it as much as the blood was weeping from his hands. Slowly, very slowly, pieces of understanding started to settle into place in Henry's mind. The tears—they were for him. The pain—it was his pain.

Surely he didn't count enough to warrant *that* . . . ? He was the spoiled one, the one who had gotten to stay home, well-fed, too much of a prig to get into any *interesting*, worthwhile trouble. But here was Abba bearing his pain just as much as he'd wept and kept watch for Henry's little brother. And he was doing it freely, without even being asked, even though Henry hadn't run away, or thought he hadn't run away, or whatever it was that had made him too privileged and self-righteous to deserve that kind of fuss.

And if Abba was doing it freely, *that* must mean—that must mean that he *wanted* to. That he didn't begrudge having Henry around.

"I'm sorry, Abba!" he cried, throwing himself against his father's chest, and Abba's arms immediately squeezed tight around him. "I must have hurt your feelings so much! What have I accused you of?"

His father held him, and held him. And they cried. They cried for each other's pain, and they cried for their own pain that finally had a companion to help carry it.

"And now," said Abba, after they had wept their fill—or rather "their empty" I suppose, but somehow Henry felt a good deal less empty than before—"May I share something I'm really excited about with you?"

"Sure," said Henry, puzzled.

And then Abba took Henry by the hand and turned him back toward the same plot of dirt he'd been working on. Henry felt his face growing red with embarrassment.

"Oh—" he stammered. "*That*. That's just . . . I mean . . ."

Abba put two fingers under Henry's chin to stop him, and then turned his attention back to the dirt, his face glowing with the sort of excitement that one *must* contain by holding back a smile, because a full smile would leave enough of an opening for the joy to explode into utter intelligibility.

"You have no idea what I'm growing here," said Abba with a hushed exuberance.

Henry looked at the row. Abba was right. He had no idea what it could be, but surely it couldn't be all that special if Henry was the one who had been tending it. And yet—Abba wasn't the sort to lie or mislead; he wasn't feigning that excitement just to make Henry feel good, as anyone else might do. So then—so then . . . Henry's brow wrinkled in confusion. Abba laid a hand on his shoulder and spoke plainly.

"Will you grow it with me?"

"Oh," said Henry, flummoxed, "but—but isn't it wrong that I like working for you? I mean because everyone keeps saying 'it's not by works'?"

"Henry," Abba repeated gently but earnestly, with a rather hurt look in his eyes, "I want to share this with you."

Henry scuffed a toe in a wide semicircle in the dirt, feeling very uncomfortable but feeling it rather impolite to say so.

"It's just—" he faltered finally, "—it's just people have always seemed to say it was wrong of me. You know—that I made it all about me—about pride, or feeling good about myself—or that I was replacing you with work. I mean, how do I know I wouldn't be doing it for the wrong reasons? And besides, wouldn't it be arrogant of me to think *I'd* be worthy to work on something important to you?"

"I didn't ask you to be worthy of it; I asked you to *do* it."

"Well . . . yes, but . . ."

"Don't do it because you're worthy; do it for me."

"But—but if I do it, people will notice—and wouldn't that be showing off?"

"Don't do it for them; do it for me."

"But Abba, if I start thinking I'm worthy—"

"My son is worthy to do anything I ask. And when he does, I am pleased."

"Oh, you don't have to say *that*," said Henry, alarmed. "I wasn't—you know—fishing for a compliment or anything. I may be arrogant, but I'm not *so* arrogant yet as to think I could be pleasing to you."

"What do you think of me?" asked Abba, and Henry heard the hurt in his voice again. "Even *you* are pleased by these young gardeners who come to you, whether they do things right or not. And am I really so stingy and hard-fisted that I may not do the same?"

Henry gaped for a moment, lost for words.

"I'm sorry," he said. "I didn't mean it that way."

"I know," said Abba. "But that's what it means."

"I'm sorry," Henry said again. "That's unfair to you, I know. I suppose I'm just so used to being afraid—"

"I know," Abba put in before Henry could finish.

"I mean," Henry went on, "I've been so used to being afraid of my own . . . I don't know; afraid of myself. And so I thought—"

"—you'd run away from me?" Abba finished for him.

"What?" breathed Henry.

"You're so afraid of doing it for the wrong reasons that you're almost convinced it would be better to not do what I asked at all. You're so afraid to love me insincerely that you haven't looked at me for weeks and weeks. Yes, you were burying yourself in the work—but I was right here all the same. And I was right here when you were trudging home at the end of the day, thinking you were alone. It wasn't working, or not working, that kept you from seeing me. It was that you were too ashamed to look. But Henry: I am not ashamed. Look at me," he commanded, as Henry hung his head. Abba gently lifted the boy's chin, and waited until Henry held his gaze. "*I* am not ashamed of you. And I *know you*."

Henry let out his breath slowly, and then sat down on the ground, overwhelmed.

"Well, thank you," he managed. "Although I don't think I'll be able to remember all of this all the time."

"Oh you won't," said Abba good-naturedly. "But I'll be right here. You'll water this ground with a good many more tears, but there will be fruit."

"Fruit?" said Henry curiously, snapping out of his torpor to look in surprise from Abba to what he'd assumed was more barley and back again. "What *are* you growing here?"

"Ah," said Abba with a secret sort of grin, "Wouldn't you like to know?"

After a few moments Henry found that he was grinning back, and he grabbed his spade, but Abba laid a hand on his shoulder.

"First, though," said Abba, "come with me to the house. I believe your brother has prepared quite a feast for you."

Part 2:

But I've Got Questions

1

Perilous Parables

(Does God love me less if I'm good?)

One of Jesus' most beloved parables is the parable of the lost sheep. In it, a single sheep wanders away from a flock of one hundred. Instead of shrugging off the missing one as a negligible loss or more trouble than it's worth, the shepherd actually leaves the other ninety-nine where they are and goes to find it. And Jesus, the Good Shepherd who went off into danger to find us, says that the shepherd then carries it home on his shoulders, happier about that one sheep he found than about the ninety-nine others who were never lost.[3] Even more beloved, perhaps, is the story of the prodigal son.[4] Like the lost sheep, he wanders off—albeit a lot farther and with a lot more sass—and is received back with joy by the very father he dishonored: a scene that is moving even now and would have been nigh unthinkable then, when a father would have been well within his rights to kill such a son. After 2,000 years, these stories still stand as some of the most beautiful and poignant depictions of God's relentless love. For a few of us, though, (and even fewer of us will admit it), these are also some of the parables that trouble us the most.

In certain hearts and minds, these parables raise a puzzling question: does God love me less if I'm good? Some of us who grow up in the church are taught early on to "be a good girl (or boy)," to obey the rules, and to care deeply about right and wrong—and we're later blindsided by the fact that it's not just our non-Christian neighbors, but other Christians and even Jesus himself who seem to fault us for it. Why would Jesus, the very one

3. Luke 15:4–7; see also Matt 18:12–14.

4. See Luke 15:11–32.

who taught us to love what is good and hate what is evil,[5] then relegate us to the status of boring, unloved ninety-ninth sheep instead of special, beloved one-hundredth sheep—just for trying to do what he said? Are we automatically the "older brother" in the Lost Son story simply if we grew up in the church and never went through an intense rebellious phase—or even just if we're Christians at all, as many imply and even teach?

Part of our problem comes from the fact that we don't always get how parables work. And we can get ourselves into trouble, or at least absurdity, when we use something in a way it was never meant to be used, as anyone who has shoveled a driveway with a spatula can attest.[6] Parables are deliberately simple stories aimed at making a specific point. As such, they're meant to be limited: the details aren't meant to be picked apart and worked out into specific one-to-one comparisons.

Consider the parable of the sower:[7] in it, Jesus describes people's hearts using the images of a footpath, rocky soil, weedy soil, and good soil—and describes what happens to the seeds that fall on each. (Spoiler: only the seeds on good soil make it.) His point is that there are a lot of things that can keep people from really receiving God's Word and being transformed by it . . . but while the details are meaningful to dig into, the images in these stories can't rationally be taken all the way to the extreme endpoints of what *could* be inferred.

For instance, when Jesus says the devil snatches the Word away from those who don't understand like a bird snatches up and eats a seed, he doesn't mean they have absolutely *no* memory of the Word (even though the seed in the analogy is completely gone), and it doesn't mean that the devil has power over God's Word, or will end up with a tummy-ache from eating it. In describing four types of soil, Jesus doesn't mean there are four, and only four, types of people in the world. And when, for the sake of clear and simple illustration, he describes them separately, he doesn't mean that people's problems are exclusive to their "type," as if "rocky soil"—those who are prone to giving up when the going gets tough—never experience the "worries and pleasures" of life that characterize the "weedy soil." In describing what happens to the seeds planted on the various soils, Jesus is not saying rocks can't be moved, weeds can't be pulled, or good soil is perfect—and there would be very little point in telling the parable if that was the case. All

5. See Amos 5:15; Rom 12:9; 1 Thess 5:21–22.

6. I haven't done this, but I did grow up with stories of my dad's childhood neighbors, who used to cut their grass with scissors.

7. Matt 13:3–23; Mark 4:3–20; Luke 8:5–15.

of those ideas *could* be derived from the details he used, but they're not the ideas he intends to convey.

More to the point, consider our sheep friends again. If every single detail of a parable was supposed to be matched to something in real life, you'd think the numbers would be important. In that case, Jesus would be giving us important mathematical information when he compares the one lost sheep to the ninety-nine others: either "lost people" are relatively rare, only about one in a hundred; or the value of a "sinner" is over ninety-nine times greater than that of "righteous persons who do not need to repent." But that parable, along with the story of the lost son, is actually part of a group of three parables, with the one in the middle being about a woman who loses (and finds) one of her ten silver coins.[8] So in this group of related parables, where we have a flock of a hundred sheep, a pocketful of ten coins, and a pair of brothers, what is the ratio we're meant to understand? Are sinners as rare as one in a hundred or as common as 50 percent of the population? Or what is the relative value of the beloved lost compared to the not-so-beloved never-lost? One to ninety-nine? One to nine? . . . One to one?

To follow a detail all the way down the bunny trail of possible inferences is to push the bounds of the parable's job. A parable is a deliberate oversimplification for the same reason that a diagram is an oversimplification: it helps you see clearly the important parts. If we were trying for an exact depiction of, say, an engine, we would use a photograph instead, but in a diagram we deliberately suppress some of the real-life details so you can understand the big picture—and the details we do use are understood to be representative. We accept that the engine isn't *actually* see-through or cut in half; we know that the colors may be different, that the arrows showing energy flow won't be there in real life, and that when tools are included in the picture, we shouldn't expect to find them floating in midair next to the engine.

Further, a diagram of an engine is intended to tell you about the engine, not the whole airplane. (So now it's an airplane engine, apparently.) A parable addresses a specific idea or question—a piece of reality—as clearly and simply as possible. Frequently, however, we think of parables as frameworks, as though they're supposed to give us a paradigm for the whole world.

And so we look at a story like The Prodigal Son and try to divide all of humanity into either "older" sons or "younger" sons. We may not think about the fact that quite a lot of people might not closely fit the mold of either son—or that Jesus' point wasn't to give us a classification system, but

8. See Luke 15:8–10.

to give us an illustration of God's love. To do so, he gave us a small number of starkly contrasted, almost caricatured characters—literary stick figures—*not* because he sees people that way or because he intends for us to label people, but because it makes their function in the story that much clearer and more memorable. It's not that the characters don't matter; it's that he's doing something different with them than we might assume. This is exactly why characters aren't developed in jokes either: because the point isn't how many characters there are or what they're like exactly, but how they set up the punch line. The more stark and streamlined the setup, the more powerfully the joke lands.

God's love is the punch line, and Jesus is a master storyteller (*and* master humorist). He's not trying to be a novelist, historian, or systematic philosopher with these stories, as if he hit on the idea of using parables and then realized too late they were the wrong tool for the job. We just misunderstand the job. A parable is a pin of truth stuck into the map of reality; it's not meant to be the whole map. If he had wanted to give us the whole map here, he would have used a different literary form, but Jesus used parables: a genre in which the details are meant to add up to and serve that sharp punch line—not to, say, create a fully contained world the way Tolkien does in *The Lord of the Rings*. If we're going to view Jesus' words as authoritative, we need to take into account how he meant them to be understood. Jesus uses this literary form expertly, and part of the craft of parable-making is streamlining and exaggerating to make the point land as powerfully as possible.

Like a magnifying glass, a parable's exaggeration makes the message clearer, and like an impassioned shout, it helps us remember it. If Jesus had merely said, "be careful about things that cause you to sin," probably only about four of his hearers would have remembered it, but because he said "if your right eye causes you to sin, poke it out and throw it away,"[9] I doubt anyone in his audience forgot it (and it probably made for some great dinnertime discussion among the adolescent boys present). Hyperbole is the exclamation point at the end of a parable's lesson.

So, back to the sheep at hand: this parable was told in response to people who believed that those who "wander off" are worthless. They were skeptical of Jesus' credibility because they expected God to look at the lost and say "ehh, no point going after *that* one." And so Jesus used hyperbole to make an unforgettable point about both the extravagant love of the Shepherd and the continued worth of the sheep. Even though it's only one out of a hundred, he says, and a troublesome one at that, it's not only still worth something; it is in fact staggeringly valuable: not diminished in value

9. Matt 5:29a NIRV.

because it strayed, not even priced at the expected value of a single sheep, but worth *ninety-nine* sheep and then some!

For those of us "good kids" who have long questioned our own worth based on this parable, here's how the math works out on this: infinity plus infinity is still infinity. A soul of infinite worth is equal in value to another soul of infinite worth, and *also* equal in value to ninety-nine souls of infinite worth, because infinity is still infinity no matter how many times you add or multiply it. Jesus compared the one sheep to the ninety-nine because it made his point unmistakably clear to his hearers—that the worth of a creature God loves is never lost—but in God-math, this does not imply that the worth of the other sheep was only a fraction of the lost sheep's. Fractions don't apply when infinity comes into play. And God proved that infinity is indeed at play here when, on the cross, he set our worth at the boundless value of Jesus, the eternal God incarnate.

If these parables really are talking about how our worth doesn't depend on our performance, (as we so often rightly proclaim), then it would be strange to conclude that they're also saying we're loved *less* if we don't "wander." In fact, Jesus answers this very question in the pinnacle of these stories, The Prodigal Son. The older brother's complaint sounds arrogant and legalistic, but behind it lie very real questions and very real pain: "What about me—am *I* worth something? Do you still notice me? Do you love me less for some reason? Aren't you happy that *I'm* your son too?" And the father doesn't shut down these questions—or say what we so fear he will: "Why no, you're the boring son and you're not humble enough for me to really like you." Instead the father affirms his love for the older brother and reaffirms his sonship. He doesn't say, "Hush up, Sassypants; I just got done with your brother's disrespect and I don't need it from you too!" He says, "My son, you are always with me, and everything I have is yours."

To those seeking to be rewarded for good deeds, Jesus reminds us through these words that he *is* the reward. To those worried that God doesn't like or notice us, he reaffirms our status and inheritance as his children. And for all of us, we run once again into divine math: you can't have more than everything. When he says "everything I have is yours" it's not a platitude or some materialistic consolation prize ("your brother gets *love,* but don't worry: you still get *stuff*"). It's a profound statement about how logically impossible it is to compare "how much God loves *me*" to "how much God loves *him*." God is infinite and is already ours: what do we expect could be added to or subtracted from this? This is, again, why worth *can't* be dependent on performance: love is mutual self-giving, and the infinite God determined it was worth giving himself to us. You can't get promoted *or* demoted in love when you are loved by an infinite God.

As a side note, it's also significant that Jesus doesn't say the shepherd *loves* the found sheep more; he says he's *happier* about it: he's not making a "personal remark" but rather a situational one. That is, he's not happier about that one sheep because of some quality inherent to the sheep; he's happier about what's *going on with* that sheep, in this moment, than he is about what's going on with the others.

Think of a mother who has a lot of children, all of them brilliantly academically gifted . . . and the youngest of whom is severely autistic and nonverbal. Suppose that after years of visiting speech therapists and other specialists and painstakingly encouraging her boy, he finally utters his first word at the age of six. We may well say she's prouder of that one word than of all the scholarships and academic achievements his older siblings produced—and yet we wouldn't doubt for a moment that she loves and values all her children equally. It's not that she favors her youngest over the others; it's that this gigantic little hard-won victory has a particular sweetness. Another day it will be another child, and she'll be prouder of her alcoholic daughter's shaky, shy refusal of a single drink than she is of all her other children's years of easy sobriety. Another day she'll be overjoyed that the quiet one—the one who thought all along that she never noticed him—finally believed even for a moment that he's important to her—happier than she's ever been over the others' lifelong confidence.

This dynamic is, in fact, present within the parables themselves. In the story of the sheep, the shepherd leaves the "good" sheep to go find the "bad" one. In the story of the sons, the father actually leaves the *"bad"* son at the party to go find the *"good"* one. (And the woman sweeping the house to find her lost coin doesn't leave at all, except to go invite people to celebrate at the end.) There's no group or type that receives God's attention more or deserves God's presence less than another. Good, bad, or just suffering from an abysmal sense of direction, the ones Jesus comes after are the ones who need him, period. This means that if you're feeling spiritually lonely, overlooked, or unimportant—regardless of *why*—you're exactly who he's coming for.

The point of all of these parables was never that God loves any of us less: it's that *we're* the only ones who ever say "ehh, it's not worth it." The reason there was so much rejoicing over the one sheep is that it had been restored to true relationship; the truth is that there are some sheep who keep on grazing when the Shepherd leaves on his quest and never even notice he's gone. It was never about whether or not we're good; it's always been about whether or not we want to be in relationship with him. But make no mistake: *God* wants to be in relationship with *you*.

In John 10, Jesus talks a good deal about his role as our Shepherd. The interesting thing is that he doesn't make merit-based distinctions between any of his sheep. In fact, at one point he speaks of how he would be calling not just Jews, but also Gentiles (who *certainly* wouldn't make the cut in terms of following the rules), and he says "there will be one flock and one shepherd."[10] Not: "there will be sheep I love and sheep I tolerate." Not: "there will be cool rebel sheep and frumpy stick-in-the-mud sheep." *One* flock. Throughout Scripture, this theme of God's affection for the *whole* flock is apparent. Isaiah described God's attitude this way: "He tends his flock like a shepherd: He gathers the lambs in his arms and carries them close to his heart; he gently leads those that have young."[11] In other words, whether you're a mama sheep, baby sheep, or cousin sheep, God's gentle tenderness extends to the *whole flock*. In fact, the parable of the lost sheep is one of the only places in the Bible where there is any distinction made between the sheep at all. This means that this idea we have that God plays favorites—that the church is divided up into two groups that God sees as fundamentally different, and that he varies his affection based on which group we're in and where we've been in life—doesn't hold with the rest of Scripture. It's simply not a valid interpretation of what Jesus meant by the parable. And lest we think that there's been some sort of mistake—that "I somehow slipped in under the radar with this generalized love for the flock, but he doesn't actually personally like *me*"—or that this whole "one flock" business means he must not see or care much about our individuality, Jesus specifically tells us that the Good Shepherd "calls his own sheep by name."[12] He knows you. He *intended* to call *you*, by name.

In the back of our minds, we often assume that "God so loved the world"[13] must mean that no one is special—that the love is spread out among so many that it can't be very strong or personal when it comes to an individual life, like a fortune shared among so many heirs that each one gets merely pennies. But remember this: infinity *divided by* anything is still infinity too. And our God is infinite. Far from "one flock" meaning that God's love is diluted, it means that *each one* is precious and beloved—and known. And in case we missed this earlier in his comment about calling us by name, Jesus reiterates it a few sentences later, with an all-important addition: "I am the good shepherd. I know my sheep and my sheep know me . . . and I give my life for the sheep."[14]

Try doing the math on that one.

10. John 10:16 NIRV.
11. Isa 40:11 TNIV.
12. John 10:3 NIRV.
13. John 3:16 NIRV.
14. John 10:14–15 NIRV.

"Food for Thought" Questions

Questions for Reflection/Journaling

- Am I tempted to think God likes me better than others, or less than others, or both, depending on the situation? What circumstances prompt me to make those assumptions?
- If Jesus calls his sheep by name, that means he knows and values me and my story. What reasons do I have to love him that are specific to me and my own experience?
- What does it mean to me that God set my worth at the worth of Jesus? Jesus, will you help me take one step towards believing that today?

Questions for Group Study

- What in this chapter surprised or encouraged you the most?
- As humans, we have a hard time conceptualizing infinity. What are some ways you find it helpful to think about the infinite love of God?
- Are there ways you feel you've misinterpreted these parables, or elements of them, in the past? How would you explain or correct those misunderstandings for someone else?

2

Simon Says

(Am I *doomed to love* God *less if I'm good?)*

The parables of the lost sheep, the lost coin, and the lost son, when we take them the way Jesus meant them, assure us that there is nothing—good *or* bad—that will ever make God love us less. For a long time, though, I still worried that perhaps *I* was doomed to love *God* less if I hadn't committed lots of sins. I'd read in the Bible and heard at church that the more "lost" a person had been, usually the more grateful and devoted they'd be when Jesus found them. It broke my heart to think that because I'd had relatively little time or opportunity to *get* lost (having committed my life to Jesus as quite a young child), that kind of intimacy might not be available to me. This worry particularly came to a head with the story of Jesus at the home of a Pharisee named Simon.[15]

Simon throws a dinner party in Jesus' honor, and a woman "who had lived a sinful life" comes, washes Jesus' feet with her tears, dries them with her hair, and pours incredibly expensive perfume on them. Simon assumes—whether because he'd really been wondering, or because he'd been secretly hoping for a reason to write Jesus off as a hack he didn't need to listen to—that this is evidence that Jesus must not be a real prophet. A *real* prophet, he reasons, would know how sinful this woman is and tell her to keep her grubby hands to herself. Yet with fantastic Jesus-irony, this "fake prophet" then answers the secret thoughts of Simon's heart. Again, it's with a parable. (Apparently I just have a big problem with parables.)

15. This story is found in Luke 7:36–50. Incidentally, the name Simon in those days was a bit like the name Matt is today, where one in five people you meet and *every* person your friends find on dating apps is named Matt. In fact, there were two different Simons even within Jesus' twelve Apostles, and his cross was carried by yet another Simon. This guy isn't any of those people, so don't be confused. He's his own Simon.

Anyway, Jesus asks: if a lender forgives two debts, one moderate and one huge, which borrower is going to love the lender more? "I suppose the one who had the bigger debt forgiven,"[16] says Simon. Jesus then points out the extravagant lengths of love the woman had shown for him, and the comparatively cold reception Simon had given him (which had in fact bordered on rude by the standards of that day). Jesus concludes, "I tell you, her sins—and they are many—have been forgiven, so she has shown me much love. But a person who is forgiven little shows only little love.""[17]

Now, those of us who have been behaving ourselves like we were told to suddenly prick up our ears. "Wait—will I not be able to love Jesus very much if I've never seriously strayed?" It feels like a bit of a lose-lose situation for people who want to love him well. After all, if we've been avoiding sin all our lives for the love of Jesus . . . well, doesn't that mean we've got fewer sins to deepen our love for him? And this in turn raises the horrified question, "What am I doing even *thinking* I've been 'forgiven little'—doesn't it simply prove my arrogance and small love for him that I'm even asking the question?"

After all, it's been traditionally understood that Jesus isn't *actually* saying that Simon didn't have a lot that needed to be forgiven, just as when he mentions "ninety-nine righteous persons who do not need to repent,"[18] he doesn't *actually* mean they didn't need to repent. In other places, he's very clear that he thinks all people have a sin problem. From his challenge that "The person who is sinless should be the first to throw a stone"[19] to his discussion of how victims of tragedy aren't worse sinners than anyone else,[20] he keeps revealing this uncomfortable truth: that all of us need God's forgiveness, even those we consider pretty dang respectable. So what is he up to here, with this whole "forgiven-little/forgiven-much" thing?

Well, first, let me say that if your concern is loving Jesus well, his words in this passage may not be for you. These words were spoken to someone who *didn't* want to love Jesus, and needed to be woken up to his need for Jesus. To people who *do* want to love him, Jesus speaks different words. He promises that those who seek will find. When he gives that promise he makes clear that the primary thing we'll find is *him*. He promises that those who hunger and thirst for righteousness (and his definition of righteousness

16. Luke 7:43, TNIV.

17. Luke 7:47 NLT.

18. Luke 15:7 TNIV.

19. John 8:7b GW.

20. See Luke 13:1–5.

was first and foremost to love him) will have that hunger satisfied.[21] So if you're here because you love Jesus and want to love him more, don't let this passage worry you. He's speaking to a very different situation and a very different attitude.

Let's take a moment to appreciate the brilliant thing Jesus does with Simon's situation and attitude. He doesn't say "Simon, you're wrong; now stop being so self-righteous." He doesn't leave Simon's house in a huff. He goes along with Simon's assumption, and then points out that this woman—whom Simon "should" be able to run circles around morally—has just completely shown him up, both when it comes to showing honor and when it comes to loving Jesus. (The former was a very big deal in that culture; the latter was something they hadn't yet realized was a big deal, but is actually the biggest deal there could be.) The point of the passage isn't that Simon was doomed to a less passionate relationship with Jesus: because Jesus specifically is *not* saying that Simon had been forgiven little. With expert skill, without impugning Simon's honor in any way, he gives Simon pause and lets *him* do the work of questioning this assumption that he had been "forgiven little."

In every culture and generation there are sins that are seen as worse than others. In the Victorian era, respectability and sexual chastity were important, but westerners were largely blind to the rampant injustice embedded in their culture of imperialism and conquest. In 1960s America (at least in certain parts of the culture), violence and imperialism were *the* cardinal sins, while free sex was considered "no big deal" and in fact a good thing. In ancient Israel, eating the wrong foods was a huge deal, and looking down on other races or denying your daughter an education just because she was female were totally normal; today most westerners would consider the latter two unconscionable, and largely scratch their heads over the former.[22]

We don't know what this woman's sins were, except that they were the sort that give you a reputation. (In Simon's day, she was already at a "moral" disadvantage for being a woman: women were considered more promiscuous and more prone to error, and some rabbis even taught that it was sacrilegious to teach a woman God's Word.)[23] We don't know what Simon's sins were, either, although we can assume that they probably included at least self-righteousness (from the clues in this passage) and greed (from the

21. See Luke 11:9–13 on seeking and finding him; see Matt 22:35–38 and Mark 12:28–30 on defining righteousness as love for God; see Matt 5:6 on the thirst for righteousness being satisfied.

22. Although that's changing—ask anyone who's been shamed for buying the not-environmentally-conscious-enough food that everyone's avoiding *this* week.

23. Spencer, *Beyond the Curse*, 52–57.

statement elsewhere that the Pharisees, in general, "loved money").[24] These sins apparently didn't give him a bad reputation, but that doesn't mean they were negligible in God's eyes. In fact, elsewhere in the Bible greed is called a form of idolatry,[25] which was *the* fundamental sin to the Jewish people. So who is to say that any human's definition of what is a "little sin" and what's "big" is the same as God's definition?

Of course, it may be true that Simon really *hadn't* committed as many sins as this woman, in some numeric sense. Many of us who have grown up in fairly "tame" environments are in that same boat with him—and some of us are still wondering if we're being asked to lie about that. We *want* to agree with Jesus; we *want* to say with a straight face "I am the worst sinner of all,"[26] like we're supposed to . . . but after all, it isn't always our pride that balks at this; sometimes it's simply our sense of reality. A habit of sincerely submitting one's heart to God day after day *does* in fact produce a result that looks very different from a life spent rejecting God's ways. Are we supposed to deny this?

No. God never asks us to deny truth, only to see *more* of the truth.

Some philosophers talk about the concept of "moral luck": that some of us have been put in circumstances that make it a good deal easier to stay on the right side of "the rules"—circumstances that have nothing to do with actual virtue. Some of us simply haven't been put in a situation where we would have had the *opportunity* to, say, shoot someone or sell drugs, let alone being strongly tempted to do so. On the other hand, consider the children of white supremacists: they learn very different attitudes growing up than the children of advocates for racial equality—and they never asked to be born into a home where they would be indoctrinated into sin. They have a long road ahead of them as they learn to love their neighbor, a road that will often be rocky and ugly, and it's not even a little bit their fault that they were born onto it.

God cannot in true justice credit morally right "decisions" to us that we never had a chance to make, nor consider us better than those who had very different resources and options—*even when* our resulting behavior and attitudes are clearly better. So, sure: after a lifetime of following Jesus, my "sin count" probably *does* look different than someone else's, but I don't have to feel proud *or* embarrassed admitting that. It was a lucky break for me—God's ahead-of-time grace—that I was found and saved that early. And I have just as much reason to thank God, in desperate relief, for what I was

24. See Luke 16:14.

25. See Eph 5:5; Col 3:5.

26. 1 Tim 1:15b NIRV.

spared from getting into (because I certainly didn't ask to be born into my own circumstances either, circumstances where God's beauty was too obvious to miss) as any of my fellow debtors has, no matter *how* big their debt was. God isn't asking me to deny the realities of my life, or even to inflate my estimation of my debt, but to recognize the gift I've been given.

In fact, the only quantity Jesus is *actually* asking us to count up is not our sin, but our reasons to love him. He repeatedly challenges this idea that sin is about individual infractions against the law, as people often thought of it in his day (and still do now), and speaks of it instead as a condition of the heart, affecting all of life. In speaking of adultery, he talks about lust; in speaking of murder, he talks about hatred. I can easily keep a scorecard when it comes to how many people I've killed,[27] but how do you measure lust or hatred? Sin is the quality of our lives being out of joint, of us being in wrong relationship to the One who is all good and from whom all good flows.

So in many ways, Jesus turns this idea of sins being compared numerically—or at all—on its head in this passage, leading us to ask "what is 'a lot' when it comes to being forgiven by God? What is 'a little'?" Just as God asked Job if he'd ever journeyed to the springs of the sea or given orders to the dawn,[28] we find ourselves staggered when we're required to find an authoritative definition of what is "a lot" or find a fair comparison between people. Is the greed of a rich man worse than the promiscuity of an adulteress? What if the adulteress commits adultery ten times—how do you measure the rich man's greed in order to make a comparison? What if the adulteress was poor and starving and slept with someone because he promised to take care of her—is it then less wrong than it would have been? And is the rich man's greed then *comparatively* worse because he's already rich and doesn't *need* to be greedy? The whirlwind thunders through the ages, with that inimitable divine sarcasm, "Surely you know!"[29]

The point behind Jesus' parable about the debtors is not to prompt us to compare our "sin scorecards" to each other, but for us to *stop* comparing ourselves to each other long enough to see him. He's not saying "Joke's on you, Snobby-pants! You'll never be as close to God as someone who's *really* sinful!" He's not saying that you need to beat yourself up to convince yourself how sinful you really are, or factor in all of the circumstances to calculate how your scorecard really *is* worse than someone else's.

27. It's not all *that* many (yet).

28. See Job 38:12, 16.

29. Job 38:21a NRSV.

He's showing honor to a woman whose relationship with God has just been disrespected, and he's radically affirming both God's acceptance of her and her newfound closeness with him. He's defending this tender, vulnerable, but incredibly vibrant new shoot of faith springing up in her life, and he's warning Simon that he could miss out on all of this if he keeps brushing off what Jesus has to offer. His point is not that God keeps score of the "number," "size," or "severity" of our sins—for good *or* for ill—but in fact quite the opposite: *we're* the ones who keep score, and God is the one who forgives.

OK, sure. Fine. But what about those of us who are really worried by this parable? What if we've been used to seeing our own "scorecard" as better than others'? Is our relationship with Jesus doomed? What if we've tried not to think it, but a little part of us still maintains that most of the time we haven't been all *that* bad? Is there any hope for us when we find that we need to let God deal with self-righteousness in our lives? Or is it so ingrained that the only way to root it out is to start hating and judging ourselves, as we too often assume God does?

Well first of all, anything we need to let the Lord deal with is just that: something we need to let *the Lord* deal with. The words "go fix yourself and come back when you're done" are nowhere in any of these stories. If Jesus is trustworthy (and he is), and if Jesus told us that the poor in spirit are blessed (and he did),[30] then it is both safe and sufficient to come to him in prayer saying, "Lord, I haven't got this, and I need your help." Lightning may not flash and we won't become perfected saints all in a moment, but he's promised that he *will* answer us. In fact, he will accept, defend, and care for us just as readily as he did the sinful woman in this story. He's not asking us to live in guilt, but to confidently and joyfully keep our eyes open for the many ways he will teach and transform us.

Just as importantly, when we do discover arrogance in our lives, it doesn't mean we need to learn to believe God loves us *less* than we've so far assumed, but actually *more*. First, I guarantee that it's true: *God loves you more than you think*. You're a finite human; God is infinite and eternal and the very definition of love.[31] Do you really think you've even scratched the surface, let alone have a full understanding, of God's love for you? Second, when you are loved anyway, it is impossible to stay arrogant. If I refuse to believe that God still loves me when I sin, then I still can hold out hope that I could be good on my own—that without taking any handouts, I *might* still be able to earn my way back. But when God loves me anyway, it's impossible to keep on keeping score. I'm free. When you are loved, you don't *need* to

30. See Matt 5:3.

31. See 1 John 4:8.

be arrogant—just like when you've been fully fed, you don't need to keep seeking food. When you've been filled with the loving presence of Jesus, you don't have to fill that hole inside of you with yourself.

So whether, like the woman in the story, your sins have been obvious to all for a very long time, or if, like Simon, you tend to cover up your sins with self-satisfaction—or if you're the random servant holding the cheese plate at Simon's banquet, like, "Dang: I don't want to be a Pharisee *or* a ne'er-do-well; I just want to love Jesus"—the answer for all of us is to *receive the love that Jesus gives.* The point of this passage isn't that only certain lifestyles lead to a strong love for Jesus. It's that no matter what you have or haven't done, nothing can keep you away from the love into which he welcomes you: nothing except refusing to welcome him in return.

Simon didn't *want* to love Jesus. He didn't even really welcome Jesus. Even though he "invited" Jesus to his house, he was so busy looking for reasons to reject him that he didn't bother to show him a normal level of hospitality.[32] But Jesus was inviting him. And he is inviting us too. And when we respond to Jesus' invitation, the measure of our sins doesn't matter, because when we look at Jesus, we see someone who *wants* a relationship with us, no matter how messed-up (or deceptively tame) our lives have been. And when we look at Jesus, we also see a holiness to which we can never compare. The beauty of his goodness is breathtaking, and it's so far beyond any human performance that we don't need to dig very deep in order to see the contrast. Our love will always be "little" . . . compared to his. And yet falling in love with him keeps this from being discouraging: because the very one whose lovingkindness puts ours to shame is extending that same love to us.

When I was younger, I was worried sick about this passage. I tied myself in knots, not out of pride but out of a sincere desire to love God. The Holy Spirit had been at work in me from a young age, leading me to do what was right and helping me avoid what was wrong, and now I felt cheated—and wicked to boot. If it was just my own arrogance saying I was well-behaved, that must mean I was still blind to my own sinfulness . . . and if it was true that I was well-behaved, then apparently I wouldn't ever know the fullness of what loving Jesus could be.

If that is you—if the Lord's work has produced good fruit in your life—God is incredibly pleased about that. It has been your gift to each other, and that is a beautiful and joyful thing. God doesn't want you to deny it just to

32. In that culture, with as much dust as was always on the roads, people washed their feet upon entering a home. It was common courtesy to have a servant (or whoever the lowest-ranking person in the house was) perform this chore for a guest. Jesus points out in v 44 that Simon didn't even provide water for this, let alone providing a servant to do it.

avoid making the same mistake Simon did, and certainly doesn't want you to regret it, as if you'll never be able to love as deeply as you would if you had a dramatically sordid past. God is the one who wrote your story this way, and he would not have cultivated a relationship with you from a young age *with the intention of* barring you from the possibility of a deep relationship. That would be not only nonsensical, but contrary to God's nature. He has not purposely given you "less of" himself; he has already given you everything.

So if you were saved at a young age, praise God that you were! And if not, praise God that you are now! Your story is unique to you, and that means the way you love and your specific reasons to love God are unique to you too—but it does *not mean* anything about the "amount" of your love. Just as there is no reliable measuring system for sin, there is no measuring system for love, either. A parable's job is not to introduce one. A parable's job is to put an exclamation point on truth, and the truth is that Jesus welcomes all of us—saint, sinner, or servant-with-a-cheese-plate—into a love that is immeasurable.

"Food for Thought" Questions

Questions for Reflection/Journaling

- In Jesus' parable, people's love for the lender doesn't come from whether they were "good" or "bad," but from how he changed their stories. What are my own unique reasons to love Jesus because of how he's been present in my story?
- Am I comparing myself to others in an unhealthy way, rather than learning from and praising God for the differences in our stories? What are the things in my life that I'm most tempted to compare to others?
- When I compare myself to others, does it usually make me feel superior or like trash? Lord, how do you want to reorient how I see people . . . including myself? How do you see me?

Questions for Group Study

- What part of this chapter surprised or encouraged you most?
- What are some of the ways you see people "ranking" or "weighing" sin? Are there times when it's accurate or helpful (e.g., helping a child

understand the gravity of certain choices, or assuring a guilt-ridden friend that their mistake really didn't bother you that much)? When is it unhealthy, unhelpful, or beyond human reckoning?

- How would you explain to someone what Jesus is really getting at with this parable of the moneylender?

3

For Little Girls Like Me

(What really is a Pharisee—and what if I am one?)

Growing up in the church, there was one thing above all you didn't want to be: a Pharisee.

We may not have had a clear idea of what a Pharisee actually *was*, but we were clear on one thing: they were the bad guys. They were the ridiculously self-righteous people who were always opposing Jesus and ultimately ended up rejecting the gospel. And of course, we weren't so naïve as to assume that Pharisees of a sort don't still exist today. The people who present Christianity as if it's all about condemning sinners instead of welcoming and redeeming sinners. The people who are so quick to blame a single mother for her situation, and so slow to help with childcare. The sort of people who put hateful things on signs and embarrass the "rest of" us.

For those of you who were wondering, a Pharisee was a member of a strict—one might even say elitist—sect of ancient Judaism. Imagine "that guy"— you know, the one who donated enough to get his name on the new hospital wing, who runs ultra-marathons and yet somehow still always has amazing hair, whose kids all have straight-As (and straight teeth), and whose posts about all of it on social media are numerous, glamorous, and tastefully way cooler than yours. Now double that and you're not even close. One of the requirements for joining the Pharisee sect was to have the entire Tanakh ("the Old Testament") memorized. Not to have read it. To have it memorized.

But they didn't just memorize it. They tried to follow it as precisely as they possibly could. In order to make sure they didn't accidentally break God's commands about not eating unclean animals, they would strain their drinking water in case a gnat had fallen into it. In order to make sure nothing got overlooked when it came time to tithe (to give 10 percent of one's income to the Temple), they would tithe even their herb gardens. ("It doesn't matter if God doesn't actually *need* a quarter-teaspoon of dill; it's the *principle* of it.") They were precise, they were intense, and they were impressive. Respected.

And in the biblical narrative, they're the foils for Jesus. They voice everything we thought was reasonable—that God likes good people but not bad people, that if you're a "good person" God will accept you, that you should just try harder and you'll get there—and in their opposition to Jesus, they throw into sharp relief the difference of his message. That God loves sinners. That evil must be punished, but Jesus came to rescue, not to punish, and took our punishment for us. That *everyone* is contaminated by evil, and everyone needs Jesus to rescue them.

Not only do the Pharisees help us intellectually define the gospel, they help illustrate the gospel. By being the epitome of "as good as people can possibly be" and then missing God's plan completely, they prove beyond a shadow of a doubt that human "goodness" never brings us to God. They set the stage for the counterintuitive, offensive, beautiful declaration that it's never been about human effort, but about God's mercy, and that Jesus' sacrifice is both *necessary* and *enough* for each one of us.

The more the Pharisees push back against Jesus' outrageous message, the more he points out their inconsistencies and hypocrisies, and the veneer crumbles. As the glorious drama unfolds, everyone is shown to be guilty—both those whose crimes are obvious and those whose crimes are socially acceptable: both those whose darker impulses result in disgrace and destructiveness and those who, by no virtue of their own, were born into circumstances where their darker impulses didn't have an opportunity to manifest (at least not very visibly). The whole world is shown to be piercingly worse than we'd imagined . . . and then when the truly Good One is pierced, the whole world turns out to be loved more deeply than we'd ever dreamed.

And still the Pharisees miss it. They're still more caught up in their reputations and pride than they are in what God is up to, and it causes them to reject the one thing that could actually make them right with God. As the poster-children of those who reject redemption, it's small wonder that we often look at them as irredeemable.

Hard luck if you're a Pharisee.

That's why we tend to imagine we're not among them.

And that's why it's disconcerting for little girls who grow up in the church and come to realize that they're good at following the rules.

Especially if those little girls read a lot and listen to a lot of sermons and come to the conclusion that, if Jesus said the angels rejoice more over one lost sheep that is found than over ninety-nine who never wandered away in the first place[33] . . . then God must not like well-behaved little girls very much. It's even worse if those little girls are smart, and realize they sometimes take pride in their intellect. Or if they tend to be strict, and realize they gain some security from their strictness. How many qualities can you share with a Pharisee before you *are* one?

Worse, what if you find you *are* judgmental sometimes? What if you find you *are* self-righteous? If Pharisees are irredeemable, what do you do if you find you've committed that unspeakable sin of being one?

Perhaps a better question would be, Why do we think Pharisees are irredeemable?

Well, partly it's human nature. We're predisposed to think in terms of condemnation: us versus them, good guys versus bad guys. It's part of living in a world that's broken, where Satan's constant accusations are always seeping in through the jagged cracks. That inclination doesn't suddenly go away when we hear the good news of God's mercy. For a while, it just shifts the target of our condemnation—"God doesn't like sinners" shifts to "God doesn't like people who don't like sinners"—until God's mercy can finish its slow work on our understanding and eventually dissolve condemnation's hold.

It's partly also because many Pharisees did resist Jesus' good news, and his warnings about that were fittingly sobering.[34] But it's also because there are many ways to take a statement, and taken the wrong way a lot of Christian teaching—even sound, biblical teaching—can feed this false impression. Take one sermon I heard about how Jesus "redrew the lines" of who is acceptable to God. The pastor laid out some of the lines people tend to draw: "the respectable are 'in' and the 'riffraff' are 'out'" or "the religious are in and the 'heathens' are out." I expected a fairly predictable, Sunday-School-esque conclusion—that Jesus erased the line, or that everyone who believes in Jesus is now "inside the line"—but instead he made the thought-provoking paraphrase that in Jesus "the humble are in; the proud are out." He *meant* that the humble are those who accept that they need Jesus, while the proud refuse to come to him: it still was about what we do with Jesus. But that's not the only way to understand his statement.

Or consider the words of another sound, Bible-believing pastor who wrote that "Jesus opens himself up to those who are deemed far from God. Curiously, the only ones who have a hard time finding a place of welcome

33. See Matt 18:13; Luke 15:7.

34. See Matt 23.

are those who have rejected others."[35] I now have spent enough time with Jesus to be able to say, "Really?" Really, the multitude listening to the Sermon on the Mount didn't feel deeply welcomed by him? The fact that he taught so intently not just about loving their enemies but about reconciling with their own brothers[36] seems to indicate that they'd done their fair share of rejecting people. Yet he taught them like they were worth his time: like they were welcome. Really, Jesus didn't eat with the judgmental Pharisee, Simon, just as he ate with tax collectors?[37] Sure, he challenged the man's sinful attitude . . . but then again, his presence at *their* dinner table probably challenged the tax collectors and prostitutes in exactly the way they needed, too. Did sharing a meal with Simon not count as an act of fellowship the way it had counted for others? Really, Jesus' own disciples weren't welcomed by him? They did worse than look down on others or insult their brothers; they were ready to call down fire from heaven to punish their religious and ethnic enemies (and worse, they thought they were doing it for Jesus' sake).[38] And still, he spent three years with them, not just being on "OK" terms with them but living in close quarters, breathing in the dust of the road together, eating, talking, snoring, and sharing every single day together.

These pastors were getting at something real, but what they meant isn't necessarily what everyone heard. What some of us hear in "the humble are in, the proud are out" is the word *out.* What some of us hear in "a hard time finding welcome" is *un*welcome. These words aren't exactly the same as "irredeemable". . . but neither do they produce particularly *hopeful* feelings, and I can still feel the sting for the little girl inside, wondering if she's outside of God's mercy. No one *meant* to give a little girl an existential crisis. No one *means* to make Pharisees sound irredeemable. But words are tricky and so are the impressions we get from them . . . and let's face it, we preachers need sermon illustrations and the Pharisees are *such* an easy target. (I mean, who weighs out their herb gardens? Really?)

If we look more closely at the Bible, though, the picture it gives of the Pharisees is not one of flat opposition to Jesus. The Apostle Paul, who traveled virtually the entire known world spreading Jesus' teachings—and ticked off more strict sticklers[39] for the Law than Jesus even had time to, including sticklers who were Christians—was a Pharisee. Jesus' closest friends, who deserted him to his death (and who fit very well into the category of "lost

35. Villodas, *Deeply Formed Life*, 193.

36. See Matt 5:43–48 and Matt 5:21–26.

37. See Luke 7:36–50.

38. See Luke 9:53–55.

39. I dare you to say "ticked strict sticklers" five times fast.

sheep" we often consider "the people Jesus came for") weren't the ones who came back to give him a proper burial. Pharisees did that.[40] One of those Pharisees, Nicodemus, is the reason we have the most widely quoted Bible verse in history, John 3:16[41]—and that was *before* he even bought into Jesus' message. In fact, it was *because* he didn't yet understand the gospel that we have the clearest, most distilled statement of it in the entire Bible. This one verse has helped countless people understand the gospel for 2,000 years. Far from being *written off* as hopeless for not "getting" grace perfectly, he was *written down* as a signpost to the rest of us. Later, Nicodemus stuck up for Jesus when his colleagues were doing their best to arrest Jesus and shame anyone who supported him.[42] Nicodemus's comment may have been small, and not particularly brave, and at the time largely drowned out by other voices . . . but he still *made* it, and who knows: it may have been the thing that planted enough questions in the minds of his colleagues—colleagues like Joseph of Arimathea—that they eventually became followers themselves, which we know many of them did.[43]

Not only that, but the Bible's picture of *Jesus* isn't one of flat opposition to the *Pharisees,* either. Jesus doesn't criticize every single thing they do, and he freely spends time with them. He meets secretly with one who isn't ready to meet with him publicly.[44] He dines with another so publicly that they have gate-crashers.[45] None of them had a hard time *finding* welcome; it's just that some had a hard time *receiving* welcome. And that makes a world of difference. In our pride, we often choose not to receive God's loving embrace. That's true, and that's tragic. That doesn't mean God doesn't want to

40. See John 19:38–42; see also John 3:1 which identifies Nicodemus as a Pharisee and Luke 23:50 which identifies Joseph as an upright member of the Jewish ruling council (which means he was either a Pharisee or a Sadducee—a group that, despite some theological differences, had the same problem with making a show of religion that the Pharisees had).

41. "For God so loved the world that he gave his one and only son, that whoever believes in him shall not perish but have eternal life" (TNIV).

42. See John 7:45–52.

43. See John 11:45 (where "Jews" is used synonymously with "Jewish leaders" or "people of high religious status"); John 12:42; Acts 6:7; Acts 15:5.

44. When Nicodemus visits Jesus in John 3, he comes to Jesus by night—most likely because there was such controversy surrounding Jesus that Nicodemus didn't want to risk damaging his own reputation. Remarkably, Jesus doesn't say a word to him about this, but makes time for him "where he's at."

45. This Pharisee invites Jesus to his house in Luke 7, and Jesus accepts. Not only is Jesus unafraid of what people might think of him for dining with "tax collectors and sinners" (he does this numerous times), but he's also unafraid of what people might think of him for dining with self-righteous snobs like Simon the Pharisee turns out to be.

give it. Jesus' lament over the hardhearted Pharisees wasn't that he couldn't welcome them; it was "*you refuse to come to me* to have life."[46] We exclude ourselves from God's welcome all the time, but *God* does not— and there's a silhouette of a cross stretched across history showing just how far he went to *make* us welcome.

In fact, when Jesus criticizes the Pharisees for tithing their herbs while forgetting justice and mercy, he actually *affirms* some of their practices too. We often miss this—perhaps because they were so far off base so often, or maybe because they're just so easy to dislike. Either way, we might assume he'll oppose them on everything. But he doesn't. He doesn't tell them, "You shouldn't tithe your herbs." He doesn't say, "Stop being such sticklers for detail." He says, "You should have practiced the latter, *without neglecting the former*."[47] In other words, "Keep up the good work with the herb garden! . . . Just don't kid yourself that that's *all* I want." He doesn't criticize their obedience to God's law either. American Christians have weirdly ambivalent attitudes towards obedience: we know that it's a good thing, kind of . . . but then again, our entire country is founded on rebellion, and we've got five hundred years of Protestant theology warning us that we mustn't rely on "following the rules." I spent an entire childhood and four years of Christian college hearing the silent message that I was rigid and legalistic because I *didn't* have a problem with authority. But Jesus isn't upset with the Pharisees' love for God's authority. On the contrary, he challenges them to come *more* under God's authority, because they were often much more in love with *their own* authority.

He doesn't have a problem with them being precise. He doesn't have a problem with them being intense. He doesn't have a problem with them for being sinners. He just has a problem with them using what they're good at to distract from what they're not good at. They were using easily measurable "good deeds" as a way of hiding from the much more risky, much less measurable task of letting God give them good hearts. Jesus isn't faulting them for being passionate about the things of God. He's asking them to dig deeper and make sure they really know what the things of God *are*. Jesus is not asking them to become less "who they are"; he's asking them to be all that and more.

Why is this important? Because often, we assume that pleasing God consists of suppressing who we are. When we find an aspect of our personalities that has led us into sin we assume that the trait itself is bad, and that we need to do all we can to stuff it down and stamp it out. Whether we're

46. John 5:40 TNIV, emphasis mine.

47. Matt 23:23 TNIV, emphasis mine.

"Pharisees" or "lost sheep," human beings tend to look at righteousness in terms of "don'ts."

In reality, any aspect of any personality *could* lead to wrong attitudes and actions, just like any trait *could* be an asset in doing the right thing. Extreme sensitivity can lead to either cowardice or compassion. High amounts of natural cheeriness can be used to encourage others or to completely ignore and invalidate their sorrows. Punctuality can make a person really reliable, and also really impatient with someone who is running late. And precision can lead to excellence and attentive care just as much as it can lead to mercilessness. God's aim isn't to rid us of our personal traits, but to redeem them.

We're all inclined to do what the Pharisees did. We're inclined to double down on what we're good at, and try to "keep a lid on" everything else. But that's not what God asks of us. God asks us to let the Holy Spirit transform the parts that we think are already strong, as well as the parts we think are shamefully weak. God wants the things we're good at, and wants to lead us into those risky places we're *not* good at, the ones that we've been avoiding. And so Jesus doesn't say to the Apostle Peter, "Stop being so enthusiastic about being a leader!" He says, "Be just as enthusiastic about my work in other people's lives as you are about my work in yours."[48] He doesn't tell Martha, "Stop serving!" He tells her that there are things even more important than service, things that he doesn't want her to miss, and then he eats the dinner she served.[49] And he doesn't ask the Pharisees to be any less dedicated or concerned about righteousness. He asks them to come to him to learn what loving righteousness truly means. When Jesus calls us to lay down our whole selves and let him transform us, it's not because he wants to erase those whole selves. It's because God wants us to be truly, fully ourselves, and more.

48. Obviously, this is a gigantic paraphrase. But when Jesus reinstates Peter in John 21, he asks Peter, who had been quick to tout his own loyalty to Jesus in places like Mark 10:28 and John 13:37, to "feed my lambs," indicating that while Peter *wasn't* the star of the show, his God-given leader personality was important, and that he was to use it to serve and nurture others. Later, it is Peter himself (whose nickname means "stone") who declares that *all* Christians are living stones in the spiritual home God is building (1 Pet 2:5).

49. Much time has been spent by Christians on the story in Luke 10:38–42, where Martha is distracted by the preparations needed for dinner. In this story, she asks Jesus to prioritize Mary's usefulness in the kitchen over Mary's right to learn at his feet. He refuses, telling her that Mary has made the better choice. Less often do people turn to John 12 to find Martha in the kitchen again, with apparently no rebuke from Jesus. The issue wasn't whether she should serve, but whether her focus on serving displaced Jesus in her life.

In fact, for the Pharisees that listened to him, their background as Pharisees was part of how God prepared these people to follow Jesus. Paul's ministry wouldn't have been nearly as effective without his encyclopedic knowledge of Scripture and his honed intellect, memory, and debate skills. Nicodemus might not have bothered to come and have his secret, now-famous conversation with Jesus in John 3 if he didn't have a Pharisee's dedication to making sure he was getting this whole following-God-thing right. Joseph of Arimathea, without the privilege into which he was born and the high position he held, would not have been able to lend his personal tomb to Jesus—a burial that led to compelling evidence that Jesus' bodily resurrection is an actual historical fact, evidence that wouldn't have existed had Jesus been buried as a common criminal.[50] God used Pharisees and God redeems Pharisees.

Of all people, Pharisees prove once and for all that no one is irredeemable. They proved it first as Jesus' foils. Their strictness and pride highlighted Jesus' love and acceptance of those we all judge: the murderers and the adulterers and that guy who isn't even *trying* to do better. And then, they proved it as Jesus' followers: those who had it all together and missed everything, who had rejected the only One who could save them, who had won the world and lost their own souls . . . and then miraculously had their souls resurrected. Those who repeatedly didn't get God's mercy until God's mercy got them.

I love that the two best-known pillars of the early church were Peter and Paul. What polar opposites: the impulsive blue-collar guy with no religious credentials, and the highly-educated straight-A snob! (I love it even more that the rough-around-the-edges fisherman ended up spending most of his ministry in the deeply religious city of Jerusalem, and the fussy urban super-Jew ended up tromping through dusty roads and shipwrecks to bring

50. An in-depth discussion of this evidence, and other important pieces of evidence regarding Jesus' bodily resurrection, can be found in *The Case for Christ* by Lee Strobel (and in many other books as well, but Strobel's work tends to be highly accessible). Briefly, because Jesus was buried in a tomb covered by an enormously heavy stone and not thrown into a ditch to be devoured by dogs, and because the location of the tomb was known to his followers and opponents alike, the claims of those who had seen him alive were difficult to explain away—difficult enough that his opponents had to resort to claiming that the disciples (with little motivation, resources, or courage, and no reason to later die for what they knew to be a lie) had stolen his body. It would have been much easier to open up the tomb and show everyone that the corpse was still there, but this wasn't an option because he *wasn't* there. Had Joseph not stepped up and offered his own tomb when all of the disciples deserted Jesus, we would have known a lot less about what happened to Jesus' body and his opponents would have had a much easier time coming up with a plausible explanation in their attempt to dismiss the reality of the resurrection.

the gospel to the pagan gentile world. God giggles sometimes.) We can be so fond of the story of the lost sheep, and of saying "God doesn't call the equipped; he equips the called" that sometimes the educated, rule-following Pauls among us wonder if we're any use to God. But Peter and Paul show us that God *can* and *does* use anyone, regardless of their background or personality. What's more, they show us that God doesn't just use us "in spite of" who we are. Who God made us is integral to how God uses us . . . even as he brings us into places where it's impossible for us lean on our background, personality, or personal strengths. Paul's training as a Pharisee was extremely useful in his ministry, but often in ways he never expected: ways that required him to rely on *God's use of* his background, not on that background itself.

I wasted far too much time when I was younger worrying that I was irredeemable—fearing what would happen if I *did* turn out to be guilty of pride, or of thinking myself better than others, or of placing my security in "my goodness" instead of God's. But what about when the verdict comes back guilty—as it does for each of us at times? How about we just admit that we all struggle with pride? That we're all self-righteous at times? That the human impulse has always been toward self-reliance rather than trust in God? (Even—here's the really tough one—that these struggles don't just go away when one becomes a Christian? That the battle, in fact, has just begun at that point, because before we weren't even fighting?) Why don't we face the fact that we've all committed unspeakable sins—whatever those may be in our own lives—and that this is precisely why Jesus came?

Jesus came to redeem the irredeemable and forgive the unforgivable. That's me. That's you. That's the fisherman, and the Pharisee. And in each person's story, we get to see one more facet of God's peculiar grace. Don't waste time as I did thinking that it's not for you. Jesus came for *you*. And he came for little girls like me.

"Food for Thought" Questions

QUESTIONS FOR REFLECTION/JOURNALING

- Are there aspects of my personality that I've felt are unacceptable and therefore necessary to suppress? Lord, will you show me how you want to transform these qualities into ways to know Jesus better?
- Are there aspects of my personality that I like to "fall back on" because I know I'm usually praised for them and/or because they're virtues that come easily to me? Jesus, how do you want to affirm these things in

me? How do you want to lead me beyond them into goodness that I'm not naturally "good at"?

- Are there ways I've looked down on others for not having an easy time with the same virtues that come easily to me? Where are their strengths? How can I appreciate and support them for how God has made and shaped them?

Questions for Group Study

- What in this chapter surprised or encouraged you the most?
- How has God uniquely prepared you—both through the things that people praise about you and the things that have been difficult, shame-filled, or sinful—to know Jesus, connect with him, and help others know his love too? How does God want to use your passions to bless the world?
- What is the difference between "loving God's law,"[51] (which the Bible portrays as a good thing—see Ps 119:13–16, 47, 97; Matt 4:4; Jas 1:22–25), and being legalistic? How would you encourage someone who is passionate about obeying God? How would you encourage someone who has often "failed" at "following the rules"?

51. As Christians, we are no longer under the laws of the Torah, but the Bible does say we're under the "law of Christ" (Gal 6:2).

4

God, Guilt, and Mental Health

(Where is this guilt coming from?—Part 1)

THE CHURCH IN RECENT decades has made strides in learning to talk about mental health. While openness to the conversation certainly varies among localities, denominations, and individuals, in general (and I admit this is a very broad generalization) the subject has become less taboo. However, just because people are starting to be *willing* to talk about mental health doesn't mean they always know *how* to talk about mental health, and—very importantly—they may not have a very developed understanding of how mental health interacts with a person's faith (and indeed, a person's whole life).

Your brain profile—the "way you're wired"—is one of the most profound gifts you've been given by God. It's part of what makes you who you are, and *part of what makes you so uniquely valuable*. Many of my depressive friends are deeply empathetic, far outstripping the compassion of happier people. My dad's ADD tendencies give him a seemingly boundless energy and a forgiving, easygoing, buoyancy that draws just about everyone he meets to him. My own obsessive tendencies are one of my favorite qualities about myself; I would not be the same person without the fiendish level of concentration and drive God gave me, and while many have to work to maintain an awareness of God's presence, my "sticky" brain means God is pretty much never not on my mind.

Your brain profile is inevitably going to cause you problems as well. The Fall[52] has affected every aspect of Creation, and that means that throughout

52. For those not exactly sure what that is, simply put, Christians believe that God is good and made the world good, and then when the first humans rejected God, they "broke" that goodness. Because humans were made "in the image of God," which includes being able to make real decisions and being given a measure of authority, that

history we've found that our greatest strengths are also our greatest weaknesses. There are some virtues that are going to come more easily to certain brain profiles than others, and certain vices that are going to be harder to avoid. Highly conscientious people who tend towards obsessiveness are going to have a very easy time doing lots of good deeds and a much harder time withholding judgment. There are also some truths that are going to come more naturally to certain brain profiles than others. People who are very "laid-back" may have an easy time believing in God's love and forgiveness, and a harder time remembering and being compelled by the fact that holy living matters to God.

Here's where it gets tricky for Christians when we're unaware of how people's brain profiles color their experience of the world. The quirks with which we move through the world do have a *moral* and *spiritual* aspect—after all, God created us as whole beings with physical, mental, and spiritual facets, and none of these aspects exists in a vacuum—but many of our strengths and pitfalls are also deeply rooted in *neurology*. When we attribute these things *only* to a person's moral or spiritual state, we're in danger of not only unfairly passing judgment, but also of rendering ourselves unable to truly help these brothers and sisters, and even of misdirecting them from finding help themselves—and skewing their view of God.

For instance, that insensitive man in the pew ahead of you may not just be a jerk; he may have an autism spectrum disorder that makes it very hard for him to know which nuances and phrasings are socially appropriate and which are "rude." That doesn't mean he shouldn't try to learn to be more sensitive and appropriate as a way of loving God and others, but it also doesn't mean there's something especially wrong with his faith just because he has a hard time expressing himself in ways that others feel are gentle and considerate. That fellow next to you jiggling his leg and seemingly not paying an ounce of attention during the sermon might not be uninterested in spiritual matters; he may have an attention disorder that makes sitting still the most difficult and unhelpful way for him to learn—and we may do deep violence to him and his relationship with God not to mention being supremely unhelpful in his journey of finding things that *do* help him concentrate and learn if we tell him his lack of focus is unspiritual or a sign that he doesn't love God very much. Your friend who never seems to trust God's love for her may not have a "lack of faith"; she may have a depressive

---

decision had repercussions not just for them, but for the world around them and for their descendants that now live out their legacy. That, Christians believe, is why we see so much pain and evil around us, and we call that event "the Fall of Humanity" or just "The Fall." Not to be confused with The Autumn, which is generally just delicious and full of cider.

or anxious disorder that makes her interior life—including her spiritual life—frequently a bewildering, dark, unsafe place to be. And for those of us with obsessive disorders, well, we may experience a chronic guilt that has us and everyone else wondering how we could have misunderstood the message of grace so badly.

That's not to say that everyone's guilt, or even everyone's mental-health-based guilt, comes from OCD. It just happens to be how this played out in my own life, and might be illustrative for how it's playing out in your own (or your friend's, or your child's, or your neighbor's).

The best explanation I've heard of obsessiveness comes from the book *Shadow Syndromes*:

> What happens in OCD—what *keeps* happening, over and over again with no end in sight—is exactly what happens when we feel we've made a mistake. Our brains are hardwired to detect mistakes; we could not function in our world if we did not possess this capacity. . . . For most of us, this 'mistake feeling'—and it is indeed, the biology of the brain shows, a feeling—is extremely uncomfortable. . . . The key to grasping obsessive-compulsive disorder is to understand that the brain is structured so as to make us feel *compelled* to correct our mistakes. . . . And we will feel driven by the need to do this until we have finally done it. For those of us whose brains are functioning properly . . . the episode [then] comes to an end. . . . But in obsessive-compulsive disorder, horribly, this does not happen; the alarm continues to sound.[53]

That explanation changed my life. I'd had no idea I was obsessive before then. My obsessiveness is mild; I don't compulsively check that my stove is turned off or lock and re-lock my doors. But I find myself teary every time I read this passage because I recognize the description so well.

I've struggled for a good deal of my life with that feeling that "something's wrong" or "I'm doing something wrong." In lay biological terms, my mistake button is stuck. A lot of times, this has felt like a nameless guilt—I felt bad about something, but I didn't know what. I didn't know if it was something I'd forgotten about, or something I wasn't brave enough to admit to myself, or if it was just me being "legalistic."

That last one was a big problem, because legalism is a very, very bad word in Christian circles (with good reason, because it's an attitude that's very contrary to the teachings of Jesus). And usually, if someone is chronically guilt-ridden—especially if, like me, that person has always had an easy

53. Ratey and Johnson, *Shadow Syndromes,* 285–86.

time with "following the rules"—both Christians and non-Christians alike tend to assume that legalism is to blame. (By extension, this also assumes that the guilt-ridden *person* is to blame.) It's in books, and sermons, and discussions: if you trust in Jesus' grace, you don't have to feel guilty.

In a depressingly hilarious burst of irony, that always made me feel more guilty. I knew this wasn't how Christianity was supposed to be, and I kept trying to push myself out of the pride and legalism that had (apparently) kept me from accepting God's grace. However, the problem with feeling bad about something you're not actually doing is . . . well, you can't *stop* doing something you're not actually doing. And that means there's no way to stop feeling bad. And when the thing you can't stop feeling bad about is feeling bad, that creates an infinite loop of absurdity (that probably kept the forces of hell giggling for quite a long time).

Interestingly, this was all made worse for me by the fact that my disorder is mild. The authors of *Shadow Syndromes* note that one of the hallmarks of classic OCD is that the sufferer *realizes*, even as she feels compelled to do certain behaviors, that what she's feeling is not rational. In contrast, "paradoxically, a person who suffers only very mild obsessive-compulsive disorder might in fact lose insight precisely because his obsessions and compulsions are so much less intrusive and painful that he does not recognize them as irrational, or as 'not real.'"[54] This was my problem: I didn't recognize that something wasn't normal because my thoughts and feelings just seemed so *reasonable*. It's reasonable to believe that sometimes we screw up and need to ask God and others for forgiveness. It's reasonable to assume that sometimes we're unaware of harboring wrong attitudes, and that we need to examine our hearts with God's help. It's even reasonable to suspect that the tiny, tiny whisper inside saying "but wait . . . is this guilt really true?" is sometimes just an excuse, just our ego's attempt to justify itself. That's part of why I was so helpless against this disorder for so long: it had eaten even my ability to question it.

And that's why it was such an amazing relief to find out that something wasn't right with my brain. I had spent years trying to fix whatever was wrong in my relationship with God and trying to figure out why the fixes never stayed. It made so much sense, and was so liberating, to realize that it wasn't a problem with God, per se. It wasn't even, as many could easily suspect, a problem with the way I'd been *taught* about God (which was actually quite sound and wholesome, for the most part). The problem was with a brain that could twist anything—even good teachings, even One I love with all my being—into a reason for fear.

54. Ratey and Johnson, *Shadow Syndromes*, 287.

That was always my biggest concern in dealing with this, even before I knew what I was dealing with: I didn't want people to think I struggle like this *because* I'm a Christian. So many people think that Christianity *makes* people feel guilty—something I knew wasn't true from studying the Bible and knowing Jesus since childhood—and I didn't want to give a bad name to something that means so much to me. I know that many Christians with mental health disorders find that some of their biggest challenges come from the stigma that can be associated with mental health problems in the church, and the well-meaning bad advice that people give. Thankfully, that isn't my story. I've actually met with a lot of understanding and help from my brothers and sisters in Christ. The hardest part, for me, about being a Christian with a mental health disorder is the way that psychological disorders can wrap themselves around whatever is most prominent in our lives, giving the impression (even to ourselves) that these important things in our lives are the *cause* of our distress.

It took me a very long time to be able to admit to myself that some of the things I heard growing up as a Christian *were* damaging. But by and large, the percentage of those things was quite small. Looking back, the things that were damaging weren't twisted or false teachings in the church. They were little interactions—most of them completely innocuous (and not just from Christians, and many having nothing at all to do with anything "religious")—that my obsessive brain seized and built into bastions, like a crazed oyster making great unholy pearls out of tiny, tiny grains of nothing. Most people would probably be really surprised if I were to tell them just how small of an event can affect me: the ways I feel obligated to think, the ways I resolve not to act, the little hurtful mistakes I vow never to make—in response to normal, everyday interactions.

That's not God. That's not my faith making me feel bad. That's my brain being screwy.

The encouraging part is that while those weird and unhealthy thoughts may not *result from* our interactions with God, God is *not* silent or uninvolved when it comes to their healing. I'm not saying our tendencies "go away" or ever lose their ability to be both a blessing and a curse, but I *am* saying that with help we can learn to live more healthily in the brains we were given. God can provide patient friends who tell us the truth, lovingly and repeatedly. God provides our family in Christ, some of whom in their sermons and writings and conversations can help untangle the creeper vines of our mental health where they have wound around and twisted our ideas of God. Most importantly, God walks beside us through every bend and shadowed turning of the path—a path that, for many of us, is long.

The take-aways from this discussion are several.

Your Faith Isn't Defective

First, and of first importance, your mental health struggles *do not mean that something is wrong with your faith.* They mean you live in a fallen world where even the most glorious thing about you, the amazing and unique brain God has given you, can also be one of the biggest sources of trouble in your life. But they do not mean that something is wrong with your faith. Certainly, mental health struggles can "wrap around" our faith, so to speak—they can make certain truths harder to hold on to and certain distortions of the truth seem more plausible. (And yet, it is worth noting, they can also deepen our experience of God, giving us greater compassion, greater trust, greater practice [and thus, skill] in holding onto the Truth when we cannot see or feel or understand God.) We certainly need to "unwrap" them sometimes—to consciously think through where truths are distorted in our minds, and why they're distorted, and what the truth actually is. But when we find our feelings and thoughts don't match up with what we believe, it doesn't mean we're not believing "right." Many times it means we have a mental health component to our struggles that needs to be dealt with through mental health treatment, so that it doesn't have to throw the rest of our lives—including our spirituality and our relationships—off-kilter so much. I happen to have food sensitivities that profoundly affect my emotional state: I cannot tell you how many deep, incomprehensible "spiritual" struggles have suddenly resolved with a second look at the ingredients label.

Handle Snares With Care

Depending on your own mental and neurological makeup, there are certain things, even certain good things, that will be uniquely challenging or counterproductive for you. The classic example is alcohol, which the Bible itself says is a gift from God "to make people glad,"[55] but for those with addictive personalities, stirs up a problem that far outweighs the benefit of receiving this gift "with thankfulness."[56] Know your snares.

A less-usual example is the way fasting has often been a snare to me. Fasting is a wonderful spiritual practice. It challenges our entitlement, giving us a hands-on way of humbling ourselves before God, of admitting that we have neither earned nor deserved our privilege, and putting the right One back on the thrones of our lives. It teaches us to seek God first, and to know in doing so that we do not need the comforts or even necessities of life

55. Psalm 104:15 NIRV.

56. See 1 Tim 4:4–5; also 1 Cor 10:30.

to be satisfied; it helps us to train ourselves to be in control of our impulses rather than controlled by them; it allows us to focus our minds on God, to stand in solidarity with our disadvantaged neighbors, and to be aware that there is far more than the physical realm. Its very hunger pangs serve as alarm clocks reminding us to pray.

And for people with obsessive brains, fasting can reinforce the unhealthy tendency to see God in terms of punitive rules, because now there's a hard-and-fast rule ("don't eat today," or "don't eat this specific thing") that we're imposing upon ourselves and trying not to break. It can reinforce that feeling of "not being good enough" because there are many ways to fast—fasting from a specific food or all food or a certain activity, fasting for one meal or for a day, or for one meal a day for three weeks—and who's to say that the thing *I* chose to give up isn't lame or too little or that it's not a cop-out if I only fast for a meal or two and not for the whole day? It can also reignite those fears about legalism: am I doing this with the right heart? Am I being "too religious"? Is God actually asking me to do this or is it just me? Although many times I've found fasting to be a helpful spiritual practice, I've had to (ironically) give it up for many years because I realized that with my particular tendencies and weak spots, it was actually doing more damage to my relationship with God than good.

So know yourself, and realize that knowing yourself includes knowing both the things that are helpful to your spiritual walk and the things that are supremely unhelpful. Realize also that taking care of your peculiarities isn't selfish, weak, or unspiritual, but is holy stewardship of the most fundamental resources God gave you: yourself—your body, mind, and soul. So if fasting is a snare to you, don't fast. If certain types of devotional books make it harder for you to know and love God, don't read those books for now. There are plenty of other devotional resources that *will* speak a language your mind can take in healthily and *will* help with the growth that you need right now. If there are Christian brothers or sisters whose communication style or preferred topics of discussion tend to kickstart your self-condemning tendencies, don't cut that person out of your life . . . but maybe be judicious about how much you share with them of your inner life and struggles, and be aware enough of your own emotional energy level to know when you're "up for" being around them and when you might not be. And although it may sound strange to say it, don't always listen in church.

I realize this goes against most of what we've been taught about being open to God's Spirit and being attentive to God's Word, not to mention respecting God's servants. However, preachers (and writers) are speaking to a broad audience. While what they are speaking broadly is the truth of God's Word, the specifics may not apply to you. For instance, if you've been very diligent in searching your heart and repenting when the Spirit shows you things that are out of line, and your pastor happens to preach a sermon calling people to identify their blind spots and repent, that doesn't mean that you "missed something" when you were searching your heart. It means that this is a general need for the Body of Christ. If you struggle deeply with the fear that you may be a "Pharisee" and pray for God's grace to humbly love those around you, and your pastor or devotional book or friend happens to make a generalization about a lot of Christians being "judgmental" or "pharisaical," that's not God kicking you while you're down or saying you're hopelessly bad at this. Some words just aren't for you.

It took me a long time to learn this. I was so sure that I was supposed to be "open" to whatever God's Spirit might have to say, and so trained in the idea that we're not supposed to assume the message is "for someone else" (because of how easily that becomes an excuse to ignore God's conviction) that I made no attempt to protect what turned out to be some highly vulnerable places in my heart and mind. As a result, I ended up doing some really unhealthy things. There were spiritual lies and wrong thought patterns that I didn't resist because it was a sermon that triggered them and we're "supposed to" take sermons to heart. Or I would begin picking over old sins that God had already forgiven, or picking on things that weren't really sinful (because we were supposed to be repenting of *something* and I hadn't had much time to fall into sin again since the last time I'd talked with the Lord). It was weird, when I finally realized the need to weigh the words I hear, to feel sometimes like I was shutting down my heart in church. And I'm certainly not saying "don't be open to God's voice." But God's very word says we're supposed to be using discernment *even in church,*[57] and if you find that something is being said that is going to be a snare to you—something you know your mind is going to twist, words that you can feel the devil plucking at to pull you off-balance and away from the Truth—then humbly and before God, don't take that word to heart.

Additionally, to the extent that you can, be aware of your brothers' and sisters' snares too, and take care of each other. Take time to listen to the heart behind someone's struggle. Exercise wise prudence about what's really going on for someone, and what may be helpful—or extremely unhelpful—to say. Don't assume that their struggles are a sign of spiritual weakness or sin, just because they're different from yours. And don't be so afraid of sitting with their struggles that you start spouting rote Christian "right answers" before you even understand the problem.

57. See 1 Cor 14:29.

Keep at It: God Made You Worth It

Lastly, don't give up. The journey towards mental health is long, and not every type of help will be helpful for every person. Many times it takes several tries to find the right "fit" when it comes to medications or counselors, and it's tempting to look at the first (or second) bad fit and conclude that it's hopeless. It isn't. It's also tempting to think that the goal is to be "cured." It isn't. Thank God, you will never be "cured of" your brain. Your gifts and quirks are part of who you are, and God made you who you are for a very, *very* good reason. And it's precisely because your brain is so magnificent, beautiful, and vital to God's purposes that it's worth learning to understand, care for, and work with its quirks in ways that keep you from being overcome by them.

Usually this is going to look like a cocktail of help, not one single thing that is "the" answer for you. A person's "cocktail" might be made up of any number of things, including psychological counseling,[58] spiritual direction, medication, and self-care such as dietary changes or regular exercise. Each one will look a little different. But a person's "cocktail" will virtually always include four distinct sources or types of help: *professional helpers* such as psychiatrists, counselors, and pastors; *family and friends*; *oneself*; and *God*. Each of these helpers is important and none can be substituted for another.

Although God is the ultimate source of all our help and the only one big enough to fill all of our needs, we were never intended to live in isolation from others. Often the help God gives comes *through* other people, because

58. It is worth noting the difference between psychological and pastoral counseling—and for that matter, between the different types of mental health practitioners. A person with a degree in *pastoral counseling* is trained to help people work through spiritual matters and can be very helpful to talk to, but is not necessarily trained in mental health. A *psychotherapist* is specifically trained to help people with mental health issues (some are Christians, some aren't, but either way they're trained to be respectful of your faith; occasionally you'll find one who *also* has a seminary degree in something like pastoral counseling). The umbrella term "psychotherapist" includes clinical psychologists, licensed mental health counselors (LMHC), and a whole slew of social work licensures. We can't get into all the little differences in education and licensing requirements; what is important to note is that in the US a counselor or therapist can*not* prescribe medication. That requires a medical degree, and can be done by a *psychiatrist* (who may also provide counseling services), a psychopharmacologist (a psychiatrist who does not provide counseling services), or your primary care physician. If you're looking for psychiatric help and don't know what you need, your primary care physician can be a good place to start to point you in the right direction. There are also numerous hotlines if you're in need of immediate help; in America, the National Suicide Prevention Hotline is at 1-800-273-TALK (8255) and the SAMHSA (Substance Abuse and Mental Health Services Administration) 24-hour hotline is 1-800-622-HELP (4357).

the very nature of Christian life (and life in general) is relational, with each part of the Body needing all of the others. Family and friends, although an important support system, usually do not have the training, skills, or type of relationship with you to take the place of a mental health professional; conversely, while a professional can help you understand and learn to manage your mental health, he or she cannot provide the everyday companionship and love you need from your friends. And while this is never a journey you should try to undertake alone, it *is* a journey in which you play a vital part: you do the work of seeking out help, thinking or journaling or grieving, engaging with helpful books or resources, and learning to make wise decisions about your own health.

Your brain is magnificent, and is an inextricable part of who God made you. It's also disproportionately influential, comprising only about 2 percent of your body weight but using 20 percent of your oxygen intake and even more of your carbohydrate intake. Is it any wonder that the influence it exerts on our emotional, relational, and spiritual lives may often be similarly unnoticed yet profound? In this fallen world, the things that trouble your good-yet-fallen brain may not be signs of sin in your life at all. They may simply be signs of a good-yet-fallen brain. What we then do with that—the thoughts we choose to entertain, the patterns we prayerfully relearn, the help we seek out—is where our moral and spiritual responsibility begins to come into play, and all of it—neurological, spiritual, and messy in-between—is overseen and cared about by a loving Father who knows us perfectly and walks the journey with us.

"Food for Thought" Questions

Questions for Reflection/Journaling

- What are some of the things I love about the brain and personality God gave me? What are some of the things about my brain and personality that are hard to deal with?
- What snares do I need to watch out for?
- Lord, are there ways right now—whether through professionals, friends and family, personal habits, or leaning into my relationship with you—that I can take good care of the mind you gave me?

Questions for Group Study

- What in this chapter surprised or encouraged you the most?
- What are some of the things that you've found helpful for your mental health? How have those affected your spiritual health? (Or vice versa: are there things you've done for your spiritual health that have helped your mental health?)
- What are some ways we can look out for our brothers and sisters and value their unique "wiring"?

5

It's Not That Weird

(Where is this guilt coming from?—Part 2)

The previous chapter addressed some of the neurological bases of guilt and shame. But not everything is inborn or "how your brain is wired." There are "nature" and "nurture" components to just about everything, including persistent guilt or shame.

So what about the struggles that don't stem from "nature"? Are *those* sinful? Are they symptoms, as many seem to claim, of a heart that just doesn't "get" grace, a sign that we're trying to be "justified by works"? These questions can cause incredible turmoil for some of our brothers and sisters, so we need to be careful about how we think and talk about this issue.

Churches rightly preach that salvation is "by grace alone, through faith alone."[59] We rightly declare that with Jesus, there is no need for guilt. But

59. This doctrine is based on many of Paul's writings and explanations, particularly the letters to the Romans and Galatians. (It was made famous in this phrasing by Martin Luther, but it's not a uniquely Protestant idea: he said it as a Catholic who was trying to remind his fellow Catholics of what they already believed.) It's an important part of Christian belief . . . and as soon as you mention it, someone is bound to ask "but what about James?!" James 2:17 famously says that "faith by itself, if it has no works, is dead" (NRSV). Much ink has been spilled over the interaction between faith and works—which one saves us?!—but it's really not as complicated as people make it seem. The context of *everything* God says to us, including what he says about faith and works, is relationship. Both trying to "earn" salvation by works *and* completely neglecting works reveal a lack of relationship, because both attitudes treat God like a check-box: either "I do all of the right things, so God will accept me: check," or "I prayed the 'prayer of faith' so now I'm saved. Check." But no real relationship works that way. No woman marries a man because he's good at taking out the trash: a couple is going to have marital problems if the husband thinks that's what their relationship consists of. But if he consistently ignores her when she asks him to take it out, saying "it doesn't matter; that's not why she married me," they're going to have some problems too! Love is not earned by works, but it *is* expressed by works—they're a "symptom" of

when we jump from here to the idea that "if you *do* feel guilty, maybe you don't fully believe in Jesus," we can create terrible crises of faith for people who are already suffering. The thinking goes something like this: "We're saved by trusting God's grace. But apparently I don't trust it *enough*, because I still feel guilty . . . so am I even really saved?"

First of all, if you're asking that question, you probably have nothing to worry about. Asking it means that you care—you *want* Jesus—and that you know you don't have all your ducks in a row on your own. Since Jesus promises to be found by those who are looking for him[60] and says that the spiritually helpless are blessed,[61] you pretty *exactly* fit the bill of those who throw themselves on his grace and are saved. So let's explore this, but know from the outset that your salvation is not in danger here.

When the Apostle Paul wrote to the Galatian church defending the doctrine of "grace alone," he was addressing a very specific issue: the question of whether Jesus was enough for salvation, or whether one *also* had to get circumcised and obey Jewish law. He's not actually talking about struggling with persistent feelings of guilt, nor is he accusing guilt-ridden people of "relying on works"—and it turns out there are a lot of really normal, sensible, not-sinful reasons someone may struggle.

For one thing, none of us has seen a perfect example of God's grace on this earth. Even if parents and teachers and church friends did an excellent job of modeling God's grace, none of them is *actually* God, and every metaphor breaks down at some point. All of them are going to make mistakes; none of them is going to give us a perfect blueprint of interacting with God. So all of us are going to be working through misunderstandings of grace as we grow in our relationships with God.

For instance, I happen to think that strictness is (by and large) a good thing: it's good for kids to have consistent feedback that helps them develop responsibility and a reliable sense of right and wrong. But if a caregiver is strict to the point where forgiveness and acceptance are in doubt, that will color a child's understanding. If a caregiver fails to make a distinction between mistakes and sins, treating mistakes as infractions . . . well, chances are a child is going to grow up afraid to make mistakes, and be merciless with herself over every perceived failure. Or if a caregiver doesn't accept

---

the relationship. God does indeed offer us this restored relationship completely free of charge, and nothing we have done could have earned it; all that James is pointing out is that if we don't show any *"symptoms"* of a relationship with God, we may rightly question whether the relationship is actually there.

60. See Jer 29:13; Luke 11:11–13.

61. See Matt 5:3; many translate it "poor in spirit," but the NIRV calls it "spiritually helpless."

apologies, leaving a child to wonder if and when he's been forgiven, chances are that child is going to have a hard time feeling forgiven by God too. On the other hand, if a caregiver completely throws strictness out the window, giving a child very few restrictions or consequences, chances are they're setting their child up to feel mistreated and condemned any time someone—whether a human authority or God—does require something more.

Or consider instead a child growing up with a volatile, inconsistent caregiver, as occurs in many homes affected by abuse or addiction. That child may develop a sense of conscience, but its signals will be "off." Their conscience will be full of inappropriate obligations such as "you have to keep Dad from getting angry, whatever it takes," instead of true moral standards. In fact, just about any boundary issue we grow up with will skew our sense of responsibility and fault—and *all of us* have boundary issues of one sort or another.[62] So *it's not that weird* that we sometimes struggle with inappropriate feelings of guilt.

It also makes sense when we consider the nature of learning. Frequently, we forget the role of learning: after all, the Bible and history are full of stories of people who responded to the gospel after their first hearing of it, and we all know of people who have had sudden and dramatic epiphanies. And so we often assume that once we've mentally accepted a truth, we should "know it" (with all of its logical implications falling neatly and automatically into line). Therefore, the assumption goes, any doubt or difficulty we have in *applying* that truth must be either because we don't truly believe it, or because we do believe and are refusing to live in accordance with it. But that's not how learning works.

Neurologically, we mostly learn through repetition. The basic principle of neuroplasticity (the ways in which the brain learns and changes) is "neurons that fire together wire together."[63] In other words, you can imagine the brain like a series of paths in the woods: the more often you walk down a certain path, the clearer the path will become—and the easier it will be to walk down it again. (The opposite is also true: an unused path will become overgrown and harder to find because of the lack of regular foot traffic.) This is part of why Jesus said that the merciful will receive mercy and that those

62. An indispensable book on this subject is *Boundaries: When to Say Yes, How to Say No to Take Control of Your Life* by Dr. Henry Cloud and Dr. John Townsend. Rooted deeply in Scripture and grounded in years of psychological study and practice, it is a resource that is helpful spiritually, emotionally, and relationally.

63. For fascinating and highly readable helpful information on this subject see Dr. Norman Doidge's *The Brain That Changes Itself: Stories of Personal Triumph from the Frontiers of Brain Science* as well as the works of Daniel Amen, MD.

who don't forgive others won't be forgiven by God.[64] Yes, it's a sobering call to mercy, but it's also simply a description of how things are. When we show mercy, we demonstrate to ourselves and others that God's mercy is real. Conversely, we will not experience God's forgiveness as "real" for ourselves if we keep declaring through our actions that it isn't real for others. In showing mercy, we practice the reality of God's mercy. This is also part of why we regularly celebrate Communion. Whatever your personal beliefs are about the nitty-gritty spiritual realities of the Eucharist, one of the *practical* realities is that it lets us regularly (and tangibly, and actively) practice our belief in the saving mercy of Jesus. It's the same reason that the writer of Hebrews tells us to "encourage each other every day,"[65] and why Paul tells us to "speak to one another with psalms, hymns, and songs from the Spirit."[66] With each trip down the path, the path gets clearer. And implicit in these commands—whether the command is to encourage one another or to observe the Lord's Supper—is the idea that *this is a learning process*. We wouldn't have to repeat them if learning the truth was a "one and done" thing. *It's not that weird* that we don't "get" Jesus' grace perfectly the first or even the seventh time; the very commands to practice the truth imply that we need the practice.

Of course, some of our struggles with guilt and grace come from the fact that . . . well, sometimes, quite frankly, we talk about them in stupid ways. I once heard a pastor preaching about shame. He talked how the church needs to be a place where people are safe admitting their sins and struggles, a place where people know they won't be condemned. Amen. He talked about how "Jesus was safe—*except* . . . for the hypocrite. He was not safe for the hypocrite." Good point. Jesus' teachings deeply challenge human nature, and our pet sins and judgments are not safe when they meet him. But then the pastor went on: "He *despised* people that faked a particular lifestyle, or actually carried out the Law but looked down on and despised others who didn't."[67]

Excuse me? Jesus *despised* . . . anyone? The one who came "not to condemn the world, but to save the world"[68] . . . *despised* certain individuals in that world? That isn't what the pastor meant (at least I hope not!). But it's what he said. And unfortunately, it's not an unusual thing to hear in the church.

64. See Matt 5:7; 6:14–15.

65. Heb 3:13 GW.

66. Eph 5:19 NIRV; see also Col 3:16.

67. Emphasis his. Normally I would include a citation to give credit where credit is due, but since I am calling him out I have chosen keep this pastor anonymous. Let's save the credit for nice things.

68. John 3:17b GW.

What his teaching failed to recognize is that *everyone* is hypocritical in some way. It ranges from the petty—parents teaching their children not to lie, while innocently shoving the freezer door shut, claiming "but we don't *have* any ice cream!"—to the nation-wide scandals of politicians and pastors touting "family values" and then being caught in affairs. Whether we're devoutly religious, and spend more time complaining about how others don't pray than praying ourselves, or whether we hold no religious or moral beliefs except the belief that you shouldn't judge people, and then soundly condemn "those judgmental people," *all* of us have a hypocrisy problem. All of us have looked down on those who don't conform to our ideas and ideals. *All* of us have moral beliefs, and *all* of us fail to fully live up to them. Paul expresses this universal problem succinctly: "I do the very thing I hate."[69] In fact, since we're all in the same boat here, we could even say that the common assumption that "some people are hypocritical and others aren't" is inherently hypocritical.

What this teaching also fails to recognize is that for those who are sensitive, or who have been called judgmental (whether fairly or not) or just happen to be aware of their own failings in the area of hypocrisy, this sort of language can do tremendous damage. It can give people the idea that there is a group of people Jesus despises. It can give people the idea that they need to be perfect in this *one* area before Jesus can love them. It can give people the idea that they're somehow outside of Jesus' grace, and even cause them to wonder if they're really Christians. (Ask me how I know this.)

Yes, Jesus spoke sharply to those who were hypocritical. Sometimes I need to speak sharply to my niece: because I don't want her to grow up into the kind of person who thinks it's OK to scratch her little brother's face when she's angry. But never because I despise her. We hate cancer because we love people. I hate seeing my niece act so ugly, because I love the beautiful, fantastic little human she is. And Jesus hates hypocrisy because he *loves hypocrites*. He doesn't want them to grow up into the kind of souls who think it's OK to point out their brothers' faults and ignore their own. He wants to cut the cancer out of our souls because, like all cancers, it distorts the beautiful creatures we were meant to be: ones that reflect the image and likeness of God.

Of course the pastor knew this. But he used stupid words to get his point across: words that were a product of and served to perpetuate the unquestioned culture we have in the church about all of this. We preach that "sin is sin" and that God doesn't "rank" sinners . . . but we don't often act like we mean it. We have our own personal rankings. In some churches, it's your

69. Rom 7:15 NRSV.

sexual temptations that make people question your commitment to Christ. In some, it's your politics, or your relationship with science. And in many, you'll receive the impression that if you struggle with hypocrisy—if you believe in standards you don't always carry out, or if you sometimes need an attitude adjustment towards the people around you—then you don't *truly* believe in Jesus yet. Given the way the church sometimes talks about this, *it's not that weird* that people struggle. Perhaps before we ask what's wrong with someone's faith that makes them feel despised by God, we ought to stop and ask *if we've been teaching them that God despises them.*

Lastly, it makes sense that many struggle with guilt, because one of the main things the Accuser attacks is our sense of being accepted by God. Nothing is more threatening to Satan than a Christian who knows God's love, and he'll use any low-down, underhanded trick he can—including exploiting our neurology, our past, our conversations, and the stupid things people say in church—to try to cast doubt on the efficacy of Jesus' mercy. Think about it: nothing the devil can do can *actually* harm us. When we are tempted we have the opportunity to express our love by obeying God anyway. When we suffer for being Christians, we find the joy of sharing in Jesus' sufferings; even if we are killed, we're really just given a ride Home. We are on the winning side of a war already won, and we are the bearers of God's power in the world: a thousand carrier pigeons set loose with his good news, a million seeds on the wind, spreading the Life that will sprout, spread, and crumble the kingdom of darkness into dust. We may be "jars of clay,"[70] but the treasure inside—God's very Spirit—is more powerful than we can even imagine, and Satan is *100 percent terrified.* It makes sense that he's going to throw rocks at those clay jars any time he can. And he's unfortunately clever.

He knows that if he can get us to believe that God condemns judgmental people, then we won't turn to God for help when we're having trouble loving or accepting someone. God *wants* to help us. God *likes* helping sinners: both those whose sins we judge, and those of us who sin by judging. The Holy Spirit wants to help us be there for others, supporting them in the knowledge that we have a common enemy of our souls and a common Helper. But if we think that Helper condemns us, we'll bypass that help. We'll wallow in shame, thinking we're unacceptable until we somehow produce divine love on our own. We won't be able to extend grace to others that we're not experiencing ourselves. We won't experience the kinship of fighting our battles side by side. Any way that Satan can get us believing that God condemns us, he can keep us from experiencing the joy that gives us strength for all trials. And if Satan can get us believing we're defective

70. 2 Cor 4:7.

Christians—hopelessly offensive or permanently on the wrong side of grace—then we'll often be too scared to share Jesus with nonbelievers, not because we're afraid of rejection or afraid God can't move their hearts, but because we're afraid of *ourselves*. (Ask me how I know this, too.)

It's bad enough being afraid of oneself, but I have found that ultimately, not trusting myself becomes a form of not trusting God. And that suits Satan's purposes very well. After all, why stop with making us miserable if he can also silence us and keep us from experiencing intimate friendship with God? With as high as the stakes are for him, *it's not that weird* that Satan would try to attack our security in God's love, forgiveness, and acceptance of us. And it's not that weird that this would cause us some significant struggles.

If you struggle with guilt, *it makes sense that you do.* There are a million reasons people struggle with guilt, not all of which have been exhausted above. This doesn't mean you should just accept it—far from it!—or that you shouldn't work to find its roots in your life and prayerfully reestablish your thought patterns. But neither does it mean that your guilt is your *fault* or the result of something you're "doing wrong." Most importantly, it does *not* mean that you're not saved.

Some time ago, I had a dream that I was leading people to my house, and when I rounded the final bend, it had disappeared: the landscape was entirely different, the street lined with houses I'd never seen before. "It's OK," I said to the people behind me, with some annoyance because I'd suspected this would happen, "it's just doing this because it's a dream. My house really is here." And sure enough, after I'd stubbornly closed my eyes for a few moments, my house reappeared, exactly where it should have been (with a few extra daffodils). Upon waking, I found myself wishing I acted like this in real life more often.

When your house disappears in your dream, it doesn't mean your house is gone. When all you feel is guilt and condemnation, it doesn't mean your faith is defective or your salvation is gone. It means that in the messed-up dream logic of this fallen world, sometimes we can't see the loving reality where Jesus meant for us to make our home. If that is your situation, first of all I'm sorry that it is. I've been there. Second, be patient. It doesn't mean you don't belong there, that you don't live there, or that you mistook the way to get there. And whether we're able to *feel* the truth our faith has accepted or not, there is still a Hand in ours, walking with us through all of our valleys and leading us home to the place where faith is truly sight.

The truth is that *none* of us understands grace perfectly. Even the people you look up to most, those whose great faith and understanding have shaped yours, don't have a full and complete picture of grace. Paul describes our knowledge of spiritual realities this way: "Now we see only a reflection as in a mirror; then we shall see face to face. Now I know in part; then I shall know fully, even as I am fully known."[71] And this is *Paul* we're talking about: Paul, to whom the resurrected Jesus had appeared;[72] Paul, through whom the Holy Spirit spoke nearly a third of the New Testament; Paul, who had experiences so profound he couldn't even recount them![73] If anyone could have claimed to fully "get it," it would be Paul. And yet he describes what we know so far of our loving and gracious God—*even with* the revelation of the Bible, *even with* the visions and prophecies Paul is talking about—as being a dim reflection, the way you sometimes see your own face reflected back from glass picture frames or lemonade pitchers. That is the hilarious and beautiful secret of Divine Grace: like a truly great work of art, nothing you've heard, seen, or read about it can prepare you for seeing it in person, just like you can read and study all you want to about parenting and psychology, talk to parents all you want, buy all the toys you want, and still nothing can prepare you for holding your baby in your arms for the first time.

The upshot of this, of course, is that understanding grace perfectly *cannot be* a prerequisite for receiving it. Not only would that be humanly impossible this side of eternity, but it wouldn't even be grace: if we had to attain this perfect understanding before God could accept us, then *God's* acceptance would depend on something *we* achieve, which is the exact opposite of what grace means. In fact, this subtle, unconscious belief is a sneaky backdoor way that Satan tries to convince us that God can't love us unless we fix ourselves. But the truth is and always has been that it's God who does the fixing, without any strength on our part. Our weakness isn't a barrier but a canvas for God's goodness . . . and I can't help but believe that the weaknesses of our hearts—the guilt and the misunderstandings and the painful inability to feel his love—are included in that. Like the man's blindness in John 9, these infirmities are not signs that we've sinned: they're opportunities for the healing power of Jesus to be displayed in us.

71. 1 Cor 13:12 TNIV. Before the 2011 revision, the NIV used to say "a poor reflection as in a mirror"; the ESV and others say that we see "dimly" or "darkly." In Paul's time, mirrors were often made of beaten metal; it was less like what we think of today as looking in a mirror and more like looking at a reflection in an oven door or on the side of a car.

72. Acts 9:1–6; 22:1–21; 26:9–18.

73. 2 Cor 12:1–7. Many believe that Paul himself is the "man" he talks about here, because of what he says in verse 7 about how these revelations could have caused him to become conceited. Whether it's the trip to heaven mentioned here or other revelations, he learned some pretty mind-blowing things from God.

I don't need a degree in music theory to know that Tchaikovsky's music is brilliant. The fact that I don't understand its brilliance perfectly doesn't keep me from loving it and listening to it. It doesn't even keep me from playing it, and here's the important thing to realize about that: the mistakes a musician makes while learning to play a piece of music *do not* mean that the musician doesn't believe in the beauty of the song, hasn't chosen to engage with the song, or isn't committed to playing the song well. They mean just the opposite.

If you don't understand grace perfectly yet, it doesn't mean you haven't accepted it—or aren't accepted *by* it. It doesn't mean you're hopeless, or that Jesus won't bring you into greater understanding. It means that the song is too beautiful and too transcendent for our fingers to play it right the first time.

"Food for Thought" Questions

Questions for Reflection/Journaling

- What are some of the skewed understandings of God, grace, or forgiveness that I have developed? Where did they come from? Are they truly "my fault," or is there another way to make sense of them?
- What doubts about myself cause me to avoid God? What methods do I use (hint: they're often good things!) for this avoidance? What is one thing today that I can take to God rather than keep from God?
- Lord, how are you calling me to remember and repeat the truth of your heart towards me?

Questions for Group Study

- What in this chapter surprised or encouraged you the most?
- What are the ideas you most often repeat? Are they healthy, unhealthy, or somewhere in between? Is there a truth that you want to put more into practice this week or this month?
- What do you look forward to understanding more fully as you get to know God better, (and someday perfectly, face to face)?

6

Awkward Questions

(What does Jesus really have to do with my guilt?)

Do you ever find yourself with questions you don't like to admit you have? I sure do. And sometimes they've been about what Jesus did for us, which can be a little awkward considering that the doctrines surrounding Jesus' death and resurrection are . . . well, *the* central doctrines of our faith. (Of course, it's worth pointing out that the more important something is to us, the more our questions about it bother us—so if you find yourself wrestling and struggling with your questions about God, it may actually be a *good* sign: a sign that you care.)

The first awkward question—really the problem I had with Jesus for a long time—had to do with his goodness. It wasn't that I thought his goodness would cause him to judge me; I knew he's merciful. However, I did have a problem: in addition to being told that Jesus is perfect, I was also told that he understands us because, as fully human, he's gone through all of the same things we do.[74] Now, I happen to have a brain that latches on really easily to the feeling that something's wrong (thanks, OCD). For most of my life, I've felt at least some level of guilt most of the time. This made it pretty impossible for me to reconcile this whole "Jesus gets me" claim with the "Jesus is perfect" doctrine. How could he possibly understand me if the primary thing I feel is the one thing he can't relate to? How could a God who's never experienced guilt ever know what it's like to be me? The other awkward question—and this one is kind of embarrassing—was, well . . . what's so special about Jesus dying?

74. This includes temptation. See Heb 2:17–18 and 4:15 as well as the Gospel narratives of his temptation in the wilderness recorded in Matt 4:1–11, Mark 1:12–13, and Luke 4:1–13.

After all, lots of people die. In fact, everybody dies; death is one of the few things that has a 100 percent mortality rate. And lots of people suffer, many for longer periods of time than Jesus did on the cross. (For instance, one of my favorite people in the world has been in crippling pain for over twenty-five years.) Of course, looking at the details of what his execution entailed, I can't imagine a more painful experience . . . but still, there's no guarantee that his was *the* most physically painful death in history; the Bible never says that. Physically, his death was awful, but it wasn't unique. And that feels awkward to say.

Jesus didn't *only* suffer physically—but then, he's certainly not the only one to have suffered emotionally, either. Lots of people suffer injustice—some deeply and for their entire lives. (Those of us who have been very grounded in doctrines such as "there is none righteous"[75] may balk at this statement—after all, if we all deserve hell, how can we call anything that we suffer "unjust"?—but just because we've earned God's punishment, it doesn't follow that we deserve every bad thing that happens to us. Hell is a direct result of our rebellion against God, but there are plenty of unfair things in our lives that are completely disconnected from anything we've done. In fact, a big part of the reason the Bible gives for humans deserving hell in the first place is the injustice they commit against one another.) Indeed, if we consider that sin is something that morally should not happen, something that is morally not right—in other words, something that is unjust—then *all* of us have suffered injustice, repeatedly. Lots of people even suffer betrayal, as Jesus did; we wouldn't have nearly so many divorces if betrayal wasn't shockingly commonplace—and that only covers the subset of betrayal within *marriage*, let alone the betrayals of friends and business partners and family members. Not only that, but many suffer for longer than Jesus did: many who suffer from mental illness or broken families or abuse suffer for years and years on end, not just the one day that we call the Passion. So, (although it may sound irreverent to ask it), what *is* so special about what Jesus did?

The great thing about having questions that don't get answered right away is that the longer you ask, the deeper your relationship gets. The more you knock on his door, the more you get into the habit of coming to his house. Our questions draw us to seek him; those who seek him find him[76]; and when by his grace we do come to greater understanding, it's not just that the answer means more to us than if it had come easily . . . it's that *he* means more to us. And I believe the answers to both of my awkward

75. See Rom 3:10.

76. See Luke 11:9–13; Jer 29:13.

questions—and probably a lot of our other questions too—lie in a question Jesus himself asked.

While he was on the cross, close to the point of death, Jesus cried out, "My God, my God, why have you abandoned me?"[77] If any question qualifies as an awkward, embarrassing, pounding-on-God's-door type of question, this is it. Even with the redemptive themes later in the psalm he's quoting, there is no mistaking the raw agony in this question.

Here's the thing: there's such a thing as spiritual pain. Certainly, Jesus suffered much physically and emotionally—and indeed, there *are* aspects of those that are unique by virtue of his identity. For instance, he is the only one who could have chosen *not* to have a physical body that could suffer pain, which makes his physical death unique. He also had no sin limiting his capacity to love, which means he had a greater capacity to be hurt by those he loves, which makes his emotional suffering unique. It's the spiritual pain he suffered, however, that I think is key.

Look back in Genesis at the very first murder. Cain killed his brother Abel and lied to God's face about it. God should have utterly turned away from him, and didn't.[78] Look back at David, who, after being raised from total obscurity to the royal throne (*by* God), used his God-given power to sexually exploit a woman and murder her husband: God should have utterly turned away, and didn't.[79] Look at the Israelites going into exile: they had turned their backs on God, and God should have turned his back on them, but didn't; in fact Israel's entire history is one of God refusing to ever fully turn away.[80] Ezekiel, one of the prophets sent to those very exiles, ex-

77. Matt 27:46; Mark 15:34 NLT; see also Ps 22:1, which he was quoting.

78. This story is recounted in Gen 4. Strikingly, when God gives him the "mark of Cain" in response to his fear-filled protest against his exile, it is not a mark of curse but of protection: in fact, with scandalous grace, God gives him this mark to prevent Cain from suffering the very same violence that Cain himself had committed.

79. David's rise from shepherd to king of Israel is recounted in 1 and 2 Sam, beginning in 1 Sam 16 when David, the youngest of seven brothers, is anointed as Israel's next king by the prophet Samuel. His sinful encounter with Bathsheba is recorded in 2 Sam 11, with God's rebuke through the prophet Nathan following in the next chapter. Although many times this has been portrayed very sensuously as an affair, the text doesn't actually indicate that it was consensual, nor that Bathsheba had been "trying" to seduce anyone (since flat rooftops were one of the only private and practical places to bathe in an ancient city with rudimentary-at-best plumbing). Indeed, with the power dynamic at play here—David being king, Bathsheba being not only a woman in a patriarchal society but also the wife of a foreigner whose career David controlled—it can be argued that this *could not* have been entirely consensual, and that by its very nature David's sending for Bathsheba was coercive.

80. See the establishment of the covenant with Israel in Deut 27—30, in which God clearly details the blessings that will come with following the covenant, the exile and

pressed God's outlook in this way: "Do I take any pleasure in the death of the wicked? declares the Sovereign LORD. Rather, am I not pleased when they turn from their ways and live?"[81] The Bible is full, cover to cover, of this picture of God as never being willing to give up on people, always being ready to forgive. All of the judgments on Israel were prompts calling them to come back to him, and all of the animal sacrifices year after year were so that human evil could be taken away and didn't have to count against them.

But here's where it gets sticky: it counts against *somebody*. God would be a monster if he said that all of the horrible things we do to each other and to Creation and to him just "don't count." To put it another way, any environmentalist will tell you our trash doesn't just disappear; *something* must be done with it. And just shipping it off to another poorer country doesn't cut it (even though, heaven forgive us, we do that). So this cycle of piling up sin year after year and shipping it off on these animal sacrifices, and God yet again choosing to forbear and to not turn away, can't go on indefinitely; a reckoning *has* to come. But it never had, up until that point.

That's what's different.

All those times that God should have turned away and didn't, it wasn't because "God just doesn't do that"—it was because Jesus is the one he did it to. Jesus was the only one who *didn't* receive God's patience; Jesus was the only one who *didn't* receive God's second chances; Jesus was the only one who truly and fully experienced God turning away. That is hell, and the only reason we have a chance not to experience it is because Jesus did. That is a spiritual pain I can't even imagine. (We haven't even *touched* on how much worse that pain would be for a member of the Trinity, who is one with the One rejecting him—a pain that includes not only being rejected by someone who has loved him longer and more closely than any mere human can imagine, but also knowing that his suffering breaks the heart of someone so close to him. This, again, is a way in which Jesus' *identity* deepens each aspect of his pain).

That is what is special about Jesus dying.

Here's the other thing: God doesn't operate purely theoretically. For instance, the Bible says that a husband and wife are "one;"[82] this *sounds* like a theoretical statement, but it actually enters the real world in some incredibly

---

suffering that will come in response to rejecting the covenant, and the promise that even then, there is still hope for redemption and restoration. The exile is narrated in 2 Kgs 17 and 24—25 as well as in 2 Chr 36, and virtually all of the prophetic books wrestle through this dynamic of God's people breaking their relationship with God and suffering that brokenness, and yet God still not being absent.

81. Ezek 18:23 TNIV.

82. See Gen 2:24; Matt 19:4–6.

tangible ways. Not only did God give this union a physical expression, which in turn has a physical, neurological effect on the brain, but this seemingly theoretical "oneness" also has huge and far-reaching emotional, relational, and societal effects (including, sometimes, children—who are indisputably, loudly, and stickily tangible). And this makes sense, if we think about it: God is the Creator of the whole of reality—physical, spiritual, everything—and so why would we expect God to remain in the theoretical realm? You can't say "stay in your lane" to the person who made all the lanes.

This means that when we say "Jesus bore our sins," it is not some legal fiction where God shuffled some numbers around on a divine accounting ledger, or signed some form, saying "yeah OK, sure, his death counts for them." It means in some very real way he *bore* our sins: physically, emotionally, spiritually. That turning away, that rejection by God, was not theoretical; it was something Jesus fully and consciously experienced. Which means—and it sort of blew my mind when I realized this—that Jesus *does* know what guilt feels like. He actually knows it more than I ever will, because he bore it for the whole world.

More than that, because he bore *my* sin, he knows what *my* guilt feels like: the pain, the shame, the self-horror, those times I hurt my sister's feelings or was cruel to a creature that didn't deserve it. He knows what *your* deepest regret feels like, that thing that just makes you cringe every time you think of it. He knows not just "what it's like"; he knows *that*. He bore *that* specific sin, and the guilt and pain of it; he knows that specific regret from the inside.

This has some big implications.

Do you ever secretly think something like "Jesus died for the whole world, but it wasn't really for *me;* I just kind of sneaked in with the crowd when he wasn't looking"? *That doesn't hold water with a Savior who is not theoretical.*

But the implications go further. If Jesus bore my specific guilt, this means that he and he alone knows how I feel. When a person sins, others may suffer from it, but what they feel is usually the pain of the victim, not the perpetrator. Or if someone does in some way feel a measure of my pain as a perpetrator, out of some deep compassion for me, what they are feeling is empathy, not the guilt itself. Even in the case of shared guilt—for instance, if I'd had a partner in crime who is party to and guilty of the same act as I am—what they would be feeling is their own guilt for the crime, not mine. All of these people are affected by my sin, but they experience it from the outside. *Only Jesus* knows my guilt from the inside.

This also means, incredibly, that when it comes to my specific guilt, *I* am the only one who knows what *he* feels. No one else has shared this with him, or ever will. Only I can offer him the sympathy of having "been there" when it comes to these specific events.

This is infinitely more intimate friendship than I ever expected out of Christ. These are the indelible sort of bonds that are formed between soldiers on the battlefield: shared suffering that others could not possibly know. These are the sort of bonds between a husband and wife: knowledge of the other that is not transferrable to anyone else, even by telling them. Not only did he choose to enter into the suffering of my guilt and know me as no one else could, but in breathtaking vulnerability he allows me to know, love, comfort, and sympathize with him as no one else could in regard to these events.

And what comfort I wish I could give him! I once heard someone joke, "Of *course* babies cry all the time: any discomfort they feel is literally the worst thing that has ever happened to them!" I have had occasion to experience guilt over and over in my life, and it still is one of the worst pains I have ever experienced. How much worse must it have been for Jesus, who had never gotten used to it! Teresa of Ávila speaks of keeping Jesus company in his suffering, saying that when we are suffering we should ". . . look upon Him bending under the weight of the cross and not even allowed to take breath: He will look upon you with His lovely and compassionate eyes, full of tears, and in comforting your grief will forget His own because you are bearing Him company in order to comfort Him and turning your head to look upon Him."[83] And yet I find that when it comes to guilt, as I turn to him in that spirit of camaraderie, saying "I've been there," I cannot offer him the comfort I would wish. I wish, as the one more experienced with guilt, that I could offer him a hand up, like an expert hiker guiding someone up a difficult stretch of trail, or a word of comfort, like the grim senior encouraging the freshman, "Yeah, the first semester's hard, but it gets better."

But I can't. Because I *do* know guilt, and I know it doesn't get better. Without someone to take it away, guilt doesn't fade: it festers and tortures and lives just as strong as the day it was incurred. The only comfort I can give anyone about guilt is that Jesus took it away. And there is no one to take it away for Jesus.

Of course, guilt didn't win—he rose without it—but he only rose without it because he first endured it fully, to death. So as I turn my eyes towards him bearing my guilt, the only comfort I can offer is the presence of myself . . . and here is where the mystery gets really deep: he considers my presence a comfort. The reason he intimately shared the worst moments of my life

83. Teresa of Ávila, *Way of Perfection*, 175.

with me—bearing my sin to restore me to God—is because he thought it a worthwhile exchange for having me around.

I will be trying to understand this for the rest of my life.

You're not always going to *feel* forgiven. You're not always going to be able to help your feelings of guilt or abandonment; you're not always going to feel special to God. But do not ever believe—do not entertain the thought—that you don't matter to God. Or that somehow what Jesus did doesn't count for you.

Because echoing through our very real history is history's most awkward, arresting, awe-inspiring question: the cry of a Savior on a cross feeling your guilt, experiencing your forsakenness, and literally going through hell so he could be the one to open the door, invite you home, and live with you forever. And could it be that the reason history remembers it forever as a question . . . is because *we* are being called upon to respond?

Veronica

I know not if imagination's eye
or history's stone beheld her by your road,
but if imagined, I at least know why
the saints desired through her to wipe your blood.
For that is *my* guilt bearing you quite down,
and well, too well, I know the awful weight
that you—poor innocent!—discover now,
and I at least must come commiserate.
How strange, thou Ancient One and Son of Man
that I the more experienced should be
in this alone—and so I'll take your hand;
though, unlike you, I give no remedy.
For you, the Cure, have none to take your place—
But I who know these tears shall wipe your face.[84]

84. The title of this sonnet is a reference to the church tradition about St. Veronica, the woman who is said to have wiped Jesus' face when he stumbled under his cross on the way to his execution. I wrote it because as I meditated on the ideas in this chapter, I found that I needed not just to pray or journal, but somehow to attempt to express the wonder through worship. (For those who aren't into poetry, I apologize. I find that both poetry and opera are like sin: I don't really like when someone else does it, but I can't help doing it myself).

"Food for Thought" Questions

Questions for Reflection/Journaling

- Is there a sin that I've been too afraid or ashamed to bring to Jesus? Can I do it now, knowing that he already knows firsthand the guilt and pain of that sin?
- In what ways have I been thinking of Jesus theoretically? Why? How does it change my perspective to realize that Jesus' suffering was *real?*
- What are some of my awkward questions? Can I bring them to Jesus, knowing that someone who bore such painful and personal things for me can be trusted with them?
- Lord, you have shared some very painful things with me. What good things do you also want to share together to deepen our friendship?

Questions for Group Study

- What in this chapter surprised or encouraged you the most?
- What hesitations do you have about believing that Jesus wants to be your friend that intimately? What small steps can we take this week towards believing it?
- Are there times you've wondered what's special about Jesus' sacrifice? How would you answer that question in your own words?

7

The Monkey Button

(What does Jesus have to do with my shame?)

Did you know that monkeys hate saltwater? It's true. They hate saltwater; they love juice.

So one day a scientist got it into his head to map the monkeys' brains with PET Scan imaging, as scientists tend to do. He taught the monkeys that when a screen flashed blue, they were going to get juice, but if they were offered a syringe, it would be full of saltwater. As you might expect, the pleasure centers of the brain lit up with the juice, and other areas—the kind that govern disgust and things like that—lit up with the saltwater.

Well, one day he switched it on them. The hopeful little monkeys saw the beloved blue signal . . . and got a mouthful of saltwater. *And an entirely different part of the brain lit up.* This wasn't the "Hooray, juice!" area nor the "Yuck, saltwater!" area that lit up; this was the "Hey—that's wrong!" area.[85] Before we move on to less fun topics than monkeys, let's take a moment to appreciate this. Isn't it amazing—isn't it useful and fascinating and great—that God has given our brains a mechanism to recognize "Hey, that doesn't fit"? In order to make the world a better place, in order to learn and grow, in order to correct dangerous conditions or even just simple mistakes, we first need to be able to identify when something isn't right.

When that mistake-detector finds something wrong *in who we are*, we feel what is called shame. Shame is one of the most difficult emotions it is possible to experience—and interestingly, psychologists have no agreed-upon definition of what it is.[86] In the Western world, it's seen as entirely negative: it hurts, and we don't like things that hurt; it criticizes when we

85. Ratey and Johnson, *Shadow Syndromes*, 311. This anecdote is taken from the work of E.T. Rolls at Oxford University.

86. Tracy, *Mending the Soul*, 74.

generally expect our identities and choices to be celebrated. Eastern cultures, on the other hand, see it as something that has its appropriate place in life. As a Korean colleague of mine explained it, "we view shame just like any other reward or punishment you would use to raise a child." For the purposes of this discussion, we can think of shame as a more sophisticated form of the monkeys' inner "Hey that's wrong!" button: shame is the response of the mind and soul when it seems like something in us *morally doesn't fit.*

And that makes some sense, doesn't it? Sometimes the things we do *don't* fit with who we want to be or should be. God has given us a mechanism for recognizing when that's happening—and thank God for that! Without that capacity, we'd never be motivated to change. Think of our capacity for physical pain: when you step on a nail in your yard, it's better to know "something isn't right" and have something prompting you to take care of it than to get tetanus and then lockjaw, and then die. Shame is a pain of the soul that functions the same way: something that says, "Whoa, this isn't right: let's do something about it." Yes, certainly, it hurts. But that's why it works.

The Bible indicates that our capacity for shame is important. The prophet Jeremiah repeatedly expressed great concern about those who lose that capacity.[87] Centuries later, the apostle Paul expressed this same concern, warning Timothy about people whose "consciences have been scarred as if branded with a red-hot iron."[88] The Psalms frequently call down shame on those who need its correcting power—the arrogant, the deceitful, the hate-filled, those who prey on others.[89] Psalm 83 in particular spells out why: "so that they will seek you [God]."[90] No one likes it when the check-engine light goes on. But it's an important light to have—and it's certainly better than having no idea that something is wrong until you're stranded by the side of the road.

Now, it's important to note that, just like a flashing dashboard light, healthy shame is a *signal*, not a *solution*. Unlike a dashboard light, though, this signal is *not* meant to say "just fix this and it'll all be fine." Healthy shame, as it's supposed to work, should point us back toward Jesus. Go back for a moment to that image of stepping on a nail: just obeying the pain signal to get the nail out won't fix the problem. You need a doctor to treat it. You need to clean up your yard so you don't step on another. You need friends to help

87. See Jer 3:3, 6:15, 8:12, 13:27.

88. 1 Tim 4:2 GW.

89. See Pss 25:3; 35:4, 26; 40:14–15; 70:2–3; 71:13, 24; 83:16–17; 109:28–29; 119:78; 129:5.

90. Ps 83:16 NIRV.

you while you're hobbling around, and you need other friends to help you clean up the yard, because they might see nails that you missed from where you're standing. Healthy shame is supposed to lead us to repentance, but it's much more holistic than just, "Hey stop that!" Healthy shame is meant to lead us to Jesus, to his family, and to healthier patterns of living.

I know from my own experience that my capacity for shame has helped me. I can remember thinking, "When I get to heaven, people are going to see this. They're going to know if I was *actually* compassionate, or if I just did nice things because I wanted people to think I was kind." I wasn't at all afraid that God would reject me for not having pure intentions . . . but boy, would I be embarrassed to show up in heaven like that! Thinking about facing my friends and my heroes in heaven (not to mention facing *Jesus*) while wearing my tacky intentions like ill-advised sequins was enough to make me pause for an attitude adjustment. Likewise, there have been times when the pain of past mistakes has kept me from doing something similar again.

However, not all shame is healthy.

Some of it is really, really unhealthy—the sort of thing that dominates one's life and stifles it for months or years or even a whole lifetime.

Usually that unhealthiness comes when the *pain* of shame is disconnected from the *purpose* of shame. Remember: shame is a mechanism that allows us to identify and address the things that don't fit with who God means us to be. So to be healthy, shame must be based on legitimate standards, and it must be a *temporary* pain leading to positive changes. When you're feeling bad about something that wasn't your fault, or that you've already changed, or isn't really a sin, (*or* is such a treasured sin that you'd rather live with the pain than let it go) . . . well, then shame can't do its job of prompting repentance. That's when shame becomes unhealthy—and because shame is so powerful at its job, it becomes powerfully destructive when it's *not* doing its job right.

Where Did This Shame Come From?

Unhealthy shame is powerful because it infects your identity.[91] That means it can affect virtually every area of how you move through the world, precisely because it affects your idea of *who and what you are*. And it doesn't have to come from some horribly abusive situation or a terrible trauma; there are about a million and sixteen sources of toxic shame.

91. Toxic shame is a term I'm borrowing from Steven Tracy, and I owe much of my understanding of the topic to his work.

Sometimes it comes from the voices of mockery or disapproval—and those can be from really long ago without losing much, if any, of their power. Adults don't often take middle school drama seriously, but it's a very formative time of life.[92] Someone laughing at the pettiest of things—your dorky braces or your dorky clothes, whether you answered a question right, being short for your age—can stay with you well into adulthood because it's an attack on *you* at the very time when you're forming your ideas of who you are and how you can expect the world to treat you. But as Jesus himself mentioned,[93] you have no control over things like how tall you are. When people ridicule you for these sorts of things, shame can't do its job of prompting change, because these are things that (a) we can't change anyway, and (b) are based on a false standard—one that isn't God's.

Sometimes our shame stems from our customary temptations. We've all got them: certain sins that are just way more tempting to us than they are to others. But there are two problems here: we tend to think of some sins as worse than others, and we don't always make the distinction between being tempted and sinning. So my friend may feel more shame—and be looked down on more—for having an ongoing struggle with certain sexual temptations, *even if she doesn't act on them*, than I am for *actually giving in* to my inclinations to work too much or to find my comfort and security in chocolate or to seek my glory instead of God's. Depending on how our particular ongoing temptations are viewed, we may feel a lot of shame about them—but shame can't really do anything useful about a *temptation* because there's actually nothing to repent of if you're not giving in to it. Matthew Henry, speaking of Jesus' temptation, wrote, "The best of saints may be tempted by the worst of sins. . . . This is their affliction, but while there is no consent to it, . . . it is not their sin; Christ was tempted to worship Satan."[94]

Now, I know some of you will say, "but I actually did give in to temptation." Many people experience toxic shame because they feel that "my sin is too wrong for God to forgive." But the Bible indicates that the sin of *each of us* was why Jesus had to die. That means *each of us* is responsible for murdering God's Son: and that's absolutely the worst sin there is. So if God's forgiveness is enough for anyone—your pastor, your neighbor, your librarian—then it is enough for you. This idea that "*my* sin is too bad" is simply not true, and it gets in the way of our ability to move forward by telling us repentance and forgiveness aren't possible.

92. I am, again, indebted to Steven Tracy's work for pointing this out.

93. Matt 6:27—while most translations say something like "Can worrying add a single hour to your life?" it can also be translated "Can worrying add a single cubit to your height?"

94. Henry, *Commentary*, 38. (This is from his comments on Matt 4:9).

Other times, our shame comes from false comparisons. In 1 Corinthians 12, Paul talks about how different Christians are like different parts of a body—and some of those parts are, quite frankly, flashier than others. Paul warns us against comparing ourselves based on what the world values. Sometimes people see a beautiful, dazzling smile and envy that person's perfect teeth. But guess what's keeping your every cell supplied with oxygen? (Hint: It's not the teeth.) Guess what's allowing you to read these words and taste your coffee and feel joy? It's the ugly, squishy, grayish brain, an organ that no one ever even sees because its whole existence is spent behind the scenes in your skull. There are some aspects of my life that make some people think that my gifts are "cool" gifts, and that their own are comparatively "lame." There are other aspects of my life that make me a complete joke in American society. I have a choice: either to compare myself to my friends who are gifted differently and in different life situations, and feel like a loser, or to say, "This is where I belong in the body, even if sometimes it looks like an armpit." In the beautiful body of Christ, there is no place for shame—at least, I don't know about you, but *I'm* not comfortable telling Jesus that his body is shameful!

So if I've counted correctly—and I may not have, because I'm bad at math, (which is a real shame . . .)—that leaves a million and twelve other sources of unhealthy shame. Some of it comes from the insensitive ways Christians sometimes talk, or just not having anyone around to model forgiveness and acceptance. Some of it comes from old family patterns or disappointment in ourselves we just can't let go of. Wherever it comes from, it's all related to this idea that "This is indelibly who I am, and *who I am is bad.*"

Before moving on to what to *do* with all of this, it's worth mentioning two subsets of toxic shame, because they've got some unique things going on. The first is shame stemming from trauma—and this subset really deserves an entire chapter of its own from someone with much more training than I have.[95] In brief, it results from the mind's flawed way of trying to protect us: if what happened to me is somehow my fault, then I could have avoided it, which means I have at least *some* control and can keep it from happening again. It's also a defense mechanism that others use—"if it's her fault, then it can't happen to me"—the problem being that this heaps more shame on the survivor. In addition, abusers also often blame the survivor in order to avoid their own pain about their shameful actions. This is the language of "I'm sorry *but*": "I'm sorry, but you just made me so mad;" "I'm sorry, but *you* weren't submitting." It's the language of "She tempted me; *she*

95. And it got it. It's chapter 5 of *Mending the Soul* by Steven Tracy, and I owe virtually all of the information in this paragraph to his work.

caused me to stumble," or "Come on, she totally wanted it." People who have experienced trauma and abuse are frequently carrying toxic shame from their own psychological defenses *and* the defenses of all the people around them *and* the defenses of their abuser—and none of that shame "belongs" to them. None of it is a healthy warning light about something they've done wrong. It's borrowed, and it's unfair, and if this sort of shame is part of your story, I am so sorry. I know this is a really hard discussion. Please know that the shame of what happened *doesn't belong to you.* It belongs to the one who did it, and to the One who took our shame.

The other subset—and this may sound strange—is when we're ashamed of feeling ashamed. Here's how this one works: some of us struggle deeply with shame, for any of the above reasons or even seemingly for *no* reason (as can happen in OCD, in which that monkey button gets stuck and warns that something is wrong *all the time).* Often Christians will respond to this by saying, "But Jesus forgives you, so you don't have to feel ashamed anymore." Which is true. However . . . if you still struggle, they start talking to you like you don't really "get" the gospel. I don't know how many times I've been told "But you see, it's not by works!" The implication is that something is wrong with your faith, and if you *really* believed in Jesus, you wouldn't feel this way. When I was younger, very well-meaning people helped to nearly destroy my faith because I thought, "I must not actually trust Jesus."

The Power of Shame

So why does Satan love shame so much?

Satan loves shame because it's powerfully isolating. Shame says, "You're unlovable, and you should hide." When Adam and Eve were created, the Bible says that they "were both naked, and were not ashamed."[96] After they rebelled against God, they suddenly became aware of their nakedness and they hid—*not* because they suddenly realized there was something shameful about their bodies, but because nakedness is a form of being *known.* The human body that God created, in all of its intricacy and wonder (and yes, sexuality), is not shameful. The decisions humans make are. And as soon as that first shameful decision happened in the human heart, being known was no longer joyful and comfortable. Being known felt wrong and scary, enough to make us run even from those who love us. When we live in shame, it's not that God doesn't accept us; it's that *we won't come near enough to experience* that acceptance. When we live in shame, we don't experience healing or deep relationship with Jesus, and we don't get to battle spiritually

96. Gen 2:25 NRSV.

for his kingdom—not because he doesn't have those things for us, but because he is the source of those things, and we can't bring ourselves to come to him. The gospel is *mighty,* and if Satan can get you believing "Jesus died for everyone . . . but not me" and "Jesus loves everyone . . . but not me," then he can keep you from living the joyful, victorious life God has for you.

Satan loves shame because it keeps the focus painfully on you. It's really hard to reach out to love others when your mind is consumed by how disappointing you are, or when you think you're too awful to be around people. Satan loves shame because it can get you so resentful of *un*fair shame that you're not willing to hear true correction. Satan loves shame because we easily turn to sinful means to dull the pain—substance abuse, unhealthy relationships, self-harm, and even belittling and abusing others so we can feel less worthless ourselves.

The enemy comes to steal and kill and destroy,[97] and Satan loves shame because it keeps you in pain, and it keeps you alone.

So How Does Jesus Fit In?

Some of you have probably guessed that the Christian answer to shame is going to be Jesus—but how? What does Jesus have to do with our shame? Some of you have probably also guessed that the answer is going to have something to do with Jesus dying on the cross—but how does that actually connect?

Christians believe that Jesus never did wrong, but that he bore all of our wrongs on the cross. In a letter to an ancient church, Paul described it this way: "God made him who had no sin to be sin for us, so that in him we might become the righteousness of God."[98] Did you catch that? He who "knew no sin"[99] was made to *be* sin. That is the language of identity. That is the language of traumatic loss of innocence.

Jesus was punished for our sin: he joined us in our legitimate shame.

Jesus *became* sin, had his identity invaded with all the ugliness of sin: he joined us in our identity-infecting toxic shame.

Jesus was mocked and ridiculed, beaten, and publicly exposed (which is a form of sexual abuse): he joined us in our traumatic shame.

Jesus was cut off from God[100]: he joined us in our religious shame.

97. See John 10:10a.

98. 2 Cor 5:21 TNIV.

99. This is how other translations like NRSV render the beginning of the verse.

100. Matt 27:46; Mark 15:34.

Here's the cool part: what happens when you squish two people into something that was only built for one? It breaks. Shame cannot accommodate another person who loves you, because its power to isolate is gone. By joining us in our shame, Jesus broke shame. Because he died carrying our shame, we *know* beyond a shadow of a doubt that Jesus knows how our shame feels—specifically my shame, specifically your shame—he bore *that specific* shame. And because he rose from the dead, we *know* he is stronger than that shame.

Shame says, "You're too unlovable for anyone to come near you; there's no room for love." Love says, "I'm *going* to come near you; there's no room for shame." Shame shrinks your world; Jesus brings the massive love of God into that cage and cracks it from the inside.

That's what the cross—and the empty tomb—has to do with our shame.

Jesus also affects our shame because he is Truth, and speaks truth to us by his Spirit. By his actions, Jesus proves the truth about what God thinks of us. You don't pay good money for something worthless or irredeemable; you certainly don't die for it. By sending Jesus, God set your value *at the value of God's son*. Jesus' actions prove God's definition of your identity. But this truth thing isn't just a one-time job Jesus did; he continues to speak truth as we grow. The Spirit of Jesus inside us affirms that we are God's children,[101] invites us into change when we need it, and is gentle with both our sins and our wounds.

Let me be clear about that invitation to change: it is good news. Whether we're suffering under a sinful pattern or a not-sinful-but-still-painful mindset, the truth sets us free. This means we don't have to be stuck with false beliefs that have kept us ashamed. It means we don't have to worry and wallow in shame in an attempt to discover all our hidden sins and blind spots. God already knows, already forgave us, and can be trusted tell us the truth when we need to know it. It does *not* mean that just when you're starting to poke your head out of your shame-burrow God's going to slap you back down with some list of everything you're doing wrong. Any voice that belittles and despises you is never the voice of God. Jesus already bore our punishment, so he has no need or desire to punish us further by chewing us out or holding our failures over our heads. The Spirit may gently say, "Hey, there's something wrong here," but will never follow that up with "and until you fix it you're disgusting to me." There *is* a voice that says things like that—and it often tries to masquerade as Jesus—but that is the voice that Jesus defeated on the cross.

101. Rom 8:16.

As if that wasn't enough, Jesus breaks our isolation. The Bible describes Christians as being adopted into God's family[102]—and that's a big family! When you're saved by Jesus, you share a bond unlike any other with others who have been saved. You're never alone: you belong. You're not just in a community, but in a family full of people who are imperfect just like you. And no, they're not always going to handle your wounds perfectly . . . but you have people who understand and who can walk through that imperfection with you.

What does Jesus have to do with our shame? He wears it and tears it like a too-small jacket. He refutes it in action and word. And he "places the lonely in families."[103]

But I'm Still Experiencing Shame

I'm sure we would all like to believe that Jesus comes in and handles our shame and we all live happily ever after (and Christians sometimes give that impression, God forgive us). But if that's ever the case, I'd venture to say that it's the case for a very, very small percentage of people. Most of us are revisited by shame at various points, often quite strongly. So what do we do with our toxic shame *then?*

First of all, if you are dealing with trauma-related shame, please know that it is worth addressing, and that you don't have to do it alone. You should also know that this book is not the place to find professional advice; I do not specialize in the treatment of trauma, but there are plenty of therapists and ministries that do.[104] For all of us, no matter the source of our toxic shame, there are some steps we can take that are helpful.

The first is to accept the companionship Jesus offers. Darkness shrivels in the light; shame shrivels when you let people into it. When you let people in, shame loses its most potent power, the power of isolation. So spend time with Jesus, letting him into the deep places of who you are. And take a first step of honesty: there are Christians around you who would be more than happy to hear your struggles, pray through them with you, and be there for

102. John 1:12; Rom 8:15; Gal 4:5; Eph 1:5; 1 John 3:1.

103. Ps 68:6 NLT.

104. Mending the Soul Ministries (mendingthesoul.org) is one of these ministries, started by Steven Tracy, author of the book by the same name. He notes that while therapy is helpful, it is not always his first recommendation, since not everyone has easy access to therapy. If you can find a good therapist in your area or online, that is wonderful; even if you can't, Tracy recommends taking small steps into safe community, noting that healing happens not with a single person but within community.

you, but you don't know that about them until you actually share. When you do, you'll often find that it frees others up to share too.

Another step is to consider where your identity lies—and I mean both types of "lies": consider where it is placed, and consider where it is false. Some of our shame comes from fearing what other people think of us. Well, they don't get to tell you who you are or what's in your heart. Jesus is the only place big enough and steady enough to rest the foundation of your identity. And according to the Bible, your primary identity is someone created in the image of God[105] who is loved enough by God to be worth Jesus coming to earth and dying.[106] If you have trusted your life to Jesus, the Bible goes on to give further details about your identity: you are someone who is washed clean,[107] someone who is blameless and dressed in all the righteousness of Jesus,[108] someone in whom God delights,[109] someone who is here not just for a purpose but for *God's* purpose. Paul writes, "we are God's handiwork, created in Christ Jesus to do good works, which God prepared in advance for us to do."[110] That means you are purposed for good, meaningful things. If you are a Christian, no matter how your family treated you, no matter whether you achieved all your career dreams or look like a failure, no matter how much money you have or how you look or how people perceive you—your life is one that will bring glory to God. No matter who you are, your primary identity is in relation to God. And God is someone who has always known exactly who you are, and still likes you. Don't speed past that statement. *God is someone who has always known exactly who you are, and still loves you.*[111] So consider your identity. Practice it. Look up God's word about it; journal about it: identity issues are not ones you solve all in a moment. So practice.

On a similar note, it can be important to ask Jesus to tell you the truth about your situation. Sometimes we feel so much shame that it's really painful to probe it and ask it questions—which means that if it's toxic shame, we're really likely to leave it unchallenged, to feel it without even thinking about it. Shame clouds the heart so that it's really hard for us to disentangle what's our fault and what isn't, what's appropriate to feel shame about and what isn't, or even precisely what we're feeling and what we're

105. Gen 1:27, 5:1.

106. John 3:16.

107. See 1 Cor 6:11; Titus 3:5; Heb 10:22.

108. See Isa 61:10; Zech 3:3–4; Gal 3:27; Col 1:22.

109. See Pss 147:11, 149:4; Zeph 3:17.

110. Eph 2:10 TNIV.

111. I am indebted to my friend Cathie McCoy for this insight.

feeling it about. But Jesus isn't confused by it. Jesus is Truth.[112] So ask him. Ask trustworthy friends who can patiently sort it out with you. It may be scary, but remember: Jesus isn't here to condemn you.[113] Jesus is here to comfort you about the things that aren't your fault, and forgive you for the things that are. Either way, you're safe. It's hard to let him do either, though, without clarity about which is which. Remember, all toxic shame relies on a lie, whether the lie says that something is your fault when really it wasn't, or that the sins you've committed make you unacceptable forever. So truth is a vital antidote: as Jesus put it, "the truth will set you free."[114]

Sometimes, though, we're in so much pain and confusion that we can't even do that. There are times when the shame is so loud that we can't hear anything else, true or untrue. That's when I cry out to God. When I don't have the strength for anything else, I tell God exactly how I feel, and ask "will you fight on my behalf?" It's there, in that desperate cry—not in trying to "buck up" and "think positive"—that I can connect with God's comforting presence. The truth is, we're in a spiritual battle, and the Bible's take on it is that we're commissioned to fight the battle . . . but *God's* the one who wins it for us.[115]

Finally, wait on God. Keep asking, keep seeking, keep knocking.[116] When Jesus put his hands on a blind man and then asked what he saw, the man replied that he saw people but they looked like trees walking around. Jesus didn't throw up his hands in disgust and say, "you stink at being healed!" He put his hands on him again, and continued the healing.[117] Sometimes we deal with our wounds for a really long time—and that's not something to be ashamed of. That means Jesus puts his hands on our eyes again, and again. If you continue to struggle—and you will—it doesn't mean your faith isn't working. Trust is like a tomato plant: it grows in the sunlight of God's affection. If you go out intending to make pasta sauce and there aren't enough tomatoes on your plant, you can't very well say, "there's no plant here." You can trim the tree branches that are shading it; you can water it; you can weed around it; but you can't say it's not there. This world is very broken, and some of us have really big branches shading our garden that take a long time to trim. For some of us, this may be one of those customary

112. John 14:6.

113. See John 3:17.

114. John 8:32.

115. See Exod 14:14; Zech 4:6; Eph 6:10–12.

116. See Matt 7:7–8; Luke 11:9–10. Many translators and commentators note that the Greek grammar in these passages implies not simply "ask once," but "keep asking," etc.

117. Mark 8:22–25.

struggles that's going to be with us long-term—and that *doesn't mean your faith isn't real.* As much as we hate having to still struggle, it's important to realize that the time you spend in spiritual struggle is not wasted time. That's like saying that the time spent between planting and harvesting is wasted. Or that the time a gymnast spends practicing before performing brilliantly at the Olympics is wasted.

When you are struggling with shame you're in a place where your self-reliance and any foolish pride you've developed are stripped away. When you're struggling with shame, you're acutely aware of your need for a savior. When you're in this struggle, you're able to understand more deeply the pain Jesus went through, and you can grow closer because that's something you share and "get" about each other. When you're in this struggle, you're learning compassion for other people who are flooded with shame, and who think they're struggling utterly alone (and they are all around you). When you're in this struggle, you are growing in your ability to place your trust in Jesus. We don't build muscle when the weights we lift are effortless, but when they're heavy; the time you spend struggling is exactly the time you're learning to trust him.

Jesus is not going to abandon you to your shame. And the reason I know this is that he already didn't. He would not have gone to the lengths he went to—coming to earth, living among us, being betrayed and beaten and mocked and stripped and killed—if he intended to leave you there. It is a long, hard walk, working through shame . . . but you have someone walking the road with you. So allow his truth in, take whatever small steps of trust you can into community, cry out to him—and keep crying out to him.

"Food for Thought" Questions

Questions for Reflection/Journaling

- What would happen if, just for today, I acted as though what God says in the Bible about my identity is really true?
- What in my life causes me the most shame? If it's true that Jesus bore my shame—the shame I earned and the shame I didn't—can I allow him to see me and join me in this shame?
- What one small step of honesty and trust can I take this week?

Questions for Group Study

- Which ideas in this chapter surprised or impacted you the most?
- Name three specific things God says about your identity. (And don't name them Ethel, Herman, and Sheila. That's the sort of thing *I* would do, and it will totally derail your discussion. Ask me how I know this.)
- What are some ways we can learn to be gentle with people's shame?

8

Logic Problems

(How am I supposed to view myself?—Part 1)

I HAD A PROBLEM.

Christians teach that God loves us, and that since Jesus paid the full penalty for our sins, we shouldn't feel guilty. "Feeling bad about ourselves" is one of those things we point to warningly as something that will give Christianity a bad name.

However, Christians also teach that we shouldn't be prideful or self-satisfied. "Feeling good about ourselves" is often secretly suspect. After all, we certainly don't want to deny that "all have sinned."[118] We don't want to minimize our need for Jesus, or make it all about how great *we* are instead of how great *he* is. And besides, we're warned over and over again—by pastors and atheists alike—that we're not supposed to think ourselves better than anyone else. This left me with a dilemma: how am I supposed to look at myself?

Pretty much any time you come to a Christian for help with this, at least part of their answer is going to be about seeing ourselves as recipients of mercy. Half of them are also going to quote Isaiah about how our righteousness is "like filthy rags" compared to God.[119] These answers are true—and they also don't help much if guilt is a struggle for you. I knew the "right" answers. I knew that my right standing with God was based on Jesus, not on me, and that this should be a freeing thought (and occasionally it was). But how could I know if I was trusting Jesus' righteousness *enough*, without it being tainted by my own pride? If we're not supposed to drown in shame and self-hatred, but we're also not supposed to base our confidence on ourselves, how could I know if my view of myself was humble enough?

118. Rom 3:23 NRSV.

119. Isa 64:6 TNIV.

Writers and pastors from C.S. Lewis to Tim Keller have defined humility as "not thinking less of yourself, but thinking of yourself less." Now, I want to say first of all that I think this is a very valid and insightful definition. It helps us shift our concept of humility to something more wholesome and accurate than the common misconception that it means devaluing ourselves and focusing on "how bad I am" (which in itself is a self-focused activity). But it didn't really answer the question that was in my heart.

Trying to put that definition into practice proved difficult, almost lonely—as if we're either to think poorly of ourselves (it's OK to downplay your good deeds, but no one will tell you to downplay your bad ones), or else not think of ourselves at all. It brought a bleakness to the idea of a relationship with God: who wants a relationship where, unless you're in trouble, you're ignored? In fact, how can there even *be* a relationship—a loving connection between two selves—if one of those selves doesn't matter and shouldn't be thought of? As helpful as that definition of humility is, taken to its extreme it can actually undermine our understanding of the relational nature of God. And I have a mind that excels at taking things to extremes.

Complicating the whole question more, Christians (at least where I grew up) really like to quote and preach on Matthew 7:

> Why worry about a speck in your friend's eye when you have a log in your own? How can you think of saying to your friend, "Let me help you get rid of that speck in your eye," when you can't see past the log in your own eye? Hypocrite! First get rid of the log in your own eye; then you will see well enough to deal with the speck in your friend's eye.[120]

This is an extremely helpful text, one that teaches us how to confront without condemning. (See the *Zacchaeus* chapter for a more detailed look at it.) But like anything, it can get misinterpreted—and when it's quoted a lot, and you're already anxious about where you stand with God, those misinterpretations and confused questions abound.

"What if I haven't acknowledged my own sin enough?" I began to ask, sometimes frantically. "Doesn't the whole 'log' and 'speck' size difference mean that I'm *always* more in the wrong than the other person when I see a problem? So why bother confronting anyone at all, if I haven't got a leg to stand on?" I sometimes even wondered whether it meant that addressing someone else's sin *put me* into error.

But the command to confront sin was *there*, unmistakably, just as much as the command not to judge. So I began to worry even more. If I'm to remove my "log" first, how do I know when I've removed it *enough* to

120. Matt 7:3–5 NLT.

confront someone else about their sin? How do I know if I've removed my "log" well enough, period?

The problem, of course, is that there isn't an objective measure of "enough": we may always have blind spots, and we always need to let God be at work in us. It will never be the case that we address someone's sin from a position of being perfect ourselves. An equally tough problem is that people naturally get upset when confronted, which can quickly turn into accusations that you think you're better than others, even if that's not really your attitude. So how could I obey God's commands to care about what's good and confront what isn't[121] with any kind of confidence that I wasn't just waving a big old arrogant log around? It seemed, to my confused and worried heart, that to be safe I *must* look at myself with a "never good enough" sort of eye. These two problems of humility and metaphorical logs created a problem of their own, which I expressed in my journal as the following logic puzzle:

Premise 1:

God does not want me to live in guilt, however . . .

Premise 2:

We are supposed to be aware of our own sin and not consider ourselves better than anyone else.

Conclusion:

Therefore in order to guard against self-righteousness, I must live in a state of constant guilt.

As you can see, the pieces don't even really fit into a proper logic puzzle, which is why in my journal it's followed by the words, "Where is the flaw in the logic?"

When I wrote this, I had already been limping under its implications for years. I had already asked multiple godly people about it over those years (although I'd never quite expressed it in those words), and somehow their answers never really quelled the aching question in my heart. And so this

121. See Lev 19:17; Ps 82:3; Amos 5:15; Matt 18:15; Rom 12:9; Eph 5:11 for a start.

time—knowing that I hadn't always heard clear answers in prayer before, wondering if I ought to ask any of the mentors in my life or if that would just make it worse as it usually did, unable to reach anybody just then anyway because I was half a mile from home on foot—I asked God directly.

What immediately came to mind was that the answer lay in the concept of being "not guilty but sorry." This is a concept I picked up from Cloud and Townsend's book *How People Grow* (which, if you've never heard of before, is an excellent resource that now you *have* heard of and should read). In their chapter on guilt, they explain that guilt is no longer an appropriate response for the Christian: it no longer applies, because Jesus took all of it on the cross. However, being *sorry* for the ways that our sin hurt others—having compassion and sorrow for their pain that was caused by us—*is* an appropriate response. Cloud and Townsend make the very helpful distinction that guilt is self-focused, while being sorry is others-focused.[122] What was God getting at with this answer?

As I sat down and prayed in order to wrap my noggin around this, I realized that what Jesus is calling us to—in the "log" illustration and other places—is not to focus on how we've similarly *sinned*, but to focus on how we've similarly *been forgiven*. In sharing God's Word, we are leading people to mercy, not guilt: our message is not that God condemns but that God redeems. And this, of course, was the key to confronting people lovingly and humbly without tearing myself to shreds or drowning myself in guilt: if we're *truly* in the same boat as those we confront, we *cannot* live in guilt, because we must receive the same mercy we preach.

The flaw in my logic lay in not realizing the implications of "not thinking myself better than anyone else." The idea implies equality. Of course God doesn't want me to look down on and hate myself, because God doesn't want me to look down on and hate anyone *else* either.

The other flaw in my logic lay in believing God would ever want me to interpret "trusting Jesus' sacrifice" to mean "endlessly accusing myself." I would never insist to another person, the way I insisted to myself, that *truly* accepting Jesus' grace meant obsessing about and feeling as terrible as possible about my sin, because the focus of grace isn't "do I know I'm bad?" but "do I know I'm forgiven?" I would never have counseled someone, as I counseled myself, to live in a constant state of spiritual self-doubt and disappointment, because the message of grace isn't "you're disappointing and should know it," it's "you're loved anyway." Yes, the need for forgiveness is assumed in the very concept of mercy, but mercy *cannot* logically leave us there or it wouldn't be mercy—just as the pain assumed by taking aspirin

122. See Cloud and Townsend, *How People Grow*, 171–73.

cannot logically be the end goal of the aspirin. And if I am to assume that I am in the same boat as everyone else, I cannot logically deny myself the same freedom, love, and joy that I claim God openhandedly offers to them.

OK, (says a mind like mine), so maybe we shouldn't *hate* ourselves. But surely seeing ourselves in a *positive* light would be . . . well, too much, right? After all, what about where Jesus says we're just "unworthy servants?"

This phrase comes from Luke 17, and I painfully misread it for years. (I don't know if I didn't hear much teaching on it because it's an uncomfortable passage or because others didn't understand it any better than I did.) In it, Jesus compares our good deeds to the duties of a servant with these words:

> Suppose one of you has a servant ploughing or looking after the sheep. Will he say to the servant when he comes in from the field, "Come along now and sit down to eat"? Won't he rather say, "Prepare my supper, get yourself ready and wait on me while I eat and drink; after that you may eat and drink"? Will he thank the servant because he did what he was told to do? So you also, when you have done everything you were told to do, should say, "We are unworthy servants; we have only done our duty."[123]

For a long time, this guided the way I thought of myself: no matter the love behind my actions, no matter how much I wanted to please God, there was never a way to *actually* please him. Anything I could do was only the fulfillment of a duty. God would never commend me—and even if, in divine generosity, he *did*, I should never accept that commendation, let alone feel good about it. I should keep my head down and acknowledge that any good thing I did was just a duty. This passage seemed to paint a cold and "never-good-enough" style of relationship with God—and to say that's what we should expect and even have as our goal.

This is not the image Jesus gives us of God elsewhere. In fact, the Bible says Jesus *is* the image of God, and the image he demonstrated wasn't a master ordering servants around, but a Master who stoops to wash the feet of his servants—and goes even farther, giving his body and soul to wash our hearts with his blood.[124] Even in my years of confusion over this passage, I recognized that the image I was seeing of God in it didn't match up with the actions of God I saw elsewhere. Why would Jesus talk about our standing with God so differently here? Well, because that's not what he's talking about here. At all.

The beginning of Luke 17 is one of those "junk drawer" passages, where it seems to contain just a bunch of random exhortations. The

123. Luke 17:7–10 TNIV.

124. See John 13; Phil 2.

translators who add headings to Bible passages (so that people can find the passage they want more easily) sometimes accidentally feed into this idea. The NIV heading at the beginning of Luke 17 is "Sin, Faith, Duty," which sounds exactly like that drawer in my kitchen called "Pencils, Rubber Bands, Takeout Menus, and A Couple Of Keys That May or May Not Still Go To Something." They might as well have called it, "We're Not Really Sure What He's Talking About Here." A number of other translations chop these first ten verses into three different mini-sections.

But Jesus is a much more skilled speaker than that, and Luke was a much more skilled writer than that. They didn't just throw a bunch of things into this passage because they wanted to say them and couldn't find a better place to put them. Jesus actually constructs a brilliant teaching about forgiveness here.

Forgiveness? Yes. Not how God sees us? No. Not how we're supposed to see ourselves? Nope. Not "Sin, Faith, Duty?" Not really. Warning: this is a tangent. But I promise it comes back to the point.

Jesus starts by talking about how serious sin is. Before he brings up forgiveness, he prepares his hearers for it: first by assuring them that God takes sin seriously (and will deal with sinners) and second by warning them to watch their own lives. Any teaching on forgiveness is incomplete without both of these elements. Sufferers need to know the God of justice cares about their plight, and seekers of justice need to remember that they themselves are not immune to acting unjustly.

From here, Jesus goes on to casually ask the impossible: forgive *ad infinitum*, like God does.[125] This is a big ask. The prevailing teachings in the disciples' culture taught that they should forgive someone three times, and that this was essentially the limit of forgiveness. In itself, this is pretty magnanimous. In western culture, forgiveness asks us to put aside our rights, which to us are sacrosanct; in honor-shame cultures like Jesus' culture, forgiveness asks us to put aside our sacrosanct dignity. In some honor-shame cultures, forgiveness is even considered more of a weakness than a virtue. No wonder the rabbis limited it to three times. But now Jesus is asking his disciples to forgive someone not just three times, but seven times *in a day*. Nobody can take that many blows to his dignity. No person can move her

125. This is not to say "just let sin slide." The scenario Jesus gives here is of forgiving someone who repents, not simply "letting it go" when someone won't acknowledge the hurt they've done. He's not asking you to be a doormat and just keep quiet about how you've been hurt, nor to confuse forgiveness (releasing a debt) with reconciliation (re-establishing closeness—which is *not* always wise or commanded). On behalf of imperfect teachers and preachers everywhere, I'm sorry if those were things you were taught you had to do.

heart to such tenderness and sacrifice over and over and over. Only God, who does this daily on an infinite scale, can do such a thing, and so the disciples rightly call out for help: "Lord, increase our faith!" Help us somehow to do this. Help us want to do this. Help us believe it's even possible.

Jesus responds with a promise: "If you have faith as small as a mustard seed, you can say to this mulberry tree, 'Be uprooted and planted in the sea' and it will obey you."[126] Jesus has not suddenly switched subjects, encouraging us to try and perform wacky miracles to prove our faith. He's saying that the hurt and bitterness that naturally grow when someone sins against us (and grow quite deep and strong, if you know mulberry trees) can be uprooted. Not only that, but we have authority under God to do this. It is impossible for a normal mortal to tear out the tough, thick roots of resentment, but in God we can command it to leave and it will obey us. It may take multiple commands, it may take coming to God repeatedly in helplessness and faith, but *it will obey you.*

OK, so now Jesus has asked the impossible. Jesus has asked the unreasonable, and proven he's serious about it by promising supernatural power to do it. Here's where the worst temptation comes. Here's where the human heart says, "Jesus asked me to do something amazingly hard, and I did it. I mustered up enough faith to perform *miracles* in order to obey God. *Look how dang magnanimous I am.*" And as we congratulate ourselves on how unreasonably kind we are to the person who hurt us, forgiveness itself is undermined. Now we're not loving and reconciling with them; we're secretly thinking how much better we are than they are. We're still keeping score.

Knowing the human heart, Jesus nips this in the bud. God *has* asked the impossible, he says—and you did it *because he told you to*, not because it was your natural instinct. You did this with miraculous power *because you needed* miraculous power, not because you're such a miracle of benevolence. This wasn't your idea, it was God's. And God started by forgiving *you*, so this isn't you being high-minded and generous, this is you repaying a token-sized duty towards the one who unreasonably, supernaturally *forgave you.* And so just like servants don't expect to be celebrated for just doing their job, we shouldn't view forgiveness as something "extra credit" that we do because we're scintillating fairies of goodwill; it is a non-optional part of obeying God's commands.

This passage has zilch to do with how God sees us; it has everything to do with how *we* see forgiveness. Jesus is making a very specific point in a very specific context—a mind-blowingly tough teaching on forgiveness—and he makes his point strongly because forgiveness is so unnatural

126. Luke 17:6 TNIV.

to us. He's challenging our ideas that forgiveness is optional, impossible, or something we achieve through our saintly good-guy strength.

But he's not giving us a blueprint of our relationship with God here. He's not saying that God wants a cold, indifferent relationship with us where we're just dutiful servants: never celebrated, never given special recognition, never sharing at the master's table. That would fly in the face of everything he modeled and everything he taught.

Let's first consider the list of people with whom this real-life Master shared meals (a time of intimate relationship—and a far cry from "wait on me and later you can eat"). It's a ridiculously long list. In fact, he was frequently criticized for not only whom he chose as dinner companions, but *how often* he ate with people instead of standing aloof and fasting like "holy" men were supposed to.[127] Second, consider how he flipped the script of this parable when he, the master, took what was culturally the place of the lowliest servant in the house to wash his disciples' feet. In fact, he *promised* the opposite of what this parable depicts, telling us that "It will be good for those servants whose master finds them watching when he comes. Truly I tell you, he will dress himself to serve, will make them recline at the table and will come and wait on them."[128] What Jesus actually demonstrated wasn't cold indifference but joyful, affectionate, self-demoting closeness, and he repeatedly reminded us that he came "not to be served but to serve, and to give his life as a ransom for many."[129]

This is possibly the most important piece of this logic puzzle: it makes no logical sense that Jesus would have gone to the lengths he did to save us if his *intention* was for us to then live in shame and guilt all our lives. Surely he could have done something less drastic if all he felt towards us was a cold sort of duty—if all he wanted to achieve was a utilitarian, legal form of "salvation" that "got the job done" but left us repugnant to him. In fact, we might question what "the job" would even be in that case: what would salvation even *be* without the restoration of relationship? And what would be the point of it? After all, it's not as though God *needs* us for anything, so *God* wouldn't get anything useful out of our being "saved." And an eternity in which we're constantly aware of our own repugnance, in which we're still effectively separated from the Source of all goodness and life, wouldn't be much good to *us* either.

If God *intended* to never truly be at peace with us—if the intent was to focus (and have us focus) perpetually on our failures, unworthiness, and

127. See Mark 2:15–16; Matt 11:19; Luke 7:34.

128. Luke 12:37 TNIV.

129. Matt 20:28; Mark 10:45 TNIV.

sin—then the world could have just kept going the way it was indefinitely, without Jesus coming or dying at all. An uncomfortable truce can be reached in any number of ways. If an uncomfortable truce was all God wanted, then the cross would be almost embarrassingly superfluous, like using a sledgehammer to drive a pushpin. And the idea that Jesus' sacrifice is so small and limited that God would intentionally take on human form, live, suffer, and die by crucifixion to achieve a "salvation" that was essentially meaningless is logically untenable. It is even (however unintentionally) theologically disrespectful. When the Almighty God comes *at all*—let alone *dies*—we had better pay attention. When One so good and loving suffers so deeply, we dare not minimize it.

The world-altering message of the Bible isn't *just* that we're in the same boat as our unjust, sawdusty neighbors, but that Jesus bore the blow of justice for us—the weight of all our logs as well as our specks fell on him. More than that, the Bible tells us that this wasn't just meant to "appease" God, but to reconcile us into a true relationship—the kind we'd actually want to be in. And this changes everything.

It turns out that "don't think less of yourself, think of yourself less" is better understood as a byproduct, not a goal. Think of how it is with a dislocated shoulder: while it is out of joint, I *can't* think about it less, because it hurts. When the injured limb is healed, I don't *have* to think about it: not because it isn't important, but because it's finally free to function the way it was meant to. But trying to think of it less while it's injured won't heal it, and certainly won't restore it to proper function.

So it is with guilt and humility. Trying to think of ourselves less while we're in spiritual pain won't heal us. Trying to think of ourselves as negatively as possible *definitely* won't heal us. These attitudes also—and this is terribly important to understand—won't get us to the real goal of how we were meant to function. We were meant to love well and be loved well: to be able to focus on the other without losing the self. "Humility" is the description of that loving outward gaze toward the other. But it's not in itself what gets us "back in joint" to make that outward gaze possible.

We were all born dislocated. We were all born into spiritual pain, trying—through arrogance, self-deprecation, distraction, or myriad other ways—to stabilize that insecure soul. The love of Jesus is what gets our dislocated selves back in joint, and it's only from that vantage point that we can properly gaze upon anything, including ourselves.

"Food for Thought" Questions

Questions for Reflection/Journaling

- Do I believe that God's loving mercy is for *me* just as much as it is for others?
- Where have my attempts to have the right attitude been misguided or damaging?
- God, how do you want to build both humility and security in me?

Questions for Group Study

- What in this chapter surprised or impacted you most?
- What do you think of this idea that humility can be described as a "loving outward gaze toward the other"? Are there other definitions you find more helpful?
- What are some ways we can remember that "in the same boat" means in the "boat" of God's *mercy*, not just the "boat" of sin?

9

Delightful

(How am I supposed to view myself?—Part 2)

He will take great delight in you,
in his love he will no longer rebuke you,
but will rejoice over you with singing.
—*ZEPHANIAH 3:17, TNIV*

IN THE LAST CHAPTER we built the negative case for how we're to look at ourselves: essentially, we looked at wrong answers to the question and clarified how we should *not* see ourselves. But the question remains, what is the positive case? How *does* God see us, and how does he ask us to see ourselves?

As it turns out, the church is remarkably nervous about this question. I remember once saying to a friend, "I just wish I could know that God approves of me." She responded, "I wouldn't say 'approves;' I'd probably say 'accepts.'"

My friend meant well. I suppose she was trying to uphold accurate doctrine, pointing out that not *everything* we do is approved by God (as if I ever would have thought that anyway!). Perhaps she was even trying to uphold grace by pointing out how God's love and acceptance are unconditional, even when we do things he can't approve. But what I heard was "you can never be pleasing to God; the best you can hope for is to be tolerated."

Now, I don't know about you, but that was a deeply dissatisfying answer to me. No one wants a relationship where we're disapproved of all the time! More than that, I love God, and *want* to please him. Who wants to be in a relationship where you're doomed at every turn to be disappointing and even hurtful to the one you love? What's even the point of staying in a relationship like that—wouldn't it be more loving to just leave?

Most of us would agree that relationships under conditions like this—relationships in which it is categorically impossible for one member to be happy with the other—are unhealthy and untenable. And yet we tacitly imply this all the time about the most important and holy relationship we could ever have, our relationship with God himself! This deep reluctance to talk about God's thoughts toward us in terms of "approval" persists in the church, and many of us grow up in the faith thinking this is normal and even necessary.

So is our uneasiness with this idea of "approval" warranted? Is God, in fact, "just tolerating" us? How are we to look at God while he looks at us?

In Psalm 16, we are given some clues to this question of how God sees us. Christians have long understood this psalm as a Messianic psalm: one that looks forward to and gives glimpses of the Messiah. In fact, this understanding goes back to (at least) the very first public Christian sermon, preached by the Apostle Peter in Acts 2, and to the preaching of Paul as well.[130] As Christianity dawned, the earliest Christians looked at a psalm they'd known all their lives and suddenly saw unmistakably reflected, as if the ripples had finally cleared away, the resurrection of Jesus. And if we look at Psalm 16 through that lens, it has some remarkable things to say.

Verse 3 has several possible translations, but most say something similar to my old 1984 NIV: "As for the saints who are in the land, they are the glorious ones in whom is all my delight." Does this make you squirm as much as it does me? In a culture so informal that "glory" is hard for us to take seriously, in an era that focuses so often on the failings of the church, this is an arresting statement. Other English translations call the people of God "noble," "excellent," or "majestic," which is hardly any less uncomfortable. We're not used to using such language about ourselves or each other—at least not without a tongue-in-cheek tone—and we don't often hear it without a wry sort of embarrassment. Not only that, many of our churches have emphasized the Bible's teachings on our inborn sinfulness so much (with very orthodox and well-meaning intent) that we tend to be leery of positive statements that could lead us into pride. And yet the Bible itself calls us glorious and a delight.

If this didn't challenge us enough, verse 5 says "Lord, you have assigned me my portion and my cup; you have made my lot secure."[131] I skimmed past this seemingly-innocuous, contented statement for years

130. Acts 13:34–37.

131. Ps 16:5 TNIV.

until I remembered that this is a Messianic psalm, and "cup" was how the Messiah often referred to his suffering.[132] Many other translations render it "Lord, you *are* my portion and my cup" rather than "you have assigned," but either way, the cup of God that Jesus received was specifically a cup full of God's wrath. And Jesus had no illusions about what this cup meant for him: he even begged God to go with another option if there was any other way to save us. So why would this psalm use such a positive image (think Psalm 23's famous "my cup runneth over") for something so brutal, and follow it up with such a confident statement of security—or as the NLT renders it, "You guard all that is mine"?

Well, it's because of the next verse: "The boundary lines have fallen for me in pleasant places; surely I have a delightful inheritance."[133] The image here is of the boundary stones that marked the borders of a person's property.[134] Boundary lines falling in pleasant places imply that it's the kind of place you inherit and realize you're rich and extremely lucky: that it's big, that the land is good, and that you look at your boundary stones and say "It includes that part too? *Sweet!*" But what kind of inheritance would the *Messiah* have? According to Psalm 2 (another Messianic psalm) it's "the nations."[135] It's us. What Jesus is saying here is that the "territory" he won on the cross—the people who have become his inheritance—are a delight to him, a more-than-ample reward for the cup he endured. Hebrews 12 puts this another way when it calls us "the joy that was set before him"—the goal and reward that kept Jesus going all the way to the cross.[136]

This is God's answer to the question of our identity—of how God sees us and how we should see ourselves. You are someone Jesus could not only die for, but also look at afterwards and say "Yes!!! That was totally worth it! The boundary lines have fallen for me in pleasant places." *God does not tolerate you. God delights in you.*

"But surely we're not actually supposed to *believe* this?" that all-too-familiar voice inside immediately objects. Won't seeing ourselves as

132. See the Gethsemane narrative in Matt 26:39–44, Mark 14:32–41 and Luke 22:42, as well as Jesus' responses to his disciples in John 18:11 and Matt 20:22. Jesus in fact never talks about having any other kind of cup.

133. Ps 16:6 TNIV.

134. You can see this practice in places like Deut 19:14, which prohibits moving boundary stones to skim off bits of a neighbor's land.

135. Ps 2:8. This, by the way, is another Messianic psalm, and was quoted as such multiple times by the earliest Christians: see Acts 4:24–30; Acts 13:33; Heb 1:5; Heb 5:5.

136. Heb 12:2 TNIV, NRSV. You could, I suppose, object that the "joy" spoken of here was something else . . . but what? Even Phil 2, which talks about the glory Jesus received, bases that glory on what he did to redeem us: so clearly not just Jesus' joy, but also the Father's joy and Jesus' glory are all inextricably linked with Jesus saving us.

"delightful" make us inclined to overlook our sins? Isn't it basically self-aggrandizing and arrogant? Or, if it's OK to believe it . . . at least shouldn't we believe it sort of the way we believe in flying squirrels—filed away as something we accept exists, but have no reason to think about in our daily lives—and then get back to focusing on others? Isn't focusing on how much God likes me pretty self-centered? And perhaps most importantly, with all of the verses about humbling ourselves, and with the importance of the Christian doctrine that "there is no one who is righteous, not even one,"[137] and with as ready as humans are to downplay our own faults while trumpeting the faults of others . . . well, isn't it better—safer—for us to focus primarily on our sinfulness? These are questions that come up for many of us, if we're honest. (Alright, nobody except me and one random zoologist asks about the flying squirrels.) But the other questions trouble many of us, and often instead of addressing those questions, we simply put the whole subject of God's delight in us on the back burner. We treat it as something that's there but too confusing or embarrassing or potentially hazardous to talk about, rather in the same mistaken way many Christians avoid the subject of sex. The problem, of course, with this "just ignore the question" approach is that we will still, in our actions, attitudes, and subconscious ideas, default to answering the question in *some* way—it's just going to be a way that we haven't thought through, that we haven't submitted to God's authority, and that probably comes from a lot of sources that aren't God. That's not a great way to answer any question, certainly not one as important as the question of how God sees us.

Jesus offers us a helpful roadmap for navigating these questions in the Lord's Prayer (recorded in Matthew 6 and Luke 11). He does indeed make mention of our sins: we do not need to worry that seeing ourselves through the eyes of God's delight will give us a falsely inflated or idealized image of ourselves. Of all people, the one who drank the cup has no illusions about what was in that cup. But that's not where he begins. When Jesus teaches us to pray, he doesn't have us start with "forgive us our trespasses" but with "Our Father."

Now, lest we speed past this too quickly, it's worth noticing that "Father" is not how God is addressed in the Bible up until that point. The nation of Israel as a whole is referred to poetically and metaphorically as God's son in the Hebrew Scriptures, but in general the people of Jesus' day tended to refer to themselves as the "sons of Abraham" and to God as "the God of our fathers." The traditional Hebrew prayers usually address God not as "Father" but as "Lord our God, King of the Universe." So Jesus isn't simply

137. Rom 3:10 NRSV; see also Pss 14:1–3; 53:1–3; Eccl 7:20, and Rom 3:23.

making a customary preamble to his prayer, or unthinkingly going along with church culture, as we often are when we start a prayer that way. He is making an unequivocal statement about who God is—and by extension, an unequivocal statement about who *we* are.

We are defined in terms of God. Jesus' statement about our identity is an inherently relational statement. It is not a "value judgment"—that we're good or evil, righteous or sinful—but a "*valued* judgment"—that we are by nature beloved. And this statement of identity comes before everything else in the prayer, which indicates something very important: it means that *God does not see us primarily in terms of our faults.*

This is the beautiful, unbelievable truth of Christianity: that because of Jesus, even when we do have issues we need to address with God, those are not the primary things God sees when he looks at us. We are no longer defined by our sins (which used to be the only identity we had—signs and symptoms of our estrangement from God), but by Jesus who restored our relationship. That definition is indelible, and doesn't change with our spotty track-record of learning to live in that relationship. In fact, our moral ups and downs *can't* be what define us in God's eyes, precisely because we've been redefined by someone who never changes. And we've been redefined as his beloved, in whom he delights.

So then, many of us assume, if we're defined by Jesus' work and not our own, we should think of God's delight solely in those terms, right? That is, shouldn't we see Jesus as the *only* pleasing thing about us, and not even consider that we ourselves could be at all delightful? After all, there is nothing we can add to what Jesus has already done for us, and nothing we can do to make God accept us more. We're "dressed in all the righteousness of Christ,"[138] as many put it: that is, we're declared righteous because when God looks at us, he sees Jesus who took our place. So wouldn't it contradict that message of grace to think that anything *we* do can please God? If we're accepted because God sees Jesus in our place, that means that any pleasure God takes in us is really pleasure in Jesus, right?

The problem with this is that it subtly erases our personhood. If, when we say I was "credited with Jesus' righteousness," we mean that "God can only accept me when he's looking at Jesus and not directly at me" . . . then God doesn't really accept *me,* does he? Worse, it would imply that what Jesus did wasn't *actually* enough to make me acceptable to God—that Jesus always has to hide me, like a kid stowing a muddy stray under his bed. It's a misunderstanding of Jesus' sacrifice that undermines our belief in the power of his sacrifice itself.

138. See Gal 3:27; Rom 3:22, 5:17; 2 Cor 5:17, 21.

This misunderstanding is best corrected when we return to looking at Jesus' sacrifice in terms of relationship. Many Western Christians are fond of saying that Christianity is a "relationship, not a religion," but that doesn't mean that we broken creatures automatically know how to see everything through this lens. It turns out that there are many ways in which we functionally forget this truth. Our theology gets very theoretical sometimes. (No offense to theory, but it is easily disconnected from the reality it seeks to describe, just as math is a complete mystery to me until I get into the kitchen and double the cookie recipe.)

So at the risk of annoying those who have known this by rote since they were knee-high to a flannel-graph, let's just state this clearly here: Christianity centers on relationship. The main thing Christians teach about Jesus is that he restored us to relationship with God, making a way for us to be adopted as God's children. Viewed this way, these puzzles of God's unconditional delight and our desire to please him in some meaningful way become much less puzzling.

Children are loved and accepted by good parents unconditionally. They are defined in terms of the relationship: they are the parents' beloved children, and the parents are glad about it, no matter what. At the same time, good parents are not indifferent to their children's moral actions nor to their efforts to please them. They don't rigidly withhold their affirmation to avoid giving them a "swelled head" or to make absolutely certain the kids don't think they've somehow earned the relationship. And Jesus, when talking of God as a Father, uses a "how much more" comparison: if broken people can still be good parents, *how much more* is God, who is the source and standard of all goodness, a trustworthy and loving parent?[139]

In fact, the overwhelming witness of Scripture is that God is deeply affected by what his children do. Far from the aloof and uninterested image we sometimes have—as though God must treat our deeds and moral conduct as irrelevant because we're "under grace"—the Bible talks about heaven's investment in our actions with an emotional intensity that may surprise us. The Old Testament repeatedly says that God "loves righteousness and justice" (and "hates wickedness").[140] Paul picks up this theme when he exhorts us to "live as children of the light" and "find out what pleases the Lord."[141] Jesus' parables and teachings clearly indicate instances of God's affirmation and approval, such as the well-known "well done, good and

139. See Matt 7:9–11; Luke 11:11–13.

140. See Pss 11:7; 33:5; 45:7; Isa 61:8; Jer 9:24.

141. Eph 5:8–10 TNIV.

faithful servant."[142] He even indicates that God's approval is so extravagant that it will surprise and confuse us: in Jesus' description of the final judgment, the King says to his bewildered followers that in showing kindness to others, they have clothed and fed and ministered directly to him.[143] Here, as well as in other places (such as the declaration that one who gives "even a cup of cold water" will be rewarded)[144] we get the sense that the small acts of kindness we don't even notice are celebrated in heaven and touch God's heart.

I downplayed this for many years, citing verses like where Jesus says we should consider ourselves "unworthy servants."[145] And perhaps it *is* worth taking a moment to note that in all of the passages above, it is *God* who makes a big deal out of our small gifts of love and obedience: it could get pretty gross pretty fast if we thought it was *our* job to point out and celebrate all of our own nice deeds. However, this doesn't mean we should ignore the joy God does express towards us: after all, to ignore God's heart is to ignore God. And for this one passage that *seems* at first glance to depict a cold relationship, there are dozens of others that indicate God's passion.

Jesus describes us as guests at his wedding: the kind of people you want to have around on the most important day of your life. He depicts us as sheep lovingly cared for by a good shepherd, as costly coins a woman would tear her house apart to find, and as sons, not relegated to the formality of servants but allowed (and taught) to use the closest and most familial term, "Abba" (the Aramaic equivalent of "Daddy").[146] He says to his disciples, "I no longer call you servants, because servants do not know their master's business. Instead, I have called you friends."[147] This is not the image of a God who keeps us at arm's length and withholds any approval so as not to give us a "swelled head." In fact, even in the passages where we *are* depicted as servants, there's more celebration than we might expect. In a parable of servants "just doing their job," the master *does* commend them, crying "Well done, good and faithful servant!" Going further than that, he rewards them not only with an honored position ("I will put you in charge of many things") but also with intimacy, saying "Come and share your master's

142. Matt 25:21, 23 TNIV.

143. Matt 25:34–40.

144. Matt 10:42.

145. Luke 17:10 NLT. See the previous chapter for an in-depth discussion of why I think this passage isn't really talking about our standing with God.

146. These images can be found in Matt 9:15, John 10, in the parables in Luke 15, in the Lord's Prayer in Matt 6, and many other places. Our invitation to use the special familial term "Abba" is found in Rom 8:15 and Gal 4:6.

147. John 15:15 TNIV.

happiness!"[148] In a similar parable in Luke, he even honors the servant who wasn't so good at his job: the first servant manages to get a tenfold return on his master's money but the second only manages a five-fold return, and yet he still gets an astronomical promotion, going from managing some money to ruling over five cities.[149] God's attitude towards us is repeatedly depicted as warm, involved, and passionate—and yes, pleased and proud when we respond with love towards him and others.

And this should not be a surprise to us if God really is a good Father. I was touched by the fact that my niece knew my favorite color from the age of two, and chose paint, beads, and paper for her many gifts of artwork accordingly. My sister cheers for her children when they obey her or when they're kind to each other. It's what good parents do—and they do it at every stage. They don't complain that their baby hasn't yet won a Nobel Peace Prize. They bask in the first eye contact, the first smile. Later, they clap and coo over the first "Please," and "Thank you." A little farther down the road, they celebrate the first unprompted toy-sharing as if their child really *did* win the Nobel Peace Prize. Good parents take pleasure in their children's sincere efforts, regardless of how small or insignificant they may seem to someone else. It has nothing to do with whether they're going to keep the child—nothing to do with earning "salvation by works"—and everything to do with love.

In the now-classic devotional work *My Utmost For His Highest*, Oswald Chambers asks, "Have you ever heard the Master say a hard word? If you have not, I question whether you have heard Him say anything."[150] He has a good point: sometimes the things Jesus asks of us, or the discipline our Father lovingly gives us, are hard indeed. But I also question whether we've really heard God if we've never heard him speak a *kind* word. God is depicted throughout the Bible as gracious and compassionate: a good Father; an attentive Mother.[151] Jesus, who is the "exact likeness of God's being"[152] described himself as "gentle and humble in heart."[153] In fact, the biggest progress I've made in learning to hear God has come not from some cool monk-like meditation technique or special program (which were somehow the sort of things I had expected it to come from) but from simply learning

148. Matt 25:21, 23 TNIV.

149. See Luke 19:15–19.

150. Chambers, *My Utmost for His Highest*, 230.

151. These descriptions can be found in Exod 34:6, Matt 7:9–11, and Isa 49:15, among others.

152. Heb 1:3 GW, NIRV.

153. Matt 11:29 NRSV; see also Matt 12:20; Isa 42:3; Ps 147:3.

to recognize the loving gentleness of that Voice. Yet as Brad Jersak points out in the book *Can You Hear Me?*, many of us find we have a lot more faith to hear correction from God than to hear affirmation and approval.[154] Learning to believe and receive God's delight in us is a challenge in this fallen world, and it takes time. But it's worth it, because it's true.

Rather than asking if it's appropriate to see ourselves as "delightful" to God, perhaps we should be asking a different set of questions. We worry about the possible spiritual unhealthiness of focusing on God's delighted love; do we worry equally about the unhealthiness of tacitly viewing God as cold and impossible to please? Do we realize that believing we truly are God's beloved is what leads to seeing others in terms of their belovedness too? And that being constantly annoyed and dissatisfied with ourselves invariably leads to being annoyed and dissatisfied with others? We worry about becoming self-centered; do we know that when we embrace our belovedness, people seem less like enemies or tasks, and more like children whose belovedness we can make known to them? And that this audacious, silly, illogical confidence is what frees us to love openhandedly without it becoming drudgery?

Do we realize that the most profound way to honor a God who claims to love humans beyond all reasonable measure—enough to become human, enough to die, enough to give up his own (and only) child, enough to dismantle and remove and forgive everything that stood between us and him—is to *believe* him?

"Food for Thought" Questions

Questions for Reflection/Journaling

- Do I balk at believing that God delights in me? Why? Is it fear, or habit, or something else?
- How has that resistance affected how I see myself? How has it affected how I see others?
- Lord, will you please give me a glimpse of your delight in me today? What does it look like? How does it feel?

154. See Jersak, *Can You Hear Me?*, 32–33. I must also give credit where credit is due: when I was looking for monk-like pointers on the secret to hearing God, I asked my friend Jonathan Friz (of 10 Days of Prayer) how he did it so well. "Huh," he said, as if he'd never thought about it, "I guess I meditated on his love for me. Not his love in general, but his love for me personally."

QUESTIONS FOR GROUP STUDY

- What in this chapter surprised or encouraged you the most?
- What does "delight" really mean? When have you experienced it? What is it like?
- How would you explain the balance between the ideas that "God delights in us" and "We have a real ability to please or grieve God"?

10

So Now What?

(How am I supposed to view myself?—Part 3)

If you're like me, you probably found the previous chapter frustrating. It's all well and good to talk about how God sees us and how we ought to believe what Scripture says about us, but how do we actually get there? People say things like "believe that God loves you" all the time (as if talking about it is the same thing as knowing how to do it!) but that doesn't change the fact that it's hard to get our hearts to cooperate. Our feelings, mental patterns, and inner pictures of ourselves don't just automatically match up with what God says and with what we say we believe. And the really frustrating part is, we thought we *did* believe! When we find ourselves having a hard time seeing ourselves through God's eyes and find our brothers and sisters in Christ offering well-meaning reminders to do so, we can start to wonder if something is wrong with us or our faith.

The truth is, seeing the world and ourselves in skewed ways is part of the brokenness into which we were born. Learning to see through God's eyes is a lifelong process. That's why Jesus said the Holy Spirit would guide us into all truth: because while salvation may be immediate, becoming like him isn't (otherwise he'd have to erase our personhood), and there are some truths we're not ready to understand. We certainly are born again as new creations in Christ,[155] but we are born as babies. And babies learn and grow.

So how do we grow into the habit of seeing ourselves through God's eyes? There are two extremely important general principles in answer to this question. The first is this: *we learn what we repeat*. The second is that *we learn that we're loved by being with the One who loves us*. All of the ideas

155. 2 Cor 5:17.

that follow in this chapter flow from these two principles. Before we get into talking about practical steps, however, there are several important things to bear in mind.

First of all, be honest with God. Nobody this side of heaven understands this love perfectly: God is not expecting *you* to, and isn't judging you for the fact that you don't. Besides, this is God we're talking about: *he already knows.* So there's no reason to pretend that we "get" this and then hope God doesn't notice while we scramble to catch up, like those students who surreptitiously speed-read last night's chapter under the desk while the class is discussing it. (You know who you are.) If you don't get it, raise your hand and say so. That honesty opens us up to being able to work through the things that stand in the way, hand-in-hand with God. (I may also mention that it's when I'm a crying wreck—when I admit to God that I'm scared and sad and basically a mess—that I most experience his comfort.) It's not that God *won't* or *can't* help us if we're not honest; it's that as long as we're pretending we don't need help, we will resist the help he offers us.

Second, ask God for that help. Although we have a responsibility in our own growing process, God is ultimately the one who changes our hearts—just as a farmer has a big responsibility to plow the ground and plant the seed and water the dry spots and pull the weeds, but it's God who actually brings life out of that seed. So ask. When you're struggling to understand and receive love, when you're struggling to see yourself through any eyes other than discouragement, be honest and ask. God delights to answer these sorts of prayers for his children.

Third, keep your eyes open for the little ways God is answering your prayers. It's easy for us to look at our lives, see that nothing drastic has changed, and conclude that nothing is changing at all. But that's a misunderstanding of how God generally works and how change generally works. It would be potentially devastating to a plant *and* its environment (or to an animal, or to a person) to go from seedling to full-grown in an instant. With the possible exceptions of bamboo and my gargantuan baby nephew, there's virtually no living thing that you can actually see growing before your very eyes. Instead, we watch for the little clues along the way: the shoot poking out from the dirt, the first tightly-furled leaves hinting at considering unrolling, or the "Daddy" and "HIKEE!!!" ("Hi, kitty") emerging from amidst the constant stream of babble. These are not disappointingly petty occurrences, as we often think of the small signs of our own growth, but treasured signals that something deeply important, even mysterious and sacred, is going on.

So how do we cultivate this seed, preparing the ground of our hearts to believe what God tells us about his love for us? How do we get into the habit of seeing as God sees? What follows is not an exhaustive list—I am certainly no expert!—but rather some ideas and exercises to aid in this journey of repeating the Truth and being with the One who loves us.[156] Along your road you'll no doubt find many other ways of doing this, and I'd encourage you not to overwhelm yourself, but to try a few and use the ones you find effective. You will not be able to practice all of them at once, but you may find that as God leads you through various seasons in your life, different things become helpful at different times.

Sitting With It

Start a habit of sitting regularly with your belovedness. I realize this sounds vague, and it's easy to skip past because it hardly sounds like doing anything at all. And for many of us, silence—not doing anything—is extremely uncomfortable, especially at first. But it is precisely because there are so many anxieties and insecurities and so much noise addiction drowning out the voice of Love that we need a break of silence to hear it. Not only that, but in a world that sees our value in terms of what we accomplish, stillness is powerful. Intentionally sitting and doing nothing implicitly affirms that the Love with which we are communing is True Love, love that does not depend on the things we get done or whether we succeed or fail at them. It is uncomfortable because it is against the flow of our culture's tide . . . and because it is against the flow, it is important.

I find it helpful to have a physical, visual reminder that speaks to me of God's love—not just in general, but for me personally—and to sit quietly with it for a few minutes regularly. It's not necessary to have a tangible reminder, but I find it anchors me in a time where it would otherwise be easy for my mind to anxiously flit around, wondering if I'm "doing it right." And because it's outside me, it allows me to see value and beauty that would otherwise feel too awkward to believe in if I was thinking directly of myself.

What serves as a reminder will be different for everyone. It may be a painting, a song, a particular vase of flowers. It might be the cross. If you don't have a symbol or reminder, ask God for one. (I have a friend who once said "God could tell me he loved me with a *paper clip* if he wanted to," and

156. Please note also that the following are primarily spiritual exercises, based on the assumption that the need is spiritual and relational. However, not all of the things that keep us from feeling God's love are primarily spiritual in nature. If your barrier to experiencing God's love is coming from a psychological disorder such as depression, anxiety, or obsession, or from the effects of trauma, you should seek help from a mental health professional as well. While everyone's spirituality matters and spiritual exercises can certainly help you along the way, treating mental and physical problems as if they are *only* spiritual will very often make the problem worse.

now finds paper clips everywhere.) Ask Jesus what it says about how he sees you. And then sit with it.

It might feel embarrassing; it might feel like a waste of time, but sit with it. It might feel horrifyingly vulnerable; that's OK. We all need someone from whom we don't have to hide, and Jesus is the ultimate person with whom it's safe to be vulnerable: that very vulnerability you feel may be a strong sign that you need it.

Worship

This is a powerful way to grow in our security in God—not because we're toadying in order to earn love, but because worship readjusts our eyes to reality. Worship is time spent with God, actively practicing Truth with our lips and our hearts. (It's also a solid kick in the teeth to the evil one who is lying to us, which is a nice bonus as well.) And importantly, worship presupposes justification: that is, worship assumes that things are OK between me and God.

When things aren't OK between you and someone you love, you usually don't go on with celebrating and enjoying that person until you've addressed the issue—or at least if you do, it feels dishonest and unhealthy. And yet numerous times in the Bible we see worship coming first. "Hallowed be your name" comes before "forgive us our debts."[157] After the exile, when the Israelites were coming to terms with how deeply they had messed up, God's representatives commanded the people, "Do not grieve, for the joy of the Lord is your strength."[158] The failure was real, the grief was warranted, but the bigger truth is the joy of the Lord. This foreshadowed how Jesus redefines our relationship to God: that it no longer exists in terms of human brokenness but in terms of Jesus' victorious love. No matter our sinfulness, Jesus is bigger. Worship demonstrates and practices this unbelievable Truth . . . and putting unbelievable Truths into practice helps us overcome our unbelief.

Gratitude

Like worship, the possibility of gratitude is interrupted when there's conflict with the one we're supposed to be thanking. Expressing gratitude, therefore, is a powerful way of practicing the truth that Jesus' love is bigger. Gratitude

157. Matt 6:9–12 TNIV, NRSV.

158. Neh 8:10b TNIV.

highlights and helps us notice the loving acts of God, and it expresses our loving relationship. Indeed, appreciation is part of any healthy relationship, and so when we engage in it, our relationship—and thus our ability to receive love—is strengthened, just like paving a road between two cities makes deliveries happen more easily.

Many people find it helpful to keep a gratitude journal. I like making a game of gratitude: taking everything I can think of, including those things that tempt me to dwell on the negative aspects of myself and my life, and seeing if I can turn them around into thanking God. (I learned this from my friend Cathie.) Is money tight? "Thank you, Lord, for the opportunity to depend on you, and for the surprise that is coming when I will see how you provide." Am I smarting over what my friend just said to me? "Thank you, Lord, that you're teaching me how to better deal with conflict." Am I too depressed to get out of bed? "Thank you Lord, that now more than ever I know that you love me for *me,* not for anything I do or can get done."

Being With Truth-tellers

It's important to spend time with people who tell you the truth. Many of the ideas and exercises suggested so far have been things that can be (and sometimes need to be) fairly private between you and God. It's important to remember, though, that the Christian life is not meant to be lived alone. God gave us brothers and sisters in Christ for a reason. Our perspectives on ourselves and our lives are often skewed; we need people who can see us more clearly and help correct our vision, especially when we're weary emotionally or spiritually and are trying to connect with a God whom we can't see or touch. The Bible says "if we don't love people we can see, how can we love God, whom we cannot see?"[159] and this is true in the other direction as well: we can't very well learn to receive love from an invisible, transcendent God if we don't get any practice receiving it from people we can hug and talk with and on whose shoulders we can cry. We need people who can carry God's love for us when we can't hold onto it ourselves.

Exposing the Lies

When you've got thoughts that keep picking away at you, sometimes writing them down can show just how false they are. But don't stop there. Write down next to each one what God *actually* says about it. The Bible has quite

159. 1 John 4:20b NLT.

a lot to say about what God really thinks; if you're stumped for what it has to say about a particular thought, see if there's a friend who knows. Writing down the truth right next to the lie helps make the truth stick a little more—and gives you a big stick to shake when that lie tries to stroll into your head again.

Looking at Jesus

When we do things that help us see Jesus, we automatically get a glimpse of our belovedness because he *is* Love. What helps you really see and connect with Jesus may be different from what helps someone else, but I promise you God has given you ways to see him.

I personally find it helpful to read books or listen to podcasts which address hard questions about the Christian faith. I was surprised at first that something so intellectual helped me connect so much with the heart of Jesus, but then I realized why: all intellectual questions about God are also emotional in nature, and all good answers about God are relational in nature because *God* is relational in nature.

The arts can also be very helpful in seeing Jesus. Art speaks to us in ways few other things can, and sticks with us in ways few other things can. This is part of the reason I work in Christian theatre: it's easy for us to get so used to what the Bible says that we skim over it, but seeing it quite literally brought to life—embodied in living, breathing, people—allows us to see it afresh. The TV series *The Chosen* does this admirably. Not all Christian art is up to that same standard of quality, but more and more good art is being made, and it is worth exploring.

It's also true that as we work to help others see Jesus well, we see him better ourselves. This is why writing is such a powerful activity for me, and why Christian actors can have such a powerful experience portraying the truth. The more you explain math to someone, the better you understand it yourself; the higher we hold the lantern for someone, the more light shines around our own feet too.

Find the things that help you see Jesus. If you don't know what helps you see Jesus, ask him about it, and then explore some avenues. It's alright if not all of them speak to you as powerfully as others. But seek him, because those who seek, find;[160] and those who find him, find Love.

160. See Matt 7:7; Luke 11:9; Jer 29:13.

Paying Attention to Children

I adore my niece and nephew. I adore them when they're sweet and good, and somehow I still can't help but adore them when they're naughty or crabby or being a two-person knee-high tornado. There are a lot of things that can affect how much I like myself or some of the adults I encounter, (sorry, adults!), but nothing ever changes how much I love these kids. I am a far, far cry from being perfect at loving people, but my love for these kids is absolutely unshakable.

Jesus himself used our own love for children to point to God's love. He pointed out that humankind is not just imperfect at love, but is in fact *evil*—and yet we still know how to love our kids; how much more, then, is the God of all goodness openhanded and openhearted with us?[161] We don't expect children to get everything right; we don't expect them to profit us or wait on us or even fully appreciate us. And still we delight in them: and God delights in us.

Of course, not all of us have children of our own (although many of us who don't still borrow them with some regularity as aunts or godparents or babysitters or Sunday School teachers). If you do have children in your life, pay attention. Pay attention to the children you love, because there is something there that you desperately need to see, and God frequently uses children to teach us things we never expected.

Tiny Rituals

Since we learn what we repeat—and since so many of the ideas that bombard us day in and day out are lies of the Enemy and of the world—it can be helpful to have small ways of repeating the truth. There have been seasons when I've needed to remind myself every time I start praying, "God is happy to hear from me, not annoyed that I'm not doing it right or enough." The start of my prayer time serves as the signal to say it, and saying it helps me readjust my customary outlook so that hopefully what's "customary" changes. You can use anything as the "signal"—getting in your car, pouring coffee, washing your hands[162]—and you can use whatever truth you need to repeat: "God thinks I matter." "Jesus is happy he made me." "God isn't disappointed in me." Or it may be helpful to have a short "prayer of the week" that you say at the beginning of each day. For instance, I've sometimes needed

161. See Luke 11:11–13.

162. Giving credit where credit is due, I believe I initially stole this idea from a sermon by my pastor, Bill Hodgeman.

to start every morning with, "Lord, you've said your mercies are new every morning, and I'm calling that in now; I need your mercy today." The following week, I might change it to a different truth or request on which I need to focus. You may be able to use the same prayer for longer than one week; I usually find a week is about as long as I last before I start forgetting to do it or (more likely) forgetting that it really means something. That's why it can be helpful to change it up, so that we're actually practicing the Truth, and not ignoring it as it comes out of our own mouths.

Stepping Outside Ourselves

This may sound a bit strange, but sometimes I've been able to connect to God's love for me better when I've been, well . . . not me. The theatre company I ran occasionally did exercises where we prayed in character. ("In character" just means "while pretending to be the character you'll play on stage.") It's a powerful experience on many levels, but some of the layers still surprise me.

At one rehearsal I was playing a character who is pretty nervous—the sort that figures "I don't have much to say; God doesn't really want to hear from me"—and as I knelt there, awkward and silent, I profoundly felt God's love and compassion for this person, completely unabated by the anxiety or insecurity or any of it. I knew I was seeing depths of love that this character couldn't yet see, but because I "was" that person at the time, I also experienced it as God's love for "me." And because I really was still *me* underneath it all, it also became an avenue for experiencing God's love for *me*, personally. I realized afterwards that this all happened because I didn't have my usual defenses up. It's so much easier to believe "God loves other people" than to believe "God loves *me*," and so God used this experience of "being someone else" to sneak his love past my usual hangups.

I am not suggesting (necessarily) that you go off and do weird acting exercises. I'm simply saying that "stepping outside of ourselves" can be a very helpful practice, and there are many ways to do it. In fact, Christians have been doing this for centuries with a practice called Ignatian contemplation, or "praying with the imagination" as some describe it. The practice involves thinking in detail through a story from one of the Gospels and imagining yourself as a character in the story. Pay attention to things like background noises, temperature, and smells. Is it windy? Sunny? How do you feel in your gut as you walk towards Jesus? How do your knees feel against the ground as you kneel before Jesus? You know the *words* he says from the story itself, but what do his eyes and his tone say as he speaks them?

These sorts of practices go back even farther, to God's people celebrating Sukkot, known also (depending on your translator) as the Feast of Tabernacles, The Festival of Booths, or TentFest. OK the last one I made up, but in any case, since the time of Moses, Jewish people have observed an annual week-long holiday during which they live outside in tents in order to remember the experience of their ancestors who were rescued from Egypt.[163] First, let's take a moment to applaud how fantastic the Old Testament Law was for kinesthetic learners! But then, let's also recognize the value God seems to place on "playing pretend." Apparently, God thinks that stepping into someone else's story can teach us quite a lot about our own story.

Now, different people feel differently about using their imaginations. Some people wail "I'm just not visual!" Some people feel silly or lame. Some of us (myself included) have a lot of "gut feelings" as we imagine the story, while the sights and sounds remain stubbornly undefined. Whatever way *your* imagination works, use what you've got! Just know you don't need to be *afraid* of using it. Because of course, none of us wants to be "just making things up." And some of us come from backgrounds that taught us that imagination was dangerous and warned it could lead to being deceived. But we must remember (and I'm borrowing a lot from pastor/writer Brad Jersak here) that our intellects are just as fallen as our imaginations—and our imaginations are just as redeemed as our intellects. Just as we submit our analytical brains to Jesus when we study the Bible, trusting his promise that the Holy Spirit will guide us into all truth,[164] we can submit our creative brains to him and trust that he'll meet us as we engage with his word that way. Our imaginations aren't infallible any more than our intellects are. But they *are* a part of us, and when Jesus asks us to love God with our *whole* selves—heart, soul, mind, and strength[165]—he doesn't mean for us to leave any part out. The part that daydreamed about being a firefighter or a princess, that later fantasized about romance, the part that feels silly or childish or unholy or unimportant: he wants that too. And he wants it because *he gave it to you* as a way to more wholly experience belonging to him.

Acting exercises, imaginative prayer—it doesn't even have to get as weird as that. You might journal about God's love for you as though you were writing to someone else, reminding them of God's great love for *them*. (Again, most of us find this a good deal easier to do for others than to believe for ourselves.) Or find other ways to engage your imagination in the

163. See Lev 23:42–43.

164. See John 16:13 NLT.

165. Matt 22:37; Mark 12:30; Luke 10:27, quoting Deut 6:5.

presence of Christ. As you practice letting God love you when you're "someone else," you'll get closer to letting God love you when you're *you.*

Knowing and Respecting Your Limits

Some of us who have been living with twisted pictures of God for years find that certain Christian sayings, certain preachers' styles or emphases, or certain analogies used to describe God can distort that image even more. Some of us who are carrying spiritual trauma (yes, that is a thing, and no, it's not rare) find that certain verses of the Bible or certain subjects take us right back to the feelings we had when our faith in God was injured. We are in a spiritual battle with forces of darkness that would like to drive whatever wedge they can between us and God, and this battle has been going on since the snake first lied to Eve: not a single one of us isn't carrying these wounds. So it stands to reason that, while facing our wounds is a helpful thing, it's also helpful to *not get re-injured.* Any athletic coach knows that there are some pains that you can play through and end up stronger, and other injuries where you need to get off the field *now* if you ever want to play again.

This means that in the course of our spiritual growth it may be necessary, for a season, to avoid certain preachers or podcasts. It may be helpful for a season not to engage much with certain subjects or analogies. Or to focus on other parts of the Bible for a while, rather than the verses that send you spiraling. Don't walk away from all spiritual input, certainly. But know the things that lead you closer to God, and know the things that drive you away . . . and lean *way* into the things that help rather than harm. And limit the things that *sometimes* harm.

If you're practicing listening prayer, and you find that after ten minutes, you get bogged down in worrying about how God feels about you, limit your time to eight minutes for now. If you grew up spiritually in an environment that took "self-examination" to mean exclusively "looking for sin in your heart," rather than "getting to know yourself within the warm, loving gaze of God," be intentional with how you go about this practice. You can set a timer so that your self-examination stops before falling back into old patterns, or you can spend a season where you're only "allowed" to examine your attributes that you know please God, rather than continuing to probe your sin (and you might invite a trustworthy friend into the process). If you find yourself journaling the same things over and over again and getting more and more stuck, close your journal and go for a walk.

There are times when I have been praying, in my frequent fog of nebulous spiritual angst, and I've pushed through the discomfort to something beautiful and meaningful on the other side. But there have been many more times when I've had to simply get up off of my knees and go on with my day, leaving all the discomfort unresolved, because I can tell that I'm digging myself into a hole that is not shaped or scented like God. Doing this felt "unspiritual" at first, but it was the best thing I could have done for my spiritual life—because banging our heads against a false image of God doesn't get us any closer to knowing the Real One.

We all have encountered ideas or experiences that make the truth about God's love harder to believe. A lot of them are dressed in very spiritual-looking wrappers. *Know which candy wrappers contain poison for you.* And for now, don't put them in your mouth. Someday, when your immunity is built up more, it may be different. But while you have wounds that can easily be reopened, while you have illnesses that can easily relapse, don't be embarrassed to pass that candy dish by. The Word of God is a feast, and the kingdom of God is a banquet: you will not starve if you pass up certain candies.[166]

Dogging Him

A discussion of limits wouldn't be complete without a discussion of tenacity. Even as you limit unhelpful (or helpful-in-small-doses) ways of pursuing God, this doesn't mean you need to limit your *contact with* God. Quite the opposite. It means we need to pursue God in ways that *are* helpful. And both the Bible and experience tell us we need to press on in that pursuit.

The great part is that the Bible's picture of tenacity isn't fancy or neat. It doesn't require a special kind of inner strength or the right words and ideas. Biblical tenacity is uncouth, even obnoxious. It's tenacity with tears; it lays it all out even to the point of being rude. It's the dirty beggar shouting "Jesus, have mercy on me!" well past the point where people tell him to shut up.[167] It's the pagan mom crying out for help to the prophet of a God she doesn't even worship, making enough of a scene that the disciples urge Jesus to shut her up, and then kneeling in front of him to get completely in his way.[168] It's the Psalmist saying all the things you're not supposed to say—absurdly accusing God of forsaking him, of hanging out on the sidelines when times

166. I say this as someone with (physically, not metaphorically) multiple food sensitivities, who frequently has to skip not just the candies but the doughnuts, bagels, spring rolls, and cheese tray. I'm still alive. And even a bit pudgy.

167. See Mark 10:46–52.

168. See Matt 15:21–28.

get tough, and of rejecting him[169]—and wrestling through his questions and doubts *in the presence* of God, not in a corner fearing God might overhear (nor, I might add, on the exit ramp already assuming God won't turn out to be worth it). It's Jacob wrestling with the Angel of the Lord until daybreak, and (rather impudently, I've always thought) declaring "I won't let you go until you bless me."[170] It's Jesus inviting us to bother him repeatedly with our needs, and promising that God responds to such things.[171]

None of these people were aiming to win any spirituality prizes. There isn't a "right way" to be tenacious. They were just hounding God with all the hunger of their souls until God responded. So dog him! Bother him! Cry out like a baby robin who won't stop until mama robin gives her what she needs! Don't pretend to be full when you're not. Keep bringing your emptiness to Jesus until he flies to your side. He himself has promised, "Open your mouth wide, and I will fill it."[172]

Be patient with yourself and this process. As much as we might wish for God to work an instant miracle in our hearts, the very slowness may be part of how God is demonstrating his love for you. Think about it: which is the greater act of love? To skip over the growing process, as if we're not acceptable until we're perfectly mature? Or to walk with us through it? The very fact that God allows us to take this fumbling, stumbling journey through darkness and insecurity and immaturity towards greater understanding means that *we matter* to God. God does not view you as an end-product to be achieved; God views you as *you*, and would rather be with you through the ups and the downs and the uglies than skip over your real life. Rather than bemoaning our smallness and slowness, perhaps we should be thanking God that he loves us enough to let us be small and slow. Instead of despairing that we'll never "get it," we should be praying the very honest prayer (one of my very favorites), "I do believe; help me overcome my unbelief!"[173]

We tend to look at "belief" as something you do once—the checkbox that puts you on the safe side of salvation—or as something that's an all-or-nothing opinion: you either think the world is flat or you don't. But when it counts, belief, like love, is much more alive than that. You can believe tentatively; you can believe passionately; you can believe when it's as easy

169. Pss 22:1, 10:1, 43:2.
170. Gen 32:24–30 GW.
171. Luke 18:1–8.
172. Ps 81:10b GW.
173. Mark 9:24 TNIV.

as eating cake and when it feels as bleak as a Massachusetts February. Most importantly, like love, belief can grow.

Don't be discouraged if you don't feel it right away. Don't be frustrated if the feelings don't stay. Keep seeking the One who keeps seeking you.

Belief learned in small increments is still belief.

"Food for Thought" Questions

Questions for Reflection/Journaling

- What smallness, slowness, or weakness in myself can I thank God for today?
- What is one signal of God's love (a habit, a child or friend in my life, a visual symbol, a purring cat, etc.) that I can pay attention to this week? Lord, will you please speak to me through this?
- What does it mean to me that because of Jesus, joy and love come *before* correction? Lord, how can I put this truth into practice?
- What *one* habit or exercise would be helpful to try this week?

Questions for Group Study

- Which ideas in this chapter surprised or impacted you the most?
- How might we be reminders of God's love to each other this week? How can we help each other practice this?
- Have you tried anything similar to the practices suggested in this chapter? Which ones were the most meaningful for you?

11

Feet

(How should we view sin?)

Let's face it: it's awkward talking about sin. No one wants to be that stereotype of a "Christian" bawling "sinners" out. Horror stories and hurt abound that we'd rather not repeat. And even if we're not horror-story-worthy about it, there are a lot of things we consider sinful that the wider culture doesn't, which can make us look pretty repressive.

But we struggle with talking about sin in the church, too. Half the time we're so afraid of letting sin run rampant that we run our mouths off about it without considering anyone else's feelings (or possible preexisting wounds). The rest of the time, we're so afraid of hurting people's feelings (or of reenacting the cringe-worthy condemnation we've seen too many times) that we don't say anything at all. And after all, most of the people around us seem to be decent, or at least decently behaved. Hell is increasingly unpopular to talk about, if for no other reason than it's rather embarrassing to believe in something so extreme when the average neighbor seems so . . . bland, at least, if not well-meaning. So what's the big deal with sin?

Biblically, it's a big deal because it's *an offense against a completely holy God*—but if we're honest, our increasingly informal culture is so removed from any understanding of reverence, let alone holiness, that for most of us that statement feels very abstract, if not irrelevant—and brings up uncomfortable, outdated images of an arbitrary, angry God. In our culture of self-determination we struggle with the idea that as Creator, God has just as much right to set parameters for creation as an artist has to put paint wherever she chooses on the canvas and give the finished piece whatever name she has determined. Seldom do we question the wisdom of rebelling against the manufacturer's instructions, or ask whether using our reason, will, and freedom to rebuff the One who gave us our reason, will, and freedom in the first place might be . . . well, absurd, if nothing else. We don't ask if this kind of absurdity might be a form of self-annihilation, like a tree liberating itself from its roots.

We get a little more clarity when we understand God as the source of all good—all of the freedom and fair treatment and caring attention for which we long—and realize that any movement *away* from that Source (a movement that Christian theology calls "sin") is necessarily a movement *towards* the destruction of everything we value. In our fragmented society, it's hard to generalize about what exactly "we" value, but a quick glance at social media shows that just about everyone values *something*, and values it pretty highly. Everyone has something to defend; everyone has an injustice to decry. This is what brings the "big deal" of sin home to us. The very loudness of our polarization indicates that whatever else we believe in, most of us do seem to believe that sin exists, and should be resisted. Even our entertainment is replete with revenge stories and our action movies are well-stocked with heroes who bring the greedy, the cruel, and the ruthlessly powerful to a violent end, because we recognize instinctively (and often simplistically) that people matter, and that exploiting or purposely harming them is wrong.

And yet with all of the proof around us of the destructive nature of sin, many of us don't connect ourselves or our own sins with the large-scale evil we regularly enjoy seeing eradicated in action movies. It's as if the graffiti of sin on the world convinces us, simply by its largeness, that the little pens writing our own stories in blood tell a tale of innocence.

Part of the issue here is that we're often removed from the effects of our sin. Just as most Americans buy our food pre-packaged and need give very little thought to what goes into raising a squash or a cow, or purchase items with the click of a button, without any idea what went into the invention and manufacturing of that nifty beard-comb, we're often several steps removed from our own destructiveness. Our small acts of wastefulness are shipped off through a garbage company to somewhere where it can't bother us—often to another, poorer country—where it destroys someone *else's* environment and causes hazards to someone *else's* health—someone we'll probably never meet and most of the time can completely forget exists. A thoughtlessly Anglo-centric comment may do *me* little to no discernible damage, while contributing one more brick to the weight of mental stress, emotional trauma, and even decreased life expectancy that accompanies being a Black or Indigenous person in America.[174] The ways in which we objectify women

174. This is where I reluctantly admit to my pasty heritage, and mention that I don't expect that everyone will resonate with each example in this section: I am using "we" and "me" in the very general sense as I don't have experience with each scenario. (For instance, when I wrote this, I was as yet unmarried, and so the example of abuse several

and suppress their gifts may seem negligible or normal or escape our notice entirely: we don't register how these things contribute to the erosion of a woman's attitude towards herself, and eventually to the inability to stand up for herself when that disrespect becomes physical.

Another part of the issue is that we're usually able, quite effectively, to minimize "ordinary" sins. Pornography is normal—and everywhere—in our culture, and "doesn't hurt anybody." While it's embarrassing to admit to, perhaps, it's essentially harmless . . . as long as I can ignore the fact that a high number of workers in that industry are coerced or trafficked into it, that I'm exploiting their bodies just as much as their abusers are, that even AI-generated pornography is made from pictures of real people, and that frequent porn use causes neurological and attitude changes in the viewer that are troubling at best and dangerous at worst.[175] Gossip and criticism are basically sports to many of us: at least, they can be just as enjoyable, and seem harmless (or mostly-harmless, which we tell ourselves is just as good). It seems normal and "not all that bad" to write certain people off: not everyone of course, just the aggressive/ lazy/ ignorant/ stupid/ mean/ obnoxious/ irritating/ weird/ impaired/ offensive ones, (you know . . . the ones who *deserve* to be written off). It's easy to casually hold them in contempt, while forgetting that the Bible says "do not hate your brother in your heart."[176] It's only when the culture starts pointing out certain ones of these tiny, we-thought-invisible judgments and labeling them as "racism" or "misogyny" that our cute little world gets rocked.

Evil was supposed to be "out there." It wasn't supposed to be a factor in my everyday dealings. It also wasn't supposed to be this difficult to eradicate. The true heinousness of sin is supposed to be about, say, the cruel people who use their power to crush others under their proverbial boot on purpose. It wasn't supposed to be about the secret pleasure I take in thinking how immature and nasty that client is who yelled at me for no good reason. It wasn't supposed to be about my insecurities playing out in a constant stream of belittling words towards my spouse—which, it turns out, makes me an abuser, even though it would "never progress to hitting." Whites are quick to get defensive and close their ears to the Black experience, not because it isn't true, but because it *is* true and it's overwhelming. We want injustice to be comfortably in the past, neatly blamed on mean dead people, and to think

paragraphs down was completely theoretical . . . in case you were worried about my husband.)

175. See Eberstadt and Layden, "Social Costs of Pornography." See also Doidge, "Acquiring Tastes and Loves," 102–12.

176. Lev 19:17; see also Matt 5:21–22 and 1 John 3:14–15.

that such evil is still being perpetrated now—sometimes through things *I* do (or don't bother to do)—is frequently too distressing to handle.

We want the heinousness of evil to lie in its abnormality: to horrify us because it's rare, something no normal person would do—but the truth is it's as common as dust. The heinousness lies in the nature of sin itself, that it's so far from what *should be,* not in its distance from what *usually is.* The Holocaust stands out to us because it is extreme, but that extremity was made possible by ordinary evil in ordinary people. Our self-interest. Our tendency to resent and blame others. Our ability to ignore injustice when it doesn't directly disadvantage us. Our greed, our suspicion, our desire to be better than others: a thousand natural, normal impulses that readied a culture to dehumanize and slaughter millions. The Holocaust was not built on the madness of one man; it was built on years of ordinary, unnoticed sin. Indeed, many who played a role in bringing it about had no idea what they were building through their attitudes and words, and many probably would have personally objected to it—but they had a hand in it nonetheless. Viktor Frankl, Holocaust survivor, writes, "I am absolutely convinced that the gas chambers of Auschwitz, Treblinka, and Maidanek were ultimately prepared not in some ministry or other in Berlin, but rather at the desks and in lecture halls of nihilistic scientists and philosophers."[177] Doubtless, these academics did not aim to start a genocide any more than the casually anti-Semitic common man did . . . and yet the godless, amoral ideas that the former spread; the veiled contempt that the latter harbored; the self-first tendencies that we all harbor: these laid the foundation for a horror they never meant to unleash.

The Memorial to the Murdered Jews of Europe, Berlin's Holocaust memorial, is telling in this regard. It is made up of concrete slabs laid out in a grid almost like a city map. At the edge, they're only a few inches high. As you begin to walk between them towards the center, you hardly realize the ground is sloping downward until those concrete blocks are towering around you, nearly three times your height. Evil is supposed to be obvious, alien, and elsewhere; it's not supposed to be *me*—and the more we think like that, the more easily it sneaks up on us from within.

We try to outrun it. We tell ourselves that with more education or empathy or effort, the world won't be this way. We soothe ourselves with the fairy tale that we make decisions completely freely and that we can simply choose which side of the moral scales to plop a deed on—but the truth is more disturbing than that. Sin is not a weight on one side of a scale or a tally on one side of a ledger. Sin is a disease we were all born with: something

177. Frankl, *Doctor and the Soul*, xxi.

passed down from our first parents through no decision of our own, and reinforced in every generation through countless decisions of our own. And diseases don't care about our intentions or efforts. Diseases spread destruction through us to those around us, no matter how much goodwill we have towards them. That's why you don't shake hands (no matter how warmly) when you've got the flu. That's why, no matter how "nice" we are, Christianity still teaches that each one of us is a sinner, and it is also why, no matter what particular deeds we have or haven't done, each of us still needs a savior. A deadly infection is still a deadly infection, no matter what symptoms you've exhibited so far.

Many of us don't like this. We would like to say this is just a theoretical religious concept—simply one among many ideas or models of what sin is—but in fact we see this tragedy play out every day. Pedophiles and abusers are statistically likely to have been abused themselves as children. We fairly easily accept that they are not responsible for the trauma they experienced and the inner brokenness that resulted, but we understand that they are still responsible for their own actions. We know that we had no control over the "nature" and "nurture" that still shape our behavior, and that we still have a meaningful amount of control over our behavior: enough that we are more than just automatons or puppets as we contribute to the next Holocausts, Jim Crow laws, and abuses.

It is this absolute evil hidden in even the most mundane of sinners that makes sense of why Jesus had to go through such extreme suffering to atone for it—and makes his treatment of sinners nothing short of miraculous. In John 13, Jesus (not only the King of the Universe but also the king of object lessons) gives us an unforgettable picture. The picture is so rich that theologians and pastors never tire of talking about it. It provides nearly endless food for thought because it is in fact a picture of so many things at once: of what leadership looks like done God's way, of the Christian life, of humility, of grace, and—most importantly—of his sacrificial love.

It's mere hours before Jesus' arrest, and he knows it. His disciples have arrived to celebrate Passover with him, and he strips down, wraps a towel around his waist, and washes their feet. This is striking enough in our own culture—feet are gross; men's feet that have been tromping around dusty roads in intense heat in sandals are worse—but in that culture it's even more arresting. Washing the feet of guests was a job given to the lowest-ranking slave in the household (for obvious reasons). In an honor-shame culture it's unthinkable for the leader and teacher to do this. Add to that the fact that he does it for *all* of them, including Judas Iscariot, who he knows is about to betray him, and it's not hard to see why this passage remains popular with

Christian speakers. (It's not just because it's got its own day during Holy Week!)

Although the "servant leadership" aspect of this story tends to get the most attention, Jesus also has a very important conversation with Peter in this passage that has vital implications. Peter, in this scene, is noticeably uncomfortable with Jesus' hygiene plan, and tells his Master in no uncertain terms that this is one disciple whose feet he won't be stooping to wash. Jesus gives a curious response: "If I don't wash you, you don't belong to me."[178] Ever one for extremes, Peter tells Jesus that in that case, he'd like to go whole hog and have his head and hands washed as well. Having fully acknowledged that Peter doesn't get what's going on yet, and having promised that he'll understand later, Jesus replies, "Those who have had a bath need only to wash their feet; their whole body is clean."[179]

Without anyone ever saying it explicitly, dirt has become a metaphor for sin.

This is the "later you will understand"[180] through which we should look at this passage. This is not just a story of long ago or a blueprint for us to follow. This is a picture of a Person who is still alive today and with whom we have a relationship. Perhaps we expected his cleansing to be on a grander, less intimate scale, something along the lines of the washing of the whole world in the days of Noah or the wholesale purification evoked by the words of the prophets. But just before he performs the most dramatic act imaginable on the cross to reconcile all of creation to God, Jesus also performs this most individual, personal act of cleansing. Maybe it is because the scale of the reality-rending work on the cross is so big—universe-sized, eternity-sized work that sometimes overwhelms our ability to process and connect with it—that he gives us this smaller picture, one that can more easily fit into our understanding, so that we cannot miss how he deals with us and our sin.

Look at the gentleness with which he takes our feet in his hands. He shows no disgust at touching our dirtiness. He's not afraid of it. He doesn't resent the mess, the inevitable fact that our cruddiness will get on his hands. He doesn't leave us to deal with it ourselves, seeing as they're *our* feet and *we're* the ones who got them dirty in the first place. He doesn't hesitate, worrying that we'll be offended to know that he thinks our feet need washing, wondering if we'll turn on him for it or wondering if we're worth the trouble. And his gentleness with us is not detached, something in which he

178. John 13:8b GW.

179. John 13:10 TNIV.

180. See verse 7.

has no stake, but something in which he is as invested as it is possible to be: he went through unfathomable vicarious torture and sacrifice in order to be able to do this for us.

To the one who loves Jesus, this, perhaps more than anything else, is why sin is a big deal. Every time I ask him to cleanse me of sin, I am asking him to wash my feet. It is the most intimate, loving, non-judgmental experience—and also the one that brings the most regret, aversion to sin, and sober-mindedness. For the Lord of the universe is willing to strip himself down, kneel before me, take my foot in his wounded hands and wash it clean. And I cannot, I *cannot*, ask him flippantly to do this. I cannot say "sorry" because that's what you say to get God off your back, fully intending to do the same thing again if I feel like it. When I look into the eyes of the One who washes my feet, I can't bear to knowingly put both of us in a position where I'll need to ask him to do it again. I know I will, and I know he will. But I cannot take that holy mystery of beautiful, painful grace lightly.

As it turns out, it is not just the *seriousness* of sin that Jesus shows us here. In fact, *everything* this passage says about sin is crucial to our understanding. It tells us that even those who are in relationship with Jesus will still mess up and need to be washed. It tells us that this does not mean we weren't really saved or that we need to somehow be saved again: the bath has already been achieved, it's the dust we pick up on the way that Jesus wants to deal with now. It tells us unequivocally about the heart of God towards sinners. And it tells us that we are commissioned by Jesus to wash one another's feet.

Rarely do we connect Jesus' command to "wash one another's feet" with the things this passage teaches us about sin. But it is significant that he gives us this command *after* his conversation with Peter. We almost always talk about this command in terms of humbly serving one another, but interestingly, nowhere does Jesus explicitly interpret his command here as "service." He washes his disciples' feet, has his conversation with Peter about sin, and then tells his disciples to follow his example. He didn't say, "Now that I've served you, you should also serve each other"; he said, "Now that I have washed your feet, you also should wash one another's feet."[181] He leaves the metaphor open. He is talking about both: asking us not just to serve, but to actively apply his forgiveness and grace.

Care for our brothers and sisters *has to* include care for their souls. And what a powerful picture of how to do it! Foot-washing cannot be undertaken from afar. You have to be close enough to take your fellow

181. John 13:14 TNIV, abridged. (I removed his comments about his identity for the flow of the sentence, but do still heartily affirm that he is both Lord and teacher!)

Christian's foot in your hand. Close enough that you can see if there are wounds around which you need to be particularly gentle. Close enough that some of their dirt might get on your reputation. Close enough that you have to kneel before them while you do it, and look into their eyes not from a lofty height but from below, as Jesus did. Close enough that they can kick you in the teeth—and they will sometimes. Feet are ticklish.

Being willing to risk getting kicked is, whether we like it or not, part of the job description. And when people do "kick us in the teeth" over this, we do well to prayerfully examine our own hearts and conduct to see if we have been insensitive or "off" in how we went about things, and to make every effort, "so far as it depends on you," to make peace.[182] (We can almost always learn *something* about how to communicate in ways that people can receive, even if we didn't sin against them at all.) After that, though, we also do well to remember that Jesus, too, was frequently "kicked in the teeth" for pointing out sin, and go to him for comfort and the courage to carry on. His example and presence help us to stand firm in the fact that the truth doesn't stop being true—or worth speaking—even when it makes people angry. The fault doesn't lie with the one who speaks the truth in love but with the one who refuses to listen to the truth. It's also helpful to realize that Jesus knows how we feel, and can not only heal the hurt we've received, but give us forgiveness and understanding for those who lash out at us—after all, we ourselves have frequently been the ones who have "kicked Jesus in the teeth" in defense of our own sin.

If you're someone who cares deeply about sin, it's OK that you do! In fact, that is a very, very good thing. It is not, as many make it out to be, judgmental in itself; it is in fact a crucial first step to true mercy. What we need to watch out for is smugness: the attitude of the heart in which we're secretly glad to see someone else sinning, because it means we're so many spaces ahead of them on the righteousness game-board. (That's actually the *opposite* of caring deeply about sin, because we have a vested interest in seeing them fall.)

The other thing we need to watch out for is fear. At one extreme, fear can keep us from addressing each other's dirt at all, hanging back with the righteous-sounding excuse, "It's none of my business; I'm no better, after all." At the other extreme, fear can cause us to undertake these conversations harshly or inadvisedly, because we feel so responsible to "police" our brothers and sisters and correct their behavior. But God never said we should or could fix our siblings in Christ; we can only lovingly warn them. (As God explained to the prophet Ezekiel, his job was to speak God's words

182. See Rom 12:18.

"whether they listen or fail to listen"; actually responding to God was *their* responsibility.)[183] There truly are right times and wrong times to bring things up, and we need to listen to the Holy Spirit for both the timing and the words. Sometimes people are hurting or doubting that God's love is really for them, and they need acceptance before they need correction; in such cases jumping right into confronting their "dirt" could do great spiritual damage from which it can take a long time to heal. There are also times when we need to speak up before a pattern gets repeated again. We need to be willing to wait on the Holy Spirit's timing in each circumstance, trusting that God is at work in our brothers and sisters and won't drop the ball, even without us "controlling" them. As a pastor friend of mine remarked, "I can categorically object to certain behavior on solid scriptural grounds without the need to point it out every time I see it." We need to trust God enough to shut up sometimes, as well as to lovingly speak when God says to.

Finally, it is worth pointing out that our duty towards Christians here is markedly different from our duty towards unbelievers. After all, we're only qualified to wash feet; if someone hasn't yet had a full bath yet, there's only One who can help with that. Their smelly feet are rather beside the point until they've been introduced to him. Of course, for the sake of healthy, loving relationship, it's helpful to be honest when there are interpersonal issues, and foot-washing is a good image as we remember the humility and gentleness to which Jesus calls us in this. And there will be times when we need to speak out for justice, no matter what someone believes. But in general, the fact that someone isn't a follower of Jesus—and thus hasn't signed up for the things Jesus asks of people—means that we haven't got a duty, or even a right, to hold them accountable to do those things.[184] We should still talk to people about what Jesus said, whether they're Christian or not, (and whether they're Christian or not, we should emphasize the love, compassion, and mercy of Jesus when we do), but the conversation and expectations will be very different based on whether or not that person considers Jesus to be Lord.

How are we to see sin? As a defeated but still-virulent foe—and Christians as our fellow soldiers, who look out for us as we look out for them, who tend each other's wounds and blisters, and who give each other strength to keep fighting when we've suffered a retreat. It is hard to say whether it takes more courage and love to wash someone's feet or to let someone wash ours. But we are called to do both. And as we do, we will find the sort of

183. See Ezek 2:5, 7; 3:11, 16–21; 33:1–9.

184. See 1 Cor 5:9–13, in which Paul makes a sharp distinction between believers and nonbelievers when it comes to holding people accountable for sin.

love that Jesus talked about and prayed for grows: because relational risk and relational mercy form stronger bonds than just about any other type of experience or service.

How are we to see sin? As the fatal global pandemic the great Physician gave his life to cure, and which his patients now fight: both in our own lives and in the world, as we seek to administer that same saving Life we were given.

How are we to see sin? As the filth that his pure hands tenderly wash away—and our hands as outposts of his, purified forever by him.

"Food for Thought" Questions

Questions for Reflection/Journaling

- Which aspect of the "foot-washing" described here do I find the most difficult? Being willing to confront people? Approaching people gently? Putting aside my desire to be "better-than"? Why is this hard for me?
- Is there "dirt" in my life I'm not ready to let go of? Is it worth holding on to, considering what Jesus thinks I'm worth? Why or why not?
- Jesus, thank you for washing my feet. Will you show me the gentleness and humility with which you treat me, so that I can show others the same?

Questions for Group Study

- What in this chapter surprised or encouraged you the most?
- Can you remember a time when someone confronted you gently and lovingly? What about their approach was helpful?
- What do you think of the idea that our duty toward Christians is different from our duty towards non-Christians when it comes to "foot-washing"?

12

Zacchaeus Was a Bad Little Man

(What does it really mean to judge others?)

"Why, all the souls that were were forfeit once
And He that might the vantage best have took
found out the remedy. How would you be
if He, which is the top of judgment, should
but judge you as you are? O think on that;
and mercy then will breathe within your lips
like man new made."

—WILLIAM SHAKESPEARE, *MEASURE FOR MEASURE*

WHEN I WAS A kid, the story of Zacchaeus was a popular one in Sunday School. We had a catchy little song about him and everything, but I think the real draw was the image of a short guy climbing a tree to see over the crowd.[185] It's a funny picture, the story is simple and understandable, and kids seem to sympathize with the pint-sized anti-hero, whether because of his size or because he gets picked on.

His story follows a pretty familiar motif: Jesus meets someone "where they're at;" everyone around begins to mutter about what a "sinner" that person is; Jesus reaffirms his acceptance of that person, often with a cleverness that leaves the mean mutterers speechless; the reader cheers; and Jesus rides off into the sunset. (Slowly, because he's on a donkey, if not walking.) Even readers who don't consider themselves followers of Jesus usually cheer:

185. For those of you who missed the fun in Sunday School, the story is in Luke 19:1–10.

in a world that longs for acceptance, Jesus' treatment of oft-rejected people startles us with hope.

Our culture used to feel similarly positive about Jesus' words, "Do not judge, so that you may not be judged."[186] (It was a very convenient axiom to yank out of context and wave around, because let's face it, who wants to feel judged?) Nowadays, although we *think* we still like that saying, we find we believe in quite a lot of caveats. We're wounded and cry "unsafe" when someone's judgmental mother comments on our choices, but we also expect people to boycott that actor or director or celebrity whose misconduct was exposed this week. More often than you hear "do not judge," you hear "silence is violence." We're uncomfortable and outraged (rightly so) when abuse is covered up. Amidst all of it, we feel a not-so-subtle pressure to say the right things so people know we don't approve of such abuses. Our cultural moment might better be expressed as "Make sure you judge *the right people*, so that you may not be judged." We have all sorts of fancy labels for it—"virtue-signaling," "cancel culture"—but it comes down to the age-old dilemma: there are certain behaviors we think should be condemned, and yet not a single one of us wants to be condemned ourselves. Zacchaeus may not be so simple after all.

Now, for many in America, this tension is settled with an unspoken (and often artificial) division between what is "personal" and what is "harmful." We're expected to ignore private behavior if there isn't a power dynamic—if "no one is getting hurt"—and we're expected to loudly condemn any behavior, words, or opinions that could be considered exploitative, hateful, or even just unkind. Most of this is based on a human assessment of what is worthy of condemnation (and we don't have time to get into the philosophical and theological problems with *that* kind of approach). But even those who look to God's standards have struggled with this same tension for ages.

Doesn't the Bible say God cares about justice? But then, doesn't Jesus *mean it* when he says "don't judge"? Does he mean we shouldn't categorize behavior as good or bad—that we shouldn't notice or mention it when someone is in the wrong? How then can we stand up for people who are being hurt? And if God *does* want us to care about what's right, what on earth are we supposed to do with this whole "don't judge" thing?

These questions have always been important. Our understanding of them affects our obedience to Jesus and our ability to function as a healthy community. It affects the world's perception of us—one that has all too often been an image of legalistic snobbery. But in this era, when our world is drowning in its own condemnation and crying out beyond words for both

186. Matt 7:1 NRSV; see also Luke 6:37.

justice and acceptance, it may be more important than ever for Christians to know what to do with this tension. Quite simply, the world needs us to. Every hurting sinner needs to run across someone who handles this as Jesus did.

So how *did* Jesus handle this?

One of the most beloved stories of Jesus' approach to non-judgment is found in John 8.[187] In it, Jesus is put on the spot (so that the authorities can have an excuse to condemn *him)* with the question of a woman caught in adultery. "The *law*," say Jesus' enemies, "says that women like this should be stoned. So what do *you* say?"[188]

Now, the author leaves us with a lot of unanswered questions on purpose. The law doesn't actually say "women like this should be stoned"; it says "both the adulterer and the adulteress are to be put to death."[189] Technically, the religious authorities themselves aren't following the Law of Moses here:[190] where is the adulterer? If they managed to catch this woman "in the act" as they claim . . . well first of all, how did they happen to conveniently come across this just when Jesus was around, and second, how is it that they *didn't* manage to also catch the man? Just as Jesus himself does in this passage, the author lets these questions hang unspoken in the air until we onlookers begin to realize, "Hey wait . . . there's something sketchy going on here."

When the teachers of the law don't get the hint and instead press Jesus for an answer, he invites them to go ahead and stone her, with one specification: the person who has never messed up should go first. The silence lengthens, and then one by one, starting with the oldest and wisest, the "court" empties. (There was a very enjoyable debate in the multigenerational Bible study I attended over whether the older people had had more time to *recognize* their sinfulness, or if they'd just had more time to *commit* more sins.) Once everyone has awkwardly and quietly left, Jesus asks the woman,

187. It wasn't *originally* found in John 8, but scholars generally agree that the story is authentic. We just don't know where it originally belonged.

188. John 8:5, author's own paraphrase.

189. Lev 20:10 TNIV. Note that it doesn't even prescribe stoning; this was just something they had assumed from other capital crimes in the law.

190. Which may be how they intended to trap Jesus. The text doesn't say whether they laid this trap based on his reputation for mercy or based on his habit of authoritatively teaching ideas they hadn't approved, or with some other "trick" in mind. It's possible that they were attempting to trap him on a technicality: if he says "don't stone her," he's breaking the law by sparing an adulteress; if he says "stone her," he's breaking the law by punishing the woman without punishing the man.

"has no one condemned you?" When she replies that no one has, Jesus tells her, "Then neither do I condemn you. Go now and leave your life of sin."[191]

It's an amazingly powerful story that deserves an entire book of its own to fully unpack, and it's frankly one of Jesus' most palatable examples of non-judgment. It's really easy for a modern audience to applaud his actions here, whether they consider themselves religious or not: not only does Jesus brilliantly handle this crowd, but he protects someone whom we feel deserves it. We see a woman with few legal rights surrounded by men who are flagrantly misapplying power at her expense, and we're pretty much on her side no matter *what* she's done. Jesus' words also land quite well: "Let any of you who is without sin be the first to throw a stone at her"[192] sounds quite a lot like "Oh well, no one's perfect"—which is a very popular phrase, thanks to how highly we value "not making a big deal" out of sins we consider excusable. (And let's face it, consensual sex is top on today's list of "private" things that "don't hurt anyone"—or if it does, in this case it hurt only one man in a patriarchal culture who probably treated her as lesser anyway.)[193] Jesus' affirmation "neither do I condemn you" is the icing on a very gratifying, rather comfortable cake.

And then there's Zacchaeus.

Zacchaeus was more than a "wee little man."[194] Zacchaeus was a jerk. Here is no disempowered, disenfranchised victim: most of us would probably view him with just as much disgust as his own neighbors did. As a native Israelite employed by the Romans to collect taxes, Zacchaeus was aligned with the power of the empire oppressing his own people. He was a scab, a traitor. Not only that, but in a system which put very few checks and balances on local collectors, he was free to charge his countrymen exorbitant amounts above the actual tax rates and pocket the difference—and judging by the clues we get in this story, it seems likely that he took full advantage of that. As removed as we are from first-century culture, we often think of New Testament tax collectors as petty nuisances (like we frequently view our own IRS workers) or *perhaps* as misunderstood "bad boys" (like we frequently view handsome literary thieves like Jack Sparrow or outlaws of the Old West). But Zacchaeus and his counterparts were sellouts to greed,

191. John 8:10–11 TNIV.

192. John 8:7 TNIV.

193. I am again using "we" and "us" in the very broad sense to reflect the culture around me, not to say that this paragraph represents *everyone's* attitudes or even my own.

194. Many thanks to whatever anonymous songwriter got *that* permanently stuck in the heads of many a Sunday School teacher.

power, and imperialism: the wolves of Wall Street, the Vichy government officials, the citizens who profit from the disasters of their own people.

And Jesus doesn't condemn him either.

What?! Why not?! This would be a really good time to confront injustice, wouldn't it? If nothing else, doesn't Jesus need to make a public statement about how wrong this is? Well, he does make a public statement: "Hey, hop down out of that tree; I want to come hang out with you."[195]

This is one of those times where modern standards and ancient standards align: this is just not OK. It's fine for Jesus to excuse the people we'd excuse: impoverished children stealing to survive (like Disney's Aladdin) or prostitutes selling their bodies because need or oppression forced them (like Fantine in *Les Miserables*). But *Zacchaeus?*

But Jesus isn't done making us uncomfortable. The story I find most illuminating on how Jesus handled judgment is in Luke 13, where some people tell Jesus about an atrocity that has recently been committed against some Galileans. It seems they want his take on it; possibly they want some authoritative verdict that would make sense of it all. Here's what Jesus gives them:

> Do you think that these Galileans were worse sinners than all the other Galileans because they suffered this way? I tell you, no! But unless you repent, you too will all perish. Or those eighteen who died when the tower in Siloam fell on them—do you think they were more guilty than all the others living in Jerusalem? I tell you, no! But unless you repent, you too will all perish."[196]

None of this is what anyone expected him to say. (Before we go anywhere with this, let's take a moment to applaud Jesus' genius as a communicator. As a dramatist myself, I *wish* I could construct my reversals this well! He subverts his audience's expectations *and then immediately subverts them again!* I am delightedly envious.) First, Jesus confronts the very human tendency to blame the victim. Partly because wrong actions often *do* have substantial consequences, and partly because it makes us feel safe in an unpredictable world, it's easy for us to believe that people suffer because they deserve it. This is a well-documented psychological defense mechanism, the logic being "if terrible things happen because people deserve them, then terrible things can't happen to *me*, because I don't deserve them." It's also, incidentally, one of the principles behind popular concepts such as karma. Jesus flatly contradicts this idea, defending the victims against this harsh

195. Luke 19:5, highly paraphrased.

196. Luke 13:2–5 TNIV.

oversimplification, and at the same time stripping away the psychological safety net on which his audience is relying.

At this point, we're ready for him to do what we usually do: land squarely on the side of the person who was unfairly judged, blast those snobs who judged them, and trumpet their innocence to the world. *And he doesn't.* We expect statements like "don't judge that person" or "those people were no worse than anybody else" to be followed by something about how that person wasn't really in the wrong, or how we're all trying our best in our own way. But that's not what Jesus says. He says something much scarier and much truer.

He doesn't say "they're just as innocent as you are." He says "you're in just as much danger." If we were counting on Jesus to fulfill our expectations of what a nice, kind, safe, non-judgmental person should look like . . . this is not what we were looking for.

This is the first thing to note with Jesus: to Jesus, non-judgment doesn't mean denying there's a problem. To the woman caught in adultery, he openly says that her life is characterized by sin.[197] He has no problem saying that Zacchaeus had been "lost" before his encounter with Jesus.[198] The real reason we want to defend the innocence of "victims" is that we desperately want to believe that *we're* innocent: we love statements like "they weren't worse sinners than anybody else" because they make it sound like nobody's sin is a problem. But what Jesus implies in all of these stories—indeed what he makes explicit—is that we're *not* better than anyone else, and that our sin *is* a problem. Jesus' message of mercy *depends upon* believing that some things are wrong. Unless *actual wrong* has been done, there's nothing to be merciful about. Without a belief in the wrongness of sin, it's not a message of mercy but a message of "meh."

Jesus also, apparently, didn't consider it judgmental to call for change. I might have said "Dang, this lady has had a rough day, being caught and almost killed for adultery; let's just leave her alone." But after all she's been through, Jesus still goes ahead and invites her to repent: to change her mind and change course.[199] He loves her too much to leave without showing her the exit door to her prison.

197. John 8:11.

198. Luke 19:10.

199. "Repent" can carry a lot of baggage unrelated to its actual meaning, but I use it because Jesus used it a lot and we need to understand what it means. The Greek word translated "repent" means "to turn around" or "to change one's mind." When the Bible talks about it, it means recognizing we've been wrong and choosing to change course. It doesn't actually have anything to do with "penance": beating oneself up or performing good deeds to make up for the "red in my ledger" (to quote Black Widow in Marvel's

His volume varies: with the woman, he is incredibly gentle. With the rubberneckers gossiping about recent atrocities and falling towers, he's a little more direct: probably because while the woman was already highly aware that there was a problem, this crowd was blithely oblivious to the fact that the problem had anything to do with *them*. With the Pharisees, whom he called "blind" (and other things) on many occasions,[200] he's so direct that it stings—not because they "deserved" to be judged for being so judgmental, an assumption we often make, but because they were that dangerously heedless. Mom encourages and counsels the child crying on her lap but yells at the child running into the street.

No matter the volume, though, for all who will hear, it is *good news* because a call to repentance is a call, not to punishment or self-hatred, but to wholeness. Think about it: God is love, and is the one who created wholeness and goodness to begin with. Like a physiotherapist realigning your spine, like a conductor guiding the orchestra back into rhythm, like that guy at the bike shop "trueing" your wheels,[201] our Maker is someone who brings relief by making our lives fit us better, not worse.

On the other hand, Jesus doesn't seem to consider it dangerous to meet sinners (even "oppressors") without publicly condemning their actions. Interestingly, he never invites Zacchaeus to repent at all, at least not verbally in any scene the author reports—which probably worried the crowd as much as it would have worried me. We don't *want* to see Jesus enabling and validating Zacchaeus's choices. And we shouldn't: it would be awful if Zacchaeus's greed and selfishness got to come with him when he entered God's kingdom; it wouldn't even be "grace" then but simply complicity. Thankfully, Jesus doesn't do this. But he *does* offer an invitation. It sounds delightfully backwards ("I'm coming to your house"), because he's inviting Zacchaeus not to a home but to *himself*. He's inviting Zacchaeus to experience what perfect love is like. And it is in fact Jesus' *non-judgment* (what we might call "grace") that *causes* Zacchaeus's repentance.

Now, Zacchaeus already knew that his life wasn't one a holy man would approve. And yet this holy man is there anyway—not condemning, not condoning, but not hanging back either: he's fully immersed in Zacchaeus's life as his houseguest. Apparently, Zacchaeus's bad choices aren't the only thing or even the first thing this holy man sees; apparently *someone* believes

---

Avengers).

200. See Matt 15:7–9; 23:13–39; John 9:41.

201. If you haven't had this pleasure, it's when they make your wheels perfectly circular (and perfectly *flat* circles) again, rather than whatever wonky wobbly grind-against-your-brakes shape those last few bumps or ditches or fender-benders turned them into.

that a worthwhile soul is still in there. Of course this causes a response in Zacchaeus! And this response reveals something surprising: to truly, consciously receive grace *is* to repent. By accepting someone's forgiveness, we're acknowledging that we need it—that we're in the wrong. That's the first half of repentance right there. And by choosing to accept that grace, we're also implicitly saying that we don't want to stay in the wrong. There's the second half. By calling people to repentance, Jesus is actually calling them to experience the acceptance he's been offering all along.

It's important to note that this is not only God's signature move, but also central to the gospel: Jesus doesn't wait for us to repent first. The Apostle Paul writes, "while we were still sinners, Christ died for us"[202]; elsewhere he writes that "God's kindness is meant to *lead you toward* repentance."[203] In other words, it is not our repentance that causes God to be gracious to us; it is God's kindness that makes us gratefully want to change and feel safe enough to admit we need to. Jesus didn't say "Today salvation has come to this house"[204] because Zacchaeus's sudden turnaround had earned the love of God, but because his turnaround signaled that he "got" the love of God and had willingly received it. God's kindness comes first, and then calls out to us to respond. God is not threatened—nor is God's justice threatened—by either our brokenness or our inability to fix it ourselves.

There are two things Jesus does seem to consider judgmental: keeping score, and writing people off.

When we write someone off—the fancy word is "condemn" them—we're making an unauthorized, supposedly-final verdict on who they are. We are defining them by what they've done, and giving up on their potential to be anything else. It's treating sometimes-simplistic, often-true summaries as the end of the story: "He's racist;" "She's toxic;" "He likes being obnoxious;" "She's judgmental." Now, sometimes things like this do need to be said in order to protect people, like when Jesus warned his followers that the Pharisees were "blind guides" whose seeming spiritual authority shouldn't be trusted.[205] But Jesus *defines* us differently. Jesus defines us as people he made, people he loves, people he would give anything to redeem. Condemnation is an impulse and an excuse to move *away* from a sinner; Jesus moves *towards* us to heal. In Jesus' book, sinners (even the most oppressive sinners) don't have to be collateral damage in our thirst for justice.

202. Rom 5:8b NIRV.

203. Rom 2:4b, NRSV, emphasis mine.

204. Luke 19:9 TNIV.

205. Matt 15:14.

This isn't a non-judgment that minimizes sin; it is a "moving toward" that fully acknowledges the sin and moves towards the sinner anyway.

This can't be done without the cross. Human behavior is too shattering, too hurtful. We are moderately skilled at "non-judgment" when we define it as "accepting what I already think is kind of OK," but that is not what true mercy is. Mercy means forgiving the inexcusable, not the excusable. *That* is why Jesus died: because some things really *aren't* excusable, and something had to be done about them in order for him to legitimately, without committing injustice, accept unacceptable people and forgive unforgivable acts. Without the cross, condemnation is necessary and will overtake all of us in the end; with the cross, we are freed from our sin and the condemnation it deserves, and we don't have the right to withhold that freedom from anyone.

Score-keeping is a little different. Condemnation is often based in a love for justice, even though it ends up destroying love for the sinner. When we keep score—focusing on how a person measures up (or doesn't measure up) *compared to me*—we are neither loving the sinner nor even loving what is good, but loving our own potential to win. It is, in some ways, a bloodthirsty mentality: one that assumes that my own moral survival is at stake and can be bolstered by their moral death, the way one starving man in a siege may cannibalize his neighbor. (True, Jesus never *said* "don't eat your neighbor," but . . . we're just going to assume it's covered in some of his other commands.) This is what Jesus is getting at with his "plank-and-speck" comparison. In Matthew 7 he says,

> Why do you look at the speck of sawdust in someone else's eye and pay no attention to the plank in your own eye? How can you say, 'Let me take the speck out of your eye,' when all the time there is a plank in your own eye? You hypocrite, first take the plank out of your own eye, and then you will see clearly to remove the speck from the other person's eye."[206]

He's not saying "live and let live." He's not saying "don't notice their sin" or even "don't point out their sin." After all, if judgment just meant "assessment"—an acknowledgement that someone's actions did or did not conform to a moral standard—then we couldn't even label anything as judgmental without running afoul of the same principle. And if he'd meant "never point it out," he'd have stopped his illustration sooner: he doesn't say "you've got a plank in your eye, so mind your own business;" what he essentially says is, "remove the plank from your own eye *because you also* need to remove the speck from your friend' eye."[207] The command to confront—to assess

206. Matt 7:3–5 TNIV.

207. Paraphrase and emphasis mine.

fairly and truthfully what is right and wrong—is actually *embedded in* this command not to judge. Jesus himself wouldn't have bothered teaching if he didn't think that sometimes people *do* need to be told how to live their lives.

He's saying our scorecards aren't accurate. Just like a gymnast can give a friend some pointers but needs coaches and judges to actually assess her own routine, we're "too close to the action" to truly see our own "performance" or compare it to someone else's. When we try, we're as ridiculous (and hazardous) as someone walking around with a phone pole in their eye, offering free optometry consults. We can't measure the full destructiveness of our own sin, and we can't truly determine the intentions and heart behind someone else's actions. It's worth remembering that this limited sight also means that sometimes an apparently sinful situation is actually something quite different than it seems; taking time to listen without making assumptions can keep us from well-intentioned "mercy" to sinners who aren't actually sinning, which can do its own plank-like damage.

Now, I must make a side note here, not about judgment but about this passage, because damage has inadvertently and well-meaningly been done. Many have taught that passages like the "plank-in-the-eye" illustration mean that both parties are at least somewhat at fault in any conflict. It's something that's . . . at least *frequently* true: when I get into an ugly fight with you, even if you *are* the one who took the last cookie and then gloated about it, I need to face up to my own covetousness about the cookie and the harshness of my own response. And it's often important for reconciliation, because even if I'm only 5 percent at fault, acknowledging my 5 percent can free you to start acknowledging your 95 percent. But both sides being at fault in *every* conflict? Even a cursory glance says that's absurd.

When a burglar bludgeons an old woman in order to steal her family heirlooms, no part of that is her fault. When we hear horror stories of adults molesting infants, no one even thinks to say, "well, the baby bears some responsibility too." But all too frequently, when a man takes out his long-suppressed childhood anger on his unsuspecting wife, well-meaning Christians ask her what *she* did to provoke it. When a person has grown up in an abusive household, the *last* thing they need is for us to confirm the lies they grew up with: that they somehow deserved the treatment they got . . . but that's the impression we give them when we teach that both parties are always somewhat at fault.

Yes, both parties are sinners. Yes, both parties have messed-up things inside. No, the darkness in you is not any less redeemable than the darkness in me. But we are equally sinful *in general*, not necessarily *in this particular situation*. And this distinction is crucial. It is enough for us to face the fact that we carry the same "sin gene" as those who hurt us without also blaming ourselves for getting hurt. (Thank you for accompanying me on this tangent; now back to your regular programming.)

Rather than keeping score with our fellow sinners, the Bible calls us to identify with them. This was one of the big things going wrong in that instance of the woman caught in adultery. The whole point of stoning was for people to recognize their own vulnerability to sin and punishment, so that they wouldn't incur such things.[208] It was a beyond-sobering act that the community participated in together, one which implicitly stated, "this sin is part of us, and we need to get rid of it." Instead, the Pharisees and scribes were trying to use stoning for the very opposite of its purpose: for "othering" rather than identifying. Instead of a public acknowledgement that "this could have been me" or "this sin is part of all of us," they wanted to use it to mean "*I* would never do that."

One of my favorite things about acting is the time required in another person's shoes. It is a crucial part of the process to think through why my character says, thinks, and does the things they do. Even if I disagree with a character's choices (and I often do), if I don't take the time to understand them and internalize that "under different circumstances, I could have done this too," then I'm not doing my job. It's an exercise I wish I did a little more often in real life.

The Apostle Paul describes the attitude we need this way: "If someone is caught in a sin, you who live by the Spirit should restore that person gently. But watch yourselves, or you also may be tempted."[209] In other words, remember that you're in the same boat. You may not have done what they did (yet!), but you're just as vulnerable as they were. Jesus wants you to gently help them out, not because you're so much better than them but because you *are* them. Just as you need help following Jesus, just as you desperately need people to see *you* and not just your sin, this person needs the same things from you. Paul makes it clear here that this often means helping someone correct their course—but it's always for the purpose of restoring, not rejecting (or punishing, or gloating: both of which, let's face it, can be very attractive options to the human heart).

The beautiful thing is, Jesus *wasn't* in the same boat, and yet he climbed into our storm-tossed boat anyway. He was without sin: all of the trappings of human judgment—"I'm better than you," "I would never do the things that he did," "I know she did that out of the unkindness of her heart"—all of the lies we tell ourselves to puff ourselves up . . . were *actually true* in his

208. See Deut 13:10–11. Just to be clear, I'm not advocating the practice of stoning, just thinking through how it fit into that society.

209. Gal 6:1 TNIV.

case. Unlike the Pharisees, he *was* "other"—and yet he identified with us anyway, all the way to death and beyond.

This is why we don't need to keep score: if the one perfect man in history was up for identifying with me, surely I can swallow my pride long enough to identify with my annoying neighbor. More than this, though, his identification goes in the other direction as well: Jesus passes on to us all of the merit we need and more. In light of this, trying to keep score would be as silly as a princess hoarding cake under her bed. She's got cooks and bakers at her disposal: she can have cake any time she wants to. She doesn't need to hide hers or take anyone else's—and anyway, the cake under her bed is going to get stale by the afternoon. This is what we do, though, when we think that even after everything Jesus did for us we still need to compete in order to be "better than" anyone else. Never forget: Jesus is your fresh cake.

More importantly, Jesus is the one judge we can trust. He showed he was exactly what we need when he said that God had "given him authority to judge because he is the Son of Man."[210] Now, in Jesus' day, the term "Son of Man" was a reference to a clearly supernatural figure from the book of Daniel—so it was paradoxically a claim to deity.[211] We need our judge to be no less than God. We need someone who isn't sinful like us, isn't corruptible, isn't subject to the limits and biases of a merely human perspective. And yet "Son of Man" also means that he knows what it's like to be fully human. He's not just sitting on the sidelines and criticizing. He's not, as the writer of Hebrews points out, "unable to feel sympathy for our weaknesses," but instead "has been tempted in every way, just as we are—yet he did not sin."[212]

This is all very good news! The fact that Jesus is the judge means *we don't have to be*. It means there is someone in charge who cares about justice even more than we do, who won't fail at achieving it like we do. And it means that we have a judge who is merciful: someone who can not only achieve justice but save us despite our unjust hearts and actions.

So what does it mean for us to be judgmental? Essentially, it's when we accidentally or purposely forget that our Judge is in charge, and how much he's done to redeem us. It's not about whether we assess sinful actions as sinful—we must. In fact, Jesus gave us authority to confront and forgive[213] and commanded us to do both. It's not even about how sternly we do so:

210. John 5:27 TNIV.

211. Spangler and Tverberg get into this a bit more and explain that even the term "son of" indicates that he's something different than just "a man." See Spangler and Tverberg, *Rabbi Jesus*, 48.

212. Heb 4:15 TNIV.

213. See Matt 18:15–19; Luke 17:3; John 20:23.

depending on the need, Jesus was as gentle as a lamb or as fiery as that granny across the street. (You know the one I mean.) It's about whether our intent is to restore or to reject, about whether we're identifying or "othering." It's about whether we're doing this important work of Jesus with his heart or without it. And let's be clear: the heart of Jesus only comes *from* Jesus.[214] It's not something we have to recreate so that he doesn't label us as judgmental. A river can only deliver the water that's poured into it: we only pour out God's grace and love for people because Jesus sent his spirit, the spirit of Love himself, to live in us. We only love because we've received his love; we only give grace because we receive it, over and over and over again (including for the sin of judgment) and the more we receive and respond to his love, the more natural it becomes.

Following Jesus in non-judgment is no more nor less than sharing the love we daily receive. It's about caring for people who don't always deserve it, whether or not they've repented yet, and telling the truth, whether or not they want to hear it. It's about true joy, because love is overjoyed when a person turns away from brokenness towards life. (Fake joy—the joy we get from sniping and tearing others down—is always a little sour. The "joy" we get from comparison always turns out to be stale cake.) It's about tenaciously hoping on behalf of even seemingly hopeless people, because God tells us that love "always trusts, always hopes, always perseveres,"[215] and it's about trust, for the same reason: trusting God to be at work in that person without needing us to bludgeon them, and trusting that person to have their own relationship with God, whatever it ends up looking like. It's about knowing we're in the same boat and praising the One who stills the storm.

Jesus summed up his view on judgment with the words, "The Son of Man came to seek and to save what was lost"[216]—but his ultimate statement on it is the cross itself. Here, sin is declared to be utterly, terribly, completely wrong. By undergoing torture and death in order to atone for it, Jesus implicitly states that he thinks our sin is *that bad:* bad enough to necessitate something that extreme. But by that very same suffering and death, Jesus also implicitly declares his absolute refusal to give up on us. Someday, there *will* come a day of judgment. Someday, all of the horrible things that have been done to us and by us will be dealt with by the only one who has any right to judge—either wiped away by the cross, for those who will have it, or cast into hell, for those who won't.[217] But until then, he tells us that restora-

214. See John 15:5.

215. 1 Cor 13:7 TNIV.

216. Luke 19:10 TNIV.

217. I know, I know: hell is just about the least fun Christian doctrine out there,

tion is absolutely free to anyone who will accept it. Until then, he declares with his own body that he would rather be killed himself than write any of us off. On the cross, he once and for all proved that he did not come "to condemn the world, but to save the world."[218]

"Food for Thought" Questions

Questions for Reflection/Journaling

- When have I been accused of being judgmental, or accused others of being judgmental? Was it truly judgment, or was it simply honesty about what is right and wrong?
- What need am I trying to fulfill when I judge others? (Why am I hoarding my cake?) Can I bring that need to Jesus and ask him how he wants to fill it?
- Lord, do you want to talk to me about someone I have judged? Will you please help me to understand why they may have formed those decisions or attitudes, (or give me the opportunity to hear directly from them)? Will you please give me your love for them, and ready me to be part of their healing if possible?
- In what way is it good news that on the cross, God declared sin to be completely and utterly wrong? Are there things that I need to declare as wrong, which I've been prevented from acknowledging as wrong in the past? (e.g., things that have happened to me or someone I love, or things that I know grieved God's heart, that I was discouraged from speaking up about?)

---

and it's uncool to talk about it. But Jesus talked about it more than anybody else in the Bible did, and Jesus is a lot smarter, greater, and more loving than I, so it's not my job to censor him. This is not the place to discuss at length the doctrine of hell; if you're curious, a good place to start is Lee Strobel's book *The Case for Faith*, which includes a chapter exploring the very sincere objections to the doctrines about hell and what the Bible, faith, reason, and philosophy have to say about it. The only additional remark that I will make here is that the entire point of this discussion is that it *isn't* Jesus' wish to cast anyone into hell, and that he's gone to extreme lengths to provide us a way out of it. When someone throws you a life ring, you don't complain that he didn't throw you two so that you could decide which one is more comfortable.

218. John 12:47.

Questions for Group Study

- What in this chapter surprised or encouraged you the most?
- How would you express the difference between judging someone and being truthful about what is right and wrong?
- How have you seen honest confrontation lead to repentance? How have you seen non-judgment lead to repentance?

13

Shame and Evangelism

(Will I just make things worse?)

IN THE AMERICAN CHURCH in particular, it's hard to recapture the initial joy and fervor of the first evangelists. We are constantly being told how hateful and hurtful Christians are—and unfortunately both our friends' stories and our own experiences regularly confirm how accurate such accusations can be. And many of us, if we're honest, often recognize attitudes within ourselves that don't match up with Jesus' heart.

Of course, we know that Jesus told us we'd be opposed for sharing his message . . . but we also know that sometimes we *are* "off" in our attitudes or behavior, and that he often uses other people, even non-Christians, to let us know about it. So how do I distinguish between false accusations and when I really am acting shamefully? What if I'm just too hopelessly unloving and offensive to share Jesus? Since I know I'm not perfect, wouldn't it be better if I just kept my mouth shut and didn't embarrass him?

I am not by any means an expert on evangelism. I do, however, have a lot of experience with shame and with the questions that arise because of it. So while I haven't got definitive answers or groundbreaking advice on evangelism, I do think it's worth talking through some of the objections and questions that shame raises.

I still sin and hurt people—so shouldn't I just keep my mouth shut and not embarrass Jesus?

There are several problems with this reasoning. First of all, considering anything—particularly ourselves—hopeless is a red flag signaling that we need to sit down and have a good talk with Jesus, because he's all about hope. The whole reason he came is to conquer the evil that used to have free rein in us, and to free us from it; never is it true that we are hopeless against it. And he would not have gone to such great lengths if he intended us to hide away in shame.

So if you're struggling so deeply with shame that you can't see how you can possibly be the aroma of Christ[219] to anyone, then take some time out and ask God to tell you the Truth about who you are. The Bible is full of affirming reminders of our identity—who we are to God, who we are *because* of God, and what glory Jesus intends for us—but shame and culture are both very loud. We learn what we repeat (and we regularly underestimate just how influenced we are by the messages we hear around us). It's worth taking the time to tip the scales back in favor of the Truth: to steep our souls in what the Scriptures and the Spirit say about who we are, who Jesus is, and how great God's power is that is at work among us.

Second, our message was never that *we're* exemplary, but that we're *not* exemplary, and that we're loved anyway. Jesus is the exemplary One to whom we point. As Paul put it, "What we preach is not ourselves, but Jesus Christ as Lord."[220] The message was never "We're perfect; come be like us"; it has always been "We're just as messed up as you are, and if he can accept me, then he can accept you."

So the fact that we still sin (and the fact that it shows) does not automatically disqualify us from sharing the gospel. In fact, acknowledging and apologizing for the hurts people express against Christianity—whether we were directly involved in them or not—may be one of the strongest bridges to the gospel we can offer, a healing first step without which some people might never take another. And by acknowledging our sin we demonstrate our belief that the gospel works: that we don't have to hide our sin or pretend we're perfect, because Jesus really is big enough to redeem even this.

Third, Jesus made it clear that cowardice is not an option. Look at the parable of the talents.[221] To us, the actions of the servant who buried his master's money seem sensible: he couldn't mess it up if he put it away somewhere safe. To Jesus, it was not just an act of laziness but one of distrust. In fact, the servant, in justifying his fear, actually insults the Master's good character.[222] Of course, we don't mean to say anything against God when we hang back in fear—after all, it's usually *ourselves* we distrust, not *God*—but it

219. 2 Cor 2:15.

220. 2 Cor 4:5a TNIV.

221. Matt 25:14–30.

222. Verses 24 and 25.

comes to the same thing, because we're essentially living out disbelief in the One who said he gave us "everything we need for life and for godliness."[223]

Now, I realize that "cowardice" is a strong word to use here, especially because many times we hang back not because we don't love Jesus, but because we *do* love him and don't want to give him a bad name. If that is your struggle, consider this: he loves you, too. He loves you, and he promised—in the very commission that sent us on this difficult mission—that he is with you to the end of the age.[224] Would the One who was brave unto death for us really leave us hopeless and helpless, and not carry his good work to completion in us?[225]

How do I know when I've really wronged someone by what I've said, and when they just don't like what the gospel says?

So, the idea that we'd do better to stay home and stay quiet doesn't really hold up. But what do we do when *not* staying quiet gets us into trouble? How do we know when it's "their problem"—a person's uncomfortable response to the inherent offensiveness of the cross—and when it's "our problem"—something for which we need to repent and apologize or a sign that we need to take a step back and reexamine our hearts and our approach?

Well first, we should *always* be taking time out to pray and let God examine and renew our hearts, not just when there's conflict. The love we need for people comes from Jesus, and the more time we spend with him, the more like him we'll become. Second, it's never a bad idea to listen to people and ask questions. Even if it turns out to be "their problem," respecting them by hearing them out and validating their feelings can go a long way toward softening places in their hearts where they may be holding hostilities against Jesus and his gospel.

After we listen to them, however, it is essential that we also submit every rebuke we hear to the Holy Spirit to determine if it's actually true. While God does use people's honesty to bring us to repentance when we're being arrogant or unloving, we are also living in a social media culture where demonizing others is practically a sport. In addition, Satan's primary identity is "the accuser of the saints."[226] So just because someone says you're doing

223. 2 Pet 1:3 GW.

224. Matt 28:20.

225. Phil 1:6.

226. The Hebrew word "Satan" literally means accuser or adversary; see also the description given in Rev 12:10.

something wrong, it doesn't necessarily mean you are, and we shouldn't swallow every accusation that we hear unexamined—especially since the fear that we're wronging someone can really hinder us if we're trying to share Jesus with them. The world will heap all sorts of expectations and accusations on us, and *not all of them are from God.*

One helpful thing to bear in mind is that love doesn't always mean agreeing. If that is your litmus test for whether or not you're being loving, your "test results" are going to be off. Our culture strongly implies that love means accepting everything a person thinks, believes, and does; the Bible, on the other hand, teaches that "love does not delight in evil but rejoices with the truth."[227] Look at the death of Stephen: this was an extremely loving man who had been chosen by the Jerusalem Church to help lead their charitable efforts, and whose final words were ones of forgiveness for the people murdering him.[228] He even took the effort to frame his message in words that really *meant* something to his hearers rather than rattling off a memorized script: his accusers had brought up Moses, and he brilliantly centered his entire response around Moses. From beginning to end, Stephen's actions towards those who opposed and killed him were incredibly loving—but his words were tough. Love included confronting them with truth. Or look at Jesus: he's the most loving human being ever to walk the earth, and his teachings are also the most challenging words ever spoken.

You will be told you're hateful simply for not agreeing with people. And yes, we could all use to grow in love. But do not make the mistake of thinking you're hateful based on a false definition of love. Go to God to define love, go to God for forgiveness when you lack love, and go to God for the love you need for your neighbors and enemies.

What if I don't have anything to offer?

So, good talk about not hanging back and all that . . . but what if I'm just the wrong person for the job? Of course, not all of us are called to or gifted for evangelism in, say, the way Billy Graham or the Apostle Paul was. But the question goes deeper than that. For many, it's not a question of gifting, but of identity.

There are many of us who, after years of being told that we're the "older brother,"[229] wonder if we have anything helpful to offer the "younger

227. 1 Cor 13:6 TNIV.

228. See Acts 6–7.

229. This is a reference to Jesus' story of The Lost (or "Prodigal") Son, found in Luke 15, which many people unfortunately approach rather shallowly, taking it as a

brothers" wandering out there. After all, if we grew up in the church we probably don't have a very "interesting" conversion story, and on top of feeling like we don't have very relevant or compelling experience to share, we worry that we're going to come off as stodgy, out-of-touch, judgmental, or rigidly "religious." Are we even any use when it comes to evangelism? Shouldn't God stick to using people who at least remember a time before they knew Jesus, who have some more worldly experience and are more relatable?

We forget, though, that for those of us who became Christians early, it is not we ourselves but *God* who chose to call us at a young age. *God* is the one writing our stories—and do we really think that the One who orchestrated the intricate dance of the largest stars and the tiniest quarks made a mistake in orchestrating the events of our lives? Or that he would intentionally make someone "useless"? God gave specific gifts and backgrounds to each of us, and none of us knows all of the ways he intends to use ours. Instead of wishing you were someone else or more useful, thank God that you are who you are! You might lament that you don't have the dramatic, spellbinding story of someone who went through deep darkness before meeting Jesus—but consider also what a gift it is to come of age knowing God's ways, shaped by Jesus from the beginning instead of trying to relearn how to live after decades of learning from the world. In fact, those very people you envy, who met Jesus later in life, may be lamenting the years they lost and dearly wishing they were starting off their ministry with a broader knowledge of the Bible or with more spiritual mentoring or just with a childhood of knowing they were loved.

Conversely, you may have had a much rockier road to Christ than some have had. Many people feel like their past (or present) is just too messed up for Jesus to use. Know that there are many lifelong Christians who wish they had experienced a more tangible turn towards Jesus, who want to really know the miraculous, radical difference Jesus can make in a life, and most of the time just have to take it on faith. You are gifted to know firsthand the difference Jesus makes. You are gifted to connect with hurting people and empathize with them in ways many others simply can't. You are a bridge to the gospel for somebody, just by being you. And just as God wasn't absent in the writing of anyone else's story, he's never been absent from yours either.

In *The Chronicles of Narnia*, Lucy and Edmund have very different relationships with Aslan (the lion who represents Jesus in the series). Lucy has been on his side since the beginning and knows him through the lens

---

given that people who are already Christians or grew up Christian and never had a big "rebellious phase" are the judgmental "older brother" in the story who turns out to be deeply out of sync with the Father's heart.

of long loyalty; Edmund betrayed him and was forgiven and now knows him through the lens of deep redemption. As different as these relationships with Aslan are, both of them are extremely close relationships, and both are vital to the survival and flourishing of Narnia. One doesn't get the sense that one of these relationships was more useful than the other, or that things would have worked out better for Narnia if they had both known Aslan in the same way.

I have long been intrigued and encouraged by the promise that when we emerge victorious from the long struggle for our souls, God will give each of us "a white stone with a new name written on it, a name that is known only to the person who receives it."[230] At first, it may seem odd that in the new creation there would be such secrets. But what an expression of intimacy, what an affirmation of the fundamental goodness of our individuality, that God would give us each a special name—a sign of identity showing that God both *defines* who we are and *knows* who we are in the deepest possible way—and that he would keep yours just between him and you! There are things about your relationship to God that are unique: things that are yours and yours alone. No one else knows God in exactly the same way you do, and just as you have unique ways in which you relate to God, there are unique ways in which you can help *others* relate to God. Don't ever wish away the specifics of your life! God made you who you are for a reason and a purpose; no one else is going to help someone see Jesus in the same way you are. Your story *matters*, and your gifts fit in a vital way that no one else can fill.

Remember that the Apostle Paul himself was tempted to devalue his past. But he recognized that God's plans went far beyond what he might feel he should have been, declaring that "because of God's grace I am what I am. And his grace was not wasted on me."[231]

Finally, remember that what you have to offer isn't *just* you, it's Jesus. Don't worry about who you are or where you came from. (God is the keeper of who you are anyway.) Focus instead on Jesus—whose gospel advances even by way of circumstances and people we wouldn't choose[232]—and focus on loving the people who need Jesus. Care about them. Learn their stories. People recognize love, whether or not it seems like you have anything else in common. When we are focused on Jesus and on the person in front of us—a person he wants to save—then we don't need to be sidetracked by it being "about us" or even by how "unfit" we are, but can live out his joyous words,

230. Rev 2:17b GW.

231. 1 Cor 15:10a NIRV.

232. See Phil 1:12–18; also 1 Cor 1:26–31 and 2 Cor 4:7–10.

"You who bring good news . . . lift up your voice with a shout, lift it up, do not be afraid; say . . . 'Here is your God!'"[233]

Evangelism can feel daunting—especially when we see the hurt, sometimes hostile people to whom we're speaking. Yes, we will make mistakes along the way. Yes, we will need to apologize, and we need to grieve with those who grieve—including those who have been hurt by the church, and including the Holy Spirit who grieves for their pain and for our sin. But we also need to remember two extremely important things.

First, we need to remember that Jesus is the one who will heal them. The mistakes of Christians in no way erase the need for Christ. And the fact that Christians are part of their pain does not mean we're no longer duty-bound to introduce them to the only One who can redeem their pain.[234]

Second, we need to remember that Jesus bore not just their sin and ours on the cross, but also our shame. And because of this, amazingly, *Jesus is not ashamed of us*[235]—which also means that we in turn can say with Paul "I am not ashamed of the gospel."[236]

In John 15, Jesus tells us that we will be hated and persecuted just as he was. Just before this, in that very same chapter, he tells us that he is the vine and we are the branches. The love we need for people flows from him; the courage we need to keep going flows from him; the forgiveness we need for our failures flows from him. We need to be constantly coming to him to receive his Life in exchange for our weakness. He is the One who will prune away the sinful parts in our lives, and he is the One who will make us fruitful. He is the One who, as Paul says, "has made us competent as ministers of a new covenant."[237]

233. Isa 40:9b TNIV.

234. One caveat is necessary here. I am no expert, but I believe that sometimes if we have *directly* been the cause of pain (or particularly trauma) in a person's life, we may *not* be the right person to tell them about Jesus. This is not because Jesus can't redeem our stories or bring reconciliation, nor is it to say we should live in continual shame for our past sins and mistakes. It is because, depending on where that person is in their healing process, having to interact with the one who hurt them can re-injure them. Not only is it unkind to put them in that position, it's also not what we want them to associate with the gospel. Again, I am no expert, but my advice would be: listen to God, listen to them, and be wise. If you've rebuilt your relationship, then share the gospel as the Spirit leads; be honest and humble about how your own life now demonstrates the need for a Savior, and be honest about the ups and downs of knowing him. If the person has indicated a need for space, respect that, and trust that your sovereign God has many more ways to reach your loved one than you've yet imagined. And pray. Always pray.

235. Heb 2:11.

236. Rom 1:16 TNIV.

237. 2 Cor 3:6 TNIV.

"Food for Thought" Questions

Questions for Reflection/Journaling

- Do I need to ask anyone's forgiveness for things I've done (or ways I've acted) as a Christian? Do I need to let go of anything for which I've already asked forgiveness? Lord, how do you want to use my imperfections as a bridge to the gospel?
- Am I carrying a wound from being told that I'm pushy, judgmental, or otherwise offensive for sharing my faith? Lord, what is the truth about this wound? What do you want to do with it?
- The Bible says that God has not given us a spirit of fear (2 Tim 1:7). What scares me the most about sharing my faith? "Doing it wrong"? Being rejected or embarrassed? Something else? Lord, what do you want to do with this fear?

Questions for Group Study

- What in this chapter surprised or encouraged you the most?
- God has given each of us a unique way to shine Christ's light in the world. What are some of the ways God has gifted or used you? (Or if you're not sure, what sort of ways of sharing God's love excite and inspire you?) Are there ways you can "fan that gift into flame" (2 Tim 1:6)?
- One of the most helpful things to do in evangelism is to listen to people so that we know how their hearts uniquely need Jesus. What scares us about listening (if anything)? How can we listen effectively so that we know what's appropriate (or not appropriate) to share at a given time?
- This chapter mentions the idea that the cross is "inherently offensive." Why is that? Why is that OK? What's the difference between sharing Jesus' offensive gospel unapologetically, and behaving or speaking in an offensive manner?

14

Unforgiven

(What do I do when someone won't forgive me?)

The Bible states unequivocally that people who trust in Jesus are completely forgiven by God.[238] It's also pretty clear that God has commanded us to forgive others.[239] But what about when other people don't forgive me? That one is a little murkier. It's not that the Bible has nothing to say about it, but it's one of those issues that doesn't get quite as much "stage time" (at least not as explicitly) as some other things the Bible teaches—and it doesn't get a huge amount of stage time in our preaching and teaching either.

So what do I do with the fact that, even though I know *God* forgives me, sometimes *people* don't? Does saying "God forgives me" somehow minimize their pain? Do I still need to feel guilty around them? Is there still a debt to them, even though there isn't one to God anymore? What if that debt is more than I can repay? How can I move on with my life if they won't release me through forgiveness?

First of all, these questions assume that I, as the offending party, have already taken the first steps towards reconciliation. Although there are many times that we don't realize (or don't *want* to realize) the damage we've done and need the injured party to come and point it out to us,[240] both common sense and Jesus' own teachings say that when I have wronged someone, the primary responsibility to address it lies with me. As Jesus put it, "if you are

238. See Luke 5:20–25; Acts 2:38, 10:43; Eph 1:7; 1 John 1:9, 2:12; just to scratch the surface.

239. See Matt 6:12–15; Matt 18:21–35; Mark 11:25; Luke 17:3–4; Col 3:13—again, just to scratch the surface.

240. Hence the Bible tells us to honestly confront people, see Lev 19:17; Matt 18:15–17.

offering your gift at the altar and there remember that your brother or sister has something against you, leave your gift there in front of the altar. First go and be reconciled to that person; then come and offer your gift."[241] That is, when I have wronged someone, the ball is in my court to make it right (and it's a ball that is extremely important to God).

Of course, the Bible's view of "making it right" is rather different than our concept of "saying sorry." In fact, the Bible doesn't talk much about apologizing: it talks about repentance, which is essentially reorienting the heart away from the wrong ways I've been living, toward God's ways of living. Biblical repentance may include apology, but only insofar as it reflects a true shift in the heart. Biblical repentance includes acknowledging the wrongness of my attitude or action (what the Bible calls "confession"), rejecting that sin as an option for how I live going forward, and doing whatever I can to undo the wrong I've already done. The Torah (the law book of ancient Israel, found in the first five books of the Bible) gives us numerous good examples of the latter. If you stole something, you had to return it with extra;[242] if you got into a fistfight and hurt someone, you had to compensate their lost work time and make sure they recovered.[243]

But it's not always that simple. Sometimes things can't be replaced. Sometimes people don't recover. Sometimes when I do my part for reconciliation, my injured brother or sister isn't willing to be reconciled (which is part of why Paul's instruction to live at peace with everyone includes the words "if it is possible, as far as it depends on you"[244]). And sometimes if there's been abuse or deep emotional hurt, part of making it right—actively seeking the good of the person I've wronged—includes giving that person the space and time to heal.

And so this is one of the places where the subject of forgiveness can get confusing: it doesn't always look like what we think it should, and in fact, forgiveness isn't always what we think it is. There are a number of related concepts that often get lumped in with it, but they need to be distinguished in practice—just like it's all well and good to refer to cinnamon, nutmeg, turmeric, ginger, black pepper, and chili powder all as "spices" when you're finding the right aisle at the grocery store, but you'd better know which is which when you're making apple pie (unless you're one of those hipsters

241. Matthew 5:23–24 TNIV.

242. See Exod 22:1–4, in which regulations are given for repayments for stolen livestock. See also Num 5:5–7, in which the general principle for resolving any wrong is that one must confess it and repay the value plus one-fifth to the wronged party.

243. Exod 21:18–19.

244. Rom 12:18 TNIV.

who makes chipotle-flavored everything). So let's take a look at some of the things forgiveness *isn't*.

First of all, forgiveness is not the same thing as reconciliation. Reconciliation is the ideal goal, but forgiveness is different in the same way that a wing is different from a whole bird. When you forgive me, you lay down your right to hate me, hurt me in return, look down on me, or write me off. But we're not reconciled until we're *both* willing to make the relationship healthy again. Jesus forgave his killers before he even died,[245] but he wasn't reconciled with any of them at that point because they had no interest in a relationship with him. Forgiveness takes one; reconciliation takes two.

And often, it takes time. Where there has been an offense, generally there has been a breaking of trust; trust takes time to build and it takes time to *re*build. Sometimes a person isn't all the way "there yet" in terms of being able to trust, and honestly sometimes *I'm* not there yet in terms of being trust*worthy.* Sometimes I need to undergo significant growth in order to not re-injure them. In those cases, the best way to love them may be keeping my distance for a while as I learn to interact differently—as sad and unsatisfying as that can sound. We Christians are fond of talking about redemption; we don't like to dwell as much on the cost of it. We look forward to the day when Jesus will return and restore all things, but the amount of time he's willing to take to help us get there is frankly maddening at times.[246] In my own life, I had a friend I needed to get to know all over again: true restoration and love really was possible, but the sobering reality was that we had to backtrack several years in order to start rebuilding without our old, cracked foundations.

This brings up another thing forgiveness isn't: forgiveness isn't "everything going back to the way it was." Sometimes that doesn't happen even after reconciliation: sometimes the losses we cause change a person's life indelibly, even after they've forgiven us and healed, just as removing a large rock from a river permanently alters the riverbed, even after the flurry of silt has cleared. And Lord willing, the Spirit-empowered process of repentance has also altered my character in that time. So it may often be that when we reconcile, neither one of us is quite the same person as before—which also means that the relationship won't be quite the same relationship as before. We can see this in the relationship between God and humans: the relationship we had with God in Eden before humankind sinned isn't the same relationship we have now that we've been reconciled through Jesus

245. Luke 23:34.

246. See 2 Peter 3:9a, where God is so patient that the Apostle Peter has to reassure people that God hasn't forgotten what he was up to.

(and because of the bountiful nature of our God, whose goodness is always bigger than evil, the relationship we have with God now is actually *stronger*, not weaker, than before). So if a relationship is different than before, it's not a sign that the reconciliation wasn't real.

This reveals yet another thing that forgiveness is not: forgiveness is not the same thing as being OK. You can forgive someone for breaking your leg and still remain in a cast for weeks. Just because someone is still grieving—or even if they are still reluctant to be around you—doesn't mean they do not forgive you. Sometimes space is needed in a wounded relationship, not because of unforgiveness or dislike, but because seeing the other person brings up all the difficult memories (or in some cases, particularly abusive ones, it's because seeing them threatens to bring back the unhealthy relationship patterns that are still too strong to "snap out of").

Lastly, and this is a hard one: forgiveness isn't your right. It can feel cruel and unfair when someone doesn't forgive us, and can in fact be hypocritical on their part, but at the end of the day the people we hurt don't owe us forgiveness. Forgiveness is always a free gift. I, the offender, am the one who incurred the debt: it is not logical to think that *they* owe it to *me* to wipe that debt out. Of course, if they start judging and looking down on you, slandering you, using your failure as a sort of emotional bargaining chip against you, or seeking vengeance,[247] *then* that enters the realm of sinning against you in return. In those circumstances, there *is* a measure of indebtedness in the other direction, and some cause to humbly bring it up and attempt to talk it out with them. But no one owes you forgiveness.

They owe *God* forgiveness. Each of us has been indebted to God many times in our lives, and Jesus canceled our debts with the expectation that we will pay it forward and cancel the debts that others owe us. So each and every one of us does have an obligation to *God* to forgive. But that also means that a person's decision to forgive me—even though it very much affects me—is ultimately between them and God. It is not up to me to demand it from them, and I should not act as if they're wronging me when the process isn't as fast as I'd wish. If I expect grace for my weaknesses, I must remember that they are allowed to have weaknesses too, and that God is working on

247. Note that seeking justice is different from seeking revenge or refusing to forgive. Revenge is seeking to make you hurt in return and is wrong; justice is seeking to have you acknowledge the hurt you've caused and make things right, and it's an important part of the reconciliation process. Hopefully you'll have already taken responsibility for your actions and taken steps to make things right, but sometimes of course we fail in this regard, or simply don't know the most effective way to make things right. Since the injured party knows firsthand exactly what damage was done, their voice is crucial to knowing how best to remedy or at least mitigate that damage. So don't be *too* quick to label something as vengeance.

both of us with equal patience and compassion. Just as it is not their place to judge me, it is not my place to judge how fast their story with God must go.

Forgiveness is a decision that requires repeated courage and repeated grace. It's hard work, and unfortunately, as much as we'd like to make things better, we can't demand that anyone else's healing happens on our timetable. Pushing oneself to be OK when there's still pain in the relationship usually just means stuffing down the pain and pretending it isn't there—which actually keeps the process of healing from happening because the pain isn't being dealt with and treated by Jesus the Great Physician. And so I need to leave that timetable to them and to God.

I realize that this wait can be agonizing. It often feels devastating to remain unforgiven—and forgiven or not, it is often just as difficult to have to wait for reconciliation. (In fact, the latter can be harder, because it can feel like they're *claiming* to forgive, while actually holding our failure in front of our faces.) It's hard to accept the fact that we are people who can be damaging enough to necessitate such a long time of healing. Often, we can also feel like we have to wait to accept *ourselves* until they've forgiven us, as if we're provisionally "bad" or still in the wrong until they say otherwise.

But there are several important things to recognize here. One is that we're actually *not* still in the wrong after we've repented, even if we don't feel like there's closure or resolution yet. This becomes especially important to remember if we've repented from a sin that might take a very long time to make right: we're not still actively sinning just because we haven't finished the quest to undo our damage. The guilt is over, even if the responsibility remains.

Even more importantly, Jesus and Jesus alone has ultimate authority over our lives and over who and what we are before God. When a human being will not forgive us, it does not mean we're unforgiven. It means that God has more to do in their life, just as he does in mine. That person does not dictate your worth, moral standing, or identity. God does, and he defined it in terms of the worth of Jesus, the moral standing of one totally redeemed by his cross, and the identity of a beloved child of God. Before Almighty God (inarguably the one whose opinion matters most), *you are forgiven* no matter what someone else may say.

Lastly, giving someone the space to heal and the time to rebuild trust isn't an act of shame—of saying "I'm irredeemable; I should hide my face forever"—it's an act of *faith*. It is saying "I know that despite the brokenness in this world and in my life, God can redeem it all." It is a refusal to be afraid of time, and a refusal to substitute cheap, meaningless "grace" for true redemption big enough to handle real sin and real evil head-on, with no glossing-over or sugarcoating. It is trusting that God's patience isn't useless or foolish: that if God is waiting by a garden bed, then it's not just an empty patch of dirt, and that if he is being patient with me, then a harvest *is* coming in my soul.

As much as we long for reconciliation with people we've hurt, we need to be careful not to put them in a place in our lives and hearts that only Jesus can fill. If you need *their* approval or companionship or attention or forgiveness, and can't move forward without it, then you're giving them a power that only rightly belongs to God. Besides being a form of idolatry, that creates an unfillable expectation: being a god is a burden no one but the real God can bear. If you can't get along in life without a certain person's friendship or approval, you're placing your healing in the hands of someone who is not in a position to perform that healing—first because she's a finite human being, and second because she's got significant healing of her own to do. Staking your ability to "be OK" on any other person than God just isn't fair to them—and it isn't fair to you either, because it delays your healing indefinitely.

So what *do* I do after I've confessed, repented, listened, and tried to make it right, and they still are not willing or able to reconcile?

First and foremost, I need to let Jesus define me. Some of us whose failures are more visible or less socially acceptable than others' get labeled as "bad" people—but the truth is we're all equally infected with sin. And the truth is that we are defined neither by human labels nor by the worst things we've done. *We are defined by the gospel*: the good news that Jesus has taken all of our sin and all of its guilt and died with it so we can live with him. The good news is that in Jesus there is no condemnation.[248]

When your failure is staring you in the face, this can be really hard to believe. When others are judging you, or still smarting from the things you've done, it's very hard to affirm, "This does not define me; Jesus defines me." It almost sounds wrong to proclaim this when people have been hurt so badly and sin is so real and ugly and pervasive and destructive. But the gospel doesn't stop working when sin stops being theoretical: that's when it starts.

In fact, letting Jesus' gospel define us is absolutely crucial to the process of reconciliation itself. Why? Because shame is a terrible motivator. Shame cuts us off from the very people with whom we're trying to reconcile, and saps us spiritually and emotionally. Trying to practice shame-based justice—justice based on the idea that "I am a bad person until I fix this"—will tire us out (*and* make us either resentful or incapable of relationship) long before we've had the time to make anything right. In freeing us from the

248. See Rom 8:1.

condemnation our sin deserves, the gospel frees us to love—and love is the only motivator that doesn't get tired.

Second, find people who can affirm the gospel for you. It is not always easy to believe it on our own, and shame is one of Satan's favorite weapons against our faith—not only because shame makes it harder to believe in God's forgiveness, but because it isolates us from those who are meant to encourage and strengthen our faith. When the Israelites were attacked, Moses' faith in God (expressed in raising the staff of God over the battlefield) gave them victory. When he grew too tired to do this, his brother Aaron and friend Hur brought a rock for him to sit on and then held up his hands for him, one on either side of him, until the battle was won.[249] This is not just a weird miracle story from Israel's history. This is an important model for how God *intended* the life of the Christian to be. We are not *intended* to "have it all together," as if seeking help from our brothers and sisters is only a last resort for the weak. The church has, from the beginning, been designed as an interdependent organism. Repeatedly we are told to encourage one another and build each other up,[250] not because it's a "nice thing to do" or because some people aren't as strong as they "should be," but because we are in a spiritual battle and it's *hard.* Our faith gets tired sometimes, and that's not a sign of personal weakness or lack of effort; it's a function of how hard this broken world really is. God meant us to hold each other's arms up, as a way of life. So find other people who can support you and affirm Jesus' forgiveness—and don't hesitate to do the same for them. You'll probably find, as I have, that affirming the gospel for someone else is one of the most effective ways to believe it for yourself.

Finally, we need to trust and allow God to be at work: both in our own lives and in the lives of the people we've hurt. It's tempting to try to fix all of the other person's pain—or else to resent them for still holding onto it. It's tempting to beat ourselves up, to try to "fix" ourselves, or else to deal only superficially with our sin, fearing that if we *really* let God touch it, all of the pain and insecurity it was covering up will come tumbling out and there will be nothing left of us. It's hard to believe, when people (including ourselves) still judge us, that God is actually in us, making something beautiful of our lives. In all of these things, it's easy to let the brokenness dwarf everything else. But the magnitude of the cross says otherwise. The cross laughs at anything that thinks itself bigger.

What Jesus has done in becoming human, in living a life full of pain and temptation and discouragement and embarrassment just like all of the

249. See Exod 17:8–13.

250. See Eph 5:15–20; Col 3:16; 1 Thess 5:11; Heb 3:13 for a start.

rest of us and refusing sin unlike any of us, in enduring merciless torture and death and then breaking death and evil by rising again, is so extreme that no matter what I've done or who I've become, the cross is bigger. It is bigger for you . . . and it is also bigger for the people you have hurt. The magnitude of God's redemption means that just as your sin doesn't define *your* life, your sin doesn't define *their* life either.

And so we need to leave ourselves *and* our victims in the hands of Almighty God. We need to believe Jesus' promise that he will complete his work in us.[251] We need to allow him into our shame, knowing that he both has power over it and understands it because he shared in it. And we need to allow his act of atonement—not ours—to be the basis for our hurt friend's healing.

When God is allowed to be the one who holds the keys to healing, then neither person is saddled with the impossible burden of fixing the other's brokenness. When that's the case, giving people the space to heal isn't an act of self-punishment; it's a free gift of love, because Jesus has enabled us to care about them and seek to give them everything they need for their well-being. Similarly, we are not obligated to live in guilt and shame until such time as they determine to release us: Jesus is the one in charge of our freedom, and no one can wrest those keys from him or his love from us.

We cannot—must not—refuse to be free just because things aren't resolved yet. Walking in freedom does not mean minimizing another's pain; it means releasing them from being responsible for our emotional and spiritual health, so that they, in turn, can find freedom in Jesus too. It means declaring through our lives that if the gospel is big enough for *our* brokenness, it is certainly big enough for theirs.

In this fallen world, not all things reflect the reign of Christ yet.[252] Even though Jesus has already conquered death and evil, we still find that diseases plunder us, injustice runs rampant—and sometimes, relationships remain broken despite our best efforts. But we have a promise from One who has proved himself trustworthy, that it will not always be this way: that someday "Creation itself will be liberated from its bondage to decay and brought into the freedom and glory of the children of God."[253]

251. See Phil 1:6; John 15:1–5, 8, 16.

252. See Heb 2:8, Rom 8:22–25.

253. Rom 8:21 TNIV.

"Food for Thought" Questions

Questions for Reflection/Journaling

- Whom am I letting define my worth, moral standing, or identity? Why am I letting them do that? Jesus, will you show me what it looks like to let *you* be the one to define me?
- Is there anyone I have wronged with whom I still need to make things right? What do they need from me: an apology, a repayment or replacement for something I've robbed them of, space to heal, something else? If I don't know, is there an appropriate way I can ask? Do I need to ask them directly, or ask someone close to them?
- Lord, I want to be patient with other people's healing processes, but I need comfort too. Will you please be a refuge to me and my safety "from accusing tongues" (Ps 31:20) so that I don't have to place my needs on those I've hurt? How do you want to show me your comfort today?
- Lord, will you show me a person or two with whom I can share my wounds and mistakes, and who can help "hold my arms up"?

Questions for Group Study

- Which ideas in this chapter surprised or impacted you the most?
- What is the hardest thing to accept about not being forgiven by and/or reconciled with people? What does Jesus say about this difficulty? How does he want to be present in that difficult space?
- What are some ways we can support the healing process for those who have been hurt? What are some ways we can support the healing process for those who have hurt others?
- How might one go about rebuilding damaged trust? How is Jesus integral to that process?

15

Unforgivable

(What is "the unforgivable sin," and how do I know if I've committed it?)

FEW THINGS ARE SO terrifying or confusing as the thought of an "unforgivable" sin. After all this talk about grace, is there still something I can screw up so badly that there's no coming back from it—even if I want to?

Spoiler: I believe the answer is no. I believe that one of the most important truths to remember, absorb, repeat as a mantra and write on your mirror or your hand or your friend's forehead if you need to, is that *God is not looking for an excuse to reject you.* But it's true that there are passages that bring up legitimate questions about this kind of thing. So let's take a look.

One of the biggies is Matthew 12:31–32 (and its parallel passage in Luke), when Jesus says, "I tell you, every sin and blasphemy can be forgiven—except blasphemy against the Holy Spirit, which will never be forgiven. Anyone who speaks against the Son of Man can be forgiven, but anyone who speaks against the Holy Spirit will never be forgiven, either in this world or in the world to come."[254] Add to that the chilling words in Hebrews 6, and you've got a recipe for an existential crisis: "It is impossible for those who have once been enlightened, who have tasted the heavenly gift, who have shared in the Holy Spirit . . . and who have fallen away, to be brought back to repentance."[255]

What do we do with these passages? Why does our merciful God suddenly seem so arbitrary and cruel? And how—here's the crux of it for most of us—*how do I know if I've committed this unforgivable sin?*

254. NLT.

255. Heb 6:4–6a TNIV.

Part of the problem is that both of these sins are a little ill-defined. And in the unfenced darkness of uncertainty, the imagination runs wild and fear has no limit to how big it can grow.

After all, any sin is a rejection, denial, and devaluing of God's goodness—so all sin could be considered blasphemous at root, can't it? It's *enacted* blasphemy, as it were. And all of us have fallen short of God's goodness. How far do you have to fall before it's falling *away?* That's what makes these passages so terrifying: the idea that one mistake could condemn me forever. And fear can then make us interpret these verses so extremely strictly that we can label just about *anything* as this "unforgivable" something-or-other and counter every reassurance with that relentless, "But what if . . . ?"

It is essential to note, before we go any further, that these sorts of spirals are the voice of anxiety, *never the voice of God.* And as we venture out of the spiral in search of Truth, it's essential to approach what we *don't* understand of God in light of what we *do* understand about God.

Think about who this God is. This is the one who told us to forgive "seventy times seven,"[256] in order to give the world some small picture of how endless God's own forgiveness is. This is the God who said "Do you think that I like to see wicked people die? . . . Of course not!" and called both the dyed-in-the-wool wicked and the corrupted-formerly-righteous to come back.[257] This is the same God who said that the only reason Jesus is taking so long to come back is because he's patient, "not wanting any to perish but all to come to repentance."[258] And before anyone protests, "Yeah but that's all about *becoming* a Christian, but *Christians* should know better," let's remember just how many of these passages are directed specifically to Christians, from "he will forgive us our sins and purify us from all unrighteousness"[259] to "Here I am! I stand at the door and knock!" That latter one was spoken to a church that was greedy, arrogant, and totally "meh" about Jesus, and yet Jesus still promised them, "if anyone hears my voice and opens the door, I will come in and eat with them, and they with me."[260]

And so there must be more going on here than a cursory reading of these passages might suggest. (It's probably worth saying at this point that a cursory reading of *anything* is generally going to yield only the shallowest, most easily twistable truths.) What could get this relentlessly loving, gentle God to speak this frighteningly?

256. Matt 18:22.

257. Ezek 18:23, 32 NLT.

258. 2 Pet 3:9 NRSV.

259. 1 John 1:9 TNIV.

260. Rev 3:20 TNIV.

Let's first look at what's going on in that "blasphemy" passage. Jesus had just healed a man who was possessed by a demon. Jesus cast out the spirit, restored the man's vision and speech that it had stolen for so long . . . and the Pharisees, who were already feeling testy because Jesus didn't do things their way, explained this away by saying "this man can force demons out of people only with the help of Beelzebul, the prince of demons."[261]

Now, this was an extremely stupid thing to say (as Jesus in fact pointed out).[262] And they managed to follow it up with something even stupider: demanding a sign from heaven to validate Jesus' ministry. Clearly, of course, what he had just done should have been sign enough. But what he had done *before that* should have been enough too.

See, Jesus had been doing miracles for some time. And he made it clear that while the miracles were certainly helpful to the people who received them, they were also meant to be giant, unmissable clues for anyone watching. In fact, the miracles were "witnesses." Since all testimony had to be corroborated by two witnesses, Jesus said that he was backed up by the work he did (empowered by the Holy Spirit) and the Scriptures which spoke about his coming (given through the Holy Spirit).[263] While people could have justified ignoring Jesus' own words about himself, there was no excuse for rejecting the testimony of these two witnesses—and because the Spirit was behind both of them, to accuse either one of perjury was to blaspheme against the Holy Spirit: specifically, to accuse the Holy Spirit of lying about Jesus.

In the incident we're examining, the Holy Spirit wasn't testifying through just any miracle: this was an exorcism. Theologians point out that exorcisms specifically demonstrated that "the Son of God came to destroy the works of the devil"[264] . . . which pointed ahead to Jesus' victory over evil on the cross. So those who were blaspheming the Holy Spirit's work in this instance weren't just insulting God, but preemptively rejecting what Jesus was going to do for them. They were preparing themselves to refuse to respond when Jesus died and rose on their behalf. But it gets worse.

Blasphemy implies a spoken component. These influencers were not only rejecting Jesus for themselves, but teaching others to do the same—and to feel *right* about doing the same. They weren't just smugly disregarding and devaluing the extreme sacrifice Jesus was about to make for them, but

261. Matt 12:24 GW.

262. See verses 25–28, where Jesus points out that if the forces of hell were *that* divided against one another, they wouldn't get any evildoing done at all.

263. Jesus argues this in John 5:31–40. He also casually mentions John the Baptist as a freebie third witness.

264. 1 John 3:8 NLT.

they were using their influence to push others towards hell too. They were cutting down others' saving faith in Jesus before it even had a chance to grow. Is there any reason for God *not* to be severe about this?

But even then, it wasn't unforgivable in the way we often think of the word.

I bring this up because the Apostle Paul calls himself a former blasphemer. And before we explain this away with the anxiety-induced "Yeah but," ("Yeah but he just says blasphemer; he doesn't say he blasphemed *the Holy Spirit*"), let's remember that in general, the Bible doesn't make distinctions about *types* of blasphemy. It's not as though insulting one member of the Trinity "counts" and insulting another doesn't; God is God, and so blasphemy is blasphemy. Jesus wasn't introducing different classes of "unforgivable" blasphemy and "kind-of-OK" blasphemy, but saying that the only sin that can ultimately separate someone from God is to reject the Holy Spirit's message about Jesus. This, however, is exactly what Paul had done.

While Paul is never mentioned in the Gospels, we know he was in Jerusalem at the same time Jesus was.[265] Even if he never personally opposed Jesus face to face, as a Pharisee he was deeply connected with people who did, and he almost certainly shared their stance that explained Jesus' miracles away as demonic. More to the point, very shortly after Jesus' resurrection, we see him persecuting the fledgling church to the point of imprisonment and death. The gospel was anathema to him: he was deeply opposed to the Holy Spirit's message about Jesus. Paul himself committed blasphemy against the Holy Spirit.

Therefore, this is a sin of which one can repent.

So why does Jesus say "never"? After all, "never" is a really scary word when you might be on the wrong side of it, and many of us are still hung up on it. Well, he says it because he's an ancient Jewish rabbi who's extremely good at what he does.

In ancient Jewish preaching, hyperbole was a main staple. This is why Jesus talks about things like a camel going through the eye of a needle or a sinner needing to cut off the hand that caused him to sin. He's not expecting them to get their hatchets out; he's making a point about how serious he is. It's the seriousness evoked by a mom saying "do something that dangerous

265. Paul, who is referred to as a "young man" in Acts 8, says in Acts 22:3 that he studied under Gamaliel (who was a prominent Jerusalem rabbi). That means his rabbinic training had happened in Jerusalem not too long before the book of Acts begins: almost certainly he was present during Jesus' ministry, because there simply wouldn't have been time for him to get his training in Jerusalem, happen to leave during the three years of Jesus' ministry, and then happen to come back just in time for the stoning of the very first Christian martyr.

again and you're grounded for the rest of your life" or a father saying "you lay a finger on my daughter and I'll kill you." The point is not the *informational* content but the *emotional* content.[266] I believe this gives us a clue to this passage. Jesus is getting their attention with a striking comparison. Even if people weren't *exactly* sure what the prophet Daniel had meant by the "Son of Man," they at least understood this figure to be a supernatural and holy person. With as much reverence as their culture had for heavenly beings, they probably would have been surprised that someone who spoke against the Son of Man *could* be forgiven.[267] And so Jesus uses this to impress upon the Pharisees the enormity of their bad attitude, essentially saying "even if you were to talk smack about *the Son of Man*, I could let that go, but what you're doing is *worse*." He's warning them that if the Savior is in their midst and they're ignoring even him, then there's nothing else to offer them.

And there's no point in warning someone if they're already past hope.

I believe this is what's going on in the Hebrews passage as well. Here is another Jewish writer talking to another Jewish audience, and this one was an audience that was under a lot of pressure to renounce their faith in Jesus and find an easier road. Most of them already had Jewish family and friends (in a family-oriented, honor-shame culture, no less) who were pushing them to go back to the rules and rituals of the Jewish faith—and you can imagine, coming from a religious environment that was *that* concerned with fulfilling all of the terms of God's covenant with Moses, how easily doubt would creep in about whether Jesus was really enough. Now Rome was persecuting this young church too, and the temptation to go back to a legal religion (Judaism was recognized and allowed by Rome; Christianity was not) must have been acute.

And so the writer of Hebrews, with typical ancient-Jewish flavor and flair, warns his or her audience about the seriousness of what they were

266. I like to think that there is also an emotional aspect of Jesus' response that has to do with the love within the Trinity. When I hear Jesus saying "anyone who speaks a word against the Son of Man will be forgiven, but those who blaspheme the Holy Spirit will never be forgiven," I hear an echo of my friend who heatedly told a thoughtless-tongued woman, "you can say whatever you want about me, but you DO NOT insult my mom!"

267. Dan 7:13–14 refers to "one like a son of man" who enters God's presence, is given authority, glory, and kingly power by God, and receives worship from the whole world. This is why the Jewish leaders of his day got so uncomfortable when Jesus applied this term to himself: it was a pretty blatant claim to deity. Even if his hearers didn't *quite* interpret the figure depicted in Daniel as *divine*, they still considered angelic beings as worthy of great honor. For instance, Ps 8:5 refers to human beings as "lower" than angels, and Jude 9 reminds his readers to respect heavenly beings by referring to a Jewish legend (from the apocryphal book *The Assumption of Moses*) in which the Archangel Michael doesn't dare to judge even the devil.

considering. It would have been very easy for these people to say, "well, it's the same God, it's the same moral principles: it's basically the same thing. If I leave this whole 'new covenant through Jesus' thing behind, it's not a big deal." This writer is saying "No, it's *not* 'basically the same thing,' and Jesus isn't an optional add-on. If you go back to Judaism, you're *agreeing with* and *participating in* his crucifixion. You're saying he lied about being the Son of God, and that publicly shaming and killing him to protect traditional Jewish teachings was *right.*" Exactly like Jesus' conversation did, this passage zeroes in not on the details and consequences of our sin, but on the uniqueness of Jesus.

Echoing Jesus himself, the writer of Hebrews is basically saying, "look, I have nothing else to offer you. God sending his only Son to die for our sins and rise victorious—that only happens once. If you're looking for something more, I can tell you right now, you're not going to find it. So decide." It's the sentiment evoked when Jesus asked his disciples, "do you want to leave me too?" and Peter, with his lunkheadedly poetic simplicity, just says "Where would we go?"[268]

The early Christian pastor who wrote the letter to the Hebrews isn't giving us a blueprint of becoming "unforgivable." They're warning a very tempted community about the dangers of the human heart. If we're honest, we know how easily human beings, including ourselves, can get lost in our excuses. And there is a very real danger of our hearts becoming calloused when we leave Jesus behind. After all, we face these temptations too. There are pressures in our culture to choose a more popular route—whether that's universalism ("I'm OK, you're OK!"), or agnosticism ("well, nobody really knows, do they?"), or just seeming "normal"—and there are pressures in our own hearts to choose an *easier* route: dominating rather than submitting, gossiping instead of forgiving, us-and-them instead of Jesus-died-for-us-all. And the problem with things that are easier is that . . . well, they're easier. It takes effort and courage and reliance on God to resist what people expect and resist our own temptations; it takes no effort to go with the flow. And as tough as it is to *keep* resisting pressure, it's often harder to *start* resisting again after you've given it up. The writer of Hebrews is not saying, "Fall away and God will never let you back in," but "if you fall away, there's a very good chance *you won't want* to come back in."

Jesus gives these types of warnings elsewhere too. In Luke 16, he's giving what seems to be a straightforward morality tale about how "you can't take it with you" . . . but then he adds a twist. The rich and greedy (and dead) main character begs that someone be sent back from the dead to warn his

268. John 6:67–68, author paraphrase.

equally nasty brothers, so that they won't also be tormented after death like he is. As cool of a ghost story as that would be, he's told no: his brothers already have the writings of Moses and the prophets to listen to, and that should be enough. When he insists that they need something more to catch their attention, he's told: "if they do not listen to Moses and the prophets, they will not be convinced even if someone rises from the dead."[269] At first it seemed Jesus was just challenging the Pharisees' love of money; now he adds this chilling foreshadowing that if they're not paying attention to what Moses and the prophets said about him, they're not going to believe in him even when he rises.

Now, we know that some who didn't initially believe what the Scriptures said about Jesus *did* end up being convinced after his resurrection. So was Jesus somehow wrong about his prediction here? No, because he's not making a *prediction* or giving an unbreakable principle; he's being real about how hard it is to give up our pride when we've hardened our hearts. It's the same sort of warning he gives when he talks about the "impossible" feat of a camel passing through the eye of a needle. He's saying, "it's *really* hard for a heart consumed by greed to learn to love God more"—but when the disciples, in shock, ask if salvation is just a hopeless impossibility, he replies, "With people, this is impossible. But not with God. All things are possible with God."[270]

If we're getting hung up on the "never" in these passages, we need to balance it with the other things Jesus said "never" about: particularly, "whoever comes to me *I will never* drive away."[271] If you're coming to him, then he is not driving you away. We don't serve a God who rejects people despite their sincere desire for him; we serve a God who gives people what they want, whether that's him or not.

When Jesus ends this lively discussion with the Pharisees by saying, "the words you say will either acquit or condemn you,"[272] it's because their words *revealed what they wanted.* As he says in that same passage, just like the "fruit" a tree produces tells you what kind of tree it is, our words reveal our hearts—and what their hearts wanted was to keep resisting Jesus no matter the evidence and no matter the cost. Their own words rejected relationship with the incarnate God. Therefore they would be condemned to the lack of that relationship (unless of course, something changed). The

269. Luke 16:31 TNIV.

270. Mark 10:27 NIRV; see also Luke 18:27; Matt 19:26.

271. John 6:37 TNIV, emphasis mine.

272. Matt 12:37 NLT.

Pharisees were in trouble not because of the exact words they said but because of the state of *their will.*

And that brings up a very important point: this is not a sin you can commit *by accident.* For instance, you don't one day say or think "the wrong thing" and suddenly find yourself condemned to eternity without parole. Think of it this way: you can step on the president's foot by accident, but you can't assassinate him or her by accident. You can even rashly say something to insult the president, but you don't actually commit treason until there's violent and subversive intent behind it. This "blasphemy against the Holy Spirit" is a holistic sin, involving the heart and committed will. It's not about simply saying words.

How do I know? Because you can read the Bible aloud. The Bible includes phrases like "There is no God,"[273] or even "May Jesus be cursed."[274] And yet it's totally normal to read these passages aloud, even from the pulpit. In fact, it's expected that a pastor preaching from these passages would be speaking by the Holy Spirit's power—and yet right there in the text it says, "no one speaking by the Spirit of God ever says, 'Let Jesus be cursed.'"[275] So it's not that there are magic phrases that get you saved or condemned once they come out of your mouth; it's about the state of your heart behind your words.

This means that by "blasphemy against the Holy Spirit" Jesus is *not* talking about words you said once on a dare or in a moment of weakness. He's not talking about the sincere questions you ask in periods of doubt. Or about expressing your despairing feelings when life makes no sense and connecting with God feels impossible. Or even about being angry at God. It's not about the things you say or think when you're not in your right mind or not in control of your body—and this includes moments of extreme anxiety, panic attacks, teen angst, the outbursts of disorders like Tourette's syndrome, compulsions like OCD, and the bitter things that come out of your mouth when you're tired or angry or sad or overwhelmed or in need of a sandwich. It's not talking about something that you say once and then regret (or even three times and then regret).

After all, if we're being strict, Peter's denial could be considered one of these "irredeemable" mistakes. When Jesus was on trial, Peter was nearby waiting to see what would happen, and—not once but three times—he lied to the people nearby saying he didn't even know who Jesus was. Let's look

273. Ps 14:1. The full quote is "Fools say in their hearts, 'there is no God'" (NRSV).

274. 1 Cor 12:3 NIRV. (The point in this passage is that a message like that never comes from God.)

275. 1 Cor 12:3 TNIV.

at the rap sheet here: Peter verbally denied his faith, pretending he wasn't a follower of Jesus. With his actions, he declared Jesus unworthy of loyalty: just like the Pharisees who insisted that the Holy Spirit's testimony about Jesus meant nothing. He decided his own safety and reputation were more important than the truth of who Jesus is: just like the original readers of Hebrews were tempted to do. He tried to sever his connection with Jesus in front of the watching world: a rejection we'd usually label as "falling away" from the faith. But Jesus clearly didn't look at him as irredeemable. In fact, Jesus went out of his way to redeem him and make sure he knew he was forgiven and given a fresh start.[276]

So it is completely impossible that Jesus is talking about a situation where you make one mistake (or three, or eighty-four) and suddenly you're condemned forever. He's not even talking about a situation in which you get disillusioned with the sin in the church and go through a period where you're not sure if you want to be a Christian anymore.[277] Or when you were raised Christian, maybe pray some and connect with God some, maybe even start to make your faith your own a bit, and then get distracted and ruled by the world for a long time. He's talking about a situation where people are *so* stubbornly eager for excuses not to believe in him, that eventually they fall victim to their own excuses.

But that's a very different thing than wandering, wondering, or being wounded.

Look at Jesus' track record with this. He told his disciples right before he died "you will all fall away on account of me,"[278] and yet when he rose and returned to them, there wasn't the faintest question of him rejecting them forever because of it. In fact, the entire reason he had to be abandoned and betrayed was so that he could win the salvation that would *keep them* from being rejected.

Look at the time and loving attention he gave to Thomas, precisely *because* Thomas stubbornly refused to believe in him.[279]

276. John 21:15–19.

277. In fact, in John 10 Jesus says that his "sheep" know his voice but run away from a stranger's voice. If you're putting distance between yourself and a spiritually abusive church or leader, it may well be because you *are* Jesus' sheep and you recognize that the voice you were hearing isn't his. It may make some time to trust the true Shepherd again as you disentangle from an impostor shepherd, but it doesn't mean you don't belong to Jesus or that he won't come after you.

278. Matt 26:31 TNIV.

279. See John 20:24–28.

Look at the spiritually burned-out Ephesians, who had "turned away from the love you had at first," whom Jesus encourages, warns, and calls back into love.[280]

Look at the Christians that Paul says he "turned over to Satan, so that they may learn not to blaspheme."[281] It's a severe statement, but the implication is that they're being given an unbridled experience of their own foolish decisions for a time, *so that* they can see the full bankruptcy of their ideas and return to God. Even in the heinousness of whatever they said, and even in the severity of the consequences, they're not lost forever.

Look at the first Christians, who even with the resurrected Jesus before their very eyes "worshipped him, but some doubted."[282]

The room for doubt, lack of enthusiasm, and sin is vast. These are not a spiritual death sentence.

The only spiritual death sentence in the Bible is the one it says we all were under. But Jesus already died in our place. Jesus' work on our behalf is the antidote to our toxic inner evil, and a poison is *only* incurable if you don't take the antidote. The good news of the gospel still is and always will be exactly what it's been from the beginning: that no sin is unforgivable if you will come to Jesus and hand it over to him who paid for it. The obvious and only exception is the sin of refusing to come to Jesus at all.

The warnings about *that* are fittingly severe, because what they're warning against—being without God—is the worst thing that could ever happen to anybody. But make no mistake: *that's* what the warnings are about. They're not about some big red moral "self-destruct" button you could accidentally bump that God maliciously never installed a "cancel" button for. And the severity of the warnings is like the severity of saying "anyone who doesn't get in the lifeboat will never make it to shore" or "if you abandon ship you'll definitely drown, (and be called a dolt for doing something so stupid)." It's a dire warning. It's a true warning. But the "nevers" and the "definitelys" stop applying as soon as you get back on the ship.

What about people who resist getting into the boat for a while? It happens. The panic of those drowning, distrust of the captain, the pride of strong swimmers: any of these could foil a rescue attempt. At that point, the swimmer is in the category of "anyone who doesn't get in the boat." And it's very possible that as he flounders and flails, he may go under and lose the chance to change his mind. That would be a horrible fate.

280. Rev 2:4–5 NIRV.

281. 1 Tim 1:20 NRSV.

282. Matt 28:17 TNIV.

But what if he *does* change his mind while he's still flailing? What if he resists and resists, and then finally gives up and grabs the rope thrown to him? Well, then he's going to be pulled back onto the boat. This warning is not from a vindictive captain who's going to cut the rope off just before you get to the deck; this warning is from a loving captain who doesn't want you to get into that kind of danger in the first place. He's not looking for reasons to toss you overboard. He's the one hauling you in.

I wish we had time to dig into the many other brilliant explanations and analogies people have used to explain these passages, and the countless other verses of assurance.[283] Since we don't, the long and short of it is this: If you're wondering if you can come back, *you can.* If you're wondering if you're outside the pale, condemned forever, *you're not.* If you're wondering if there is hope for your loved one, *there is.*

When the religious experts came to Jesus after this discussion of demons and blasphemy, asking for a miraculous sign, Jesus refused—and then promised the "sign of Jonah." He knew that they actually didn't want a miraculous sign: they had just seen one, and turned more viciously against him than ever for it. But someday there would be another sign: the sign they asked for and didn't want. The "sign of Jonah" was Jesus being buried and raised, just as Jonah was "buried" in the sea and "raised" back onto the shore after three days. It was the sign that would either intercede for them before the very throne of God[284] or testify against them . . . depending on what they did with it. The reason Jesus warns them is because there's still hope for them. The reason the Bible warns *us*—about anything—is because there is hope for us. And God passionately wants to give us this hope, and continues to hold it out for us no matter how long we take, and will let no one snatch it away from us.[285]

The question is not, "Oh no, what have I done?" or "What will happen to me now because of it?" The question is and always has been, "*What will I do with Jesus?*"

283. If you want to dig into this more on your own, I'd start with James 5:19–20, which makes it pretty clear that it's possible to bring someone back when they've wandered from the gospel, and maybe mull over Galatians 2, where the Apostle Peter messes up so badly that the gospel is at stake and yet he isn't booted out by Jesus (the book of Acts makes it pretty obvious that this story ended happily). If you're up for wading through some old-fashioned language, Matthew Henry's commentary on Matthew 12 is *rad.*

284. See Rom 8.

285. See John 6:28–29.

"Food for Thought" Questions

Questions for Reflection/Journaling

- What truths about God's character do I need to remember, repeat, and write on my mirror or my hand or my forehead?
- Am I angry with and/or afraid of God because of passages like this? Can I bring that anger and fear to Jesus?
- Lord, do I need healing from fear or spiritual trauma connected with these passages? How do you want to start (and/or continue) that healing in me?

Questions for Group Study

- What in this chapter surprised or encouraged you the most?
- What temptations or pressures do you face to leave Jesus behind? What makes them particularly strong? What makes their promises bankrupt?
- The Bible's warnings about rejecting Jesus can be very uncomfortable. Why would a loving God give us something so uncomfortable? What does God intend for us to do with that discomfort?

16

The Sign of Jonah

(What about when my guilty feelings don't go away?)

In Matthew 16, Jesus' enemies ask him for a sign to prove his authority from God.

Now, right before this, Jesus had just fed four thousand people with seven loaves of bread and a few small fish. The reason he had to feed them was that they'd been bringing him people to heal for three days straight, and they wouldn't go away when they saw "the mute speaking, the maimed whole, the lame walking and the blind seeing."[286] Shortly before this, he'd fed over *five* thousand, with similar resources and for similar reasons. And several chapters before all of this, Jesus had a nearly identical conversation with the Pharisees and teachers of the law . . . who bafflingly claimed that he was a servant of the devil after he'd just freed a man of demon-possession.[287]

The irony is both hilarious and annoying. Proof, apparently, doesn't always work.

In both of these conversations with his opponents, Jesus refused to prove himself further. It's a move of extraordinary self-restraint, emotional maturity, and wisdom. He knew that if they refused to believe what he'd already said and done then they would never stop looking for ways to explain him away—and instead of chasing their affections, he calls them on it.

Something inside me has always resonated with these stories. I may not be trying to disprove Jesus' ministry, but I recognize the pattern of unbelief. I've done this same thing many times: acting like there's not enough evidence for things like his love and forgiveness, when he's already given ridiculous amounts of proof for them. Why don't I just "get this" already?

286. Matt 15:31, NRSV.

287. See Matt 12:22–45.

Given stories like this, many of us wonder if God still has grace for us when we don't "just get it already." Are we going to somehow exhaust God's patience? When our guilty feelings don't go away, does it mean we never really believed? Or that somehow we're not "doing it right" when it comes to belief? What do we do with the fact that no matter how much proof we're given, we still often struggle to believe that God actually wants us, actually accepts us, actually took away our sins, and actually wants to take away our shame?

This issue doesn't just have consequences for our personal happiness or even just for our relationship with God. It silences us when we could share our hope and binds our hands when we could serve with love. Of course, you *can* still serve when you feel like you're outside God's grace, but it's service "with your head down": you can't give your whole self to people when you're ashamed of that whole self. It just doesn't work, and it's exhausting. (Ask me how I know this.) As for sharing our hope with nonbelievers . . . well, when we're afraid that we're not right with God, then we're likely to think that our speaking up will only make things worse. And Satan is fine with all of these things. It suits him only too well if we're sidelined or at least crippled in serving and sharing as Christians.

So do I just need to dig in my heels and somehow *make* myself believe? Do these stories indicate that I should just know better, and that Jesus is so fed up with my asking that he won't answer?

Well . . . no. Interestingly, immediately after this conversation in Matthew 16, Jesus has a very similar encounter with his disciples. He warns them about the "yeast of the Pharisees and Sadducees"—the teachings and attitudes of these erring influencers, which could spread and take over just like yeast in dough—but the disciples forgot to bring bread along on this trip, and they're embarrassed about it, so they assume that Jesus must be passive-aggressively pointing out their mistake.

Now, they probably *should* have known better. The miracle they had just witnessed should have been a pretty big clue that bread wasn't an issue. And they'd been with Jesus long enough that they should have known *him* better: they should have known that he not only had the power to fix their mistake, but also wasn't going to look at them in terms of lack and condemn them for it. In fact, their conclusion makes very little sense. With as often as he spoke in parables, (not to mention how weird the command to "beware of the yeast of the Pharisees"[288] would be if he *did* mean literal bread), it should have been obvious he was getting at something else. But they're so preoccupied with the fact that they screwed up that they can't see *anything*

288. Matt 16:6 NRSV.

else: not Jesus' power, not his character, not even normal conversational cues. In fact, they're *so* preoccupied that the miracle they just witnessed somehow goes right over their heads, just like it did for the Pharisees.

And I think many of us are in that boat. (The figurative one, not the one without bread. Thank goodness, *I've* brought *my* snacks.) The Pharisees forgot Jesus' miracles because they didn't *want* to believe. The disciples forgot because they were focused on their own inadequacy. And like them, we often find that although we do trust Jesus and want to obey him and deeply want to believe, our failures can loom so large that they obscure everything else. Missing bread is only a problem if it stays missing; sin is only a problem if it stays unredeemed: clearly neither of these things is going to happen with Jesus around. But frequently that's not what we see; we see that we forgot to bring him lunch.

The beautiful thing in this story is, Jesus didn't tell his disciples "you should get this already; I'm not talking to you about it anymore." He questioned their assumptions to get them thinking, and then he reasoned with them until they understood. Similarly, after Jesus' resurrection, even though Thomas *should have* gotten what was going on, (considering the fact that Jesus had regularly predicted that he would be handed over and killed and then would rise,[289] and the fact that Thomas knew the other disciples well enough to be able to trust their word, and the fact that he'd witnessed Jesus do plenty of miraculous things before), Jesus did not refuse to engage with him on it. Instead, he offered the evidence Thomas sought, and invited him not to live in doubt anymore.[290] Jesus meets us in our questions—even the ones where we should already know the answers.

Now sometimes, like the Pharisees, what we need is to *not* be answered. Jesus didn't refuse to give the Pharisees a sign because he didn't like them and thought they didn't deserve one. He refused because he knew the answer they claimed to be seeking wouldn't help them. If your GPS is broken—if it doesn't do the right thing with the information it's given—then no matter how many times you punch in the right coordinates, you won't get there. You don't need to be given the right address again; you need to fix your GPS. It wasn't *just* that the Pharisees' demand was impertinent; it wasn't *just* that he's God and he's not at our beck and call. It was that giving them a sign would have actually reinforced their unbelief. It would

289. See Matt 16:21; 17:9–12; 17:22–23; 20:17–19; 20:28; 21:33–42; 26:12; 26:31–32. This is not an exhaustive list even within the book of Matthew, and the other Gospels are full of these predictions as well; John 21:25 points out that even these are selective reports due to lack of space. In fact, Matthew 27:63 indicates that this had been prominent enough in Jesus' teaching that even his enemies knew about it.

290. John 20:24–28.

have been minimizing his former signs, basically saying "you're right, they *weren't* enough evidence." Jesus' refusal here was an act of love. The Pharisees didn't need more evidence, they needed *him*, and sometimes our faulty questions are leading us away from, not towards, him.

So sometimes we need to stop focusing on our questions and objections. For instance, when my obsessiveness gets bad, continuing to think about the issue (whether real or imagined) will only get my thinking more and more frenzied. After many years I learned that what I really need to do is not to seek an answer harder, it's to go out and take a walk: to physically change focus because mentally I can't. Or if we're still frantically asking "what do I need to repent of?" when we've already repented . . . well, the reason we may not hear an answer is that God doesn't drag forgiven sins out of the trash and make us repent again. If Jesus answered with a catalogue of our past sins it would undermine our belief in the efficacy of his forgiveness. We need Jesus far more than we need answers, and Jesus loves us enough to give us what we need—and sometimes, to *not* give us what we *don't* need.

However, sometimes when well-meaning people say things like this, they inadvertently end up glossing over real questions without solving them. And the problem with trying to put a burning question to rest is that any burning thing you tuck under the covers is eventually going to set the bed on fire. Unless you extinguish it first, you'll end up standing in a blazing house wondering why it's so hard to rest in Christ there.

To put it another way, we all know that wiggling a broken leg won't help. Although the body's pain signals say "pay attention to this," if we keep messing with it we'll actually make it worse: that's why casts were invented. Continuing to ask a faulty question won't help; it's like shaking a broken leg to get it to stop hurting. However—and this is a big "however"—if a bone isn't set first, casting it will actually cause more problems. Holding it still when it needs to be put back in place means you're going to end up with a bone that never heals right: just ignoring that there's a question at all is just as bad as harping on a question that doesn't make sense. When it comes to God's acceptance of us, perhaps we *should* "know better"—but sometimes we don't, and brushing away the very real questions that sometimes underlie our insecurities won't help. That's not how Jesus treats his disciples.

For that reason, it's worth examining some of the questions that often get brushed aside as "silly" or something we "should know already," but still continue to burn underneath. Here are just a few that come up when we're struggling with this question of why our guilt "just won't go away."

How do I know if I've really repented?

Many times when we struggle with guilt, we take it as a sign that there's something we need to make right. After all, our consciences exist for a reason, and the Holy Spirit does convict people of sin. And "the heart is deceitful above all things,"[291] so we know that sometimes we lie to ourselves and God about repentance: we say "sorry" to God because it's what you're supposed to do, but deep down we don't let go of the right to do as we please—we remain on the fence. So sometimes if we feel guilty and don't know why, we assume (with some good reason) that we must not really have repented. We assume it must mean there are sins in our lives we don't know about, or that we didn't repent sincerely, or repent "enough." Or perhaps it means we just aren't willing to dig deep enough to find out what it is we're doing wrong.

Here's where that breaks down, though: the Holy Spirit is really good at speaking, and has a lot of ways of doing it. God is not limited by your "skill," or lack thereof, in hearing him. So if you're concerned that there may be sins in your life you don't know about, you don't have to worry that God's voice won't be able to "get through," like a bad cell connection. Jesus said "ask, and it will be given to you; seek, and you will find; knock, and the door will be opened to you."[292] If *you* want to know about your blind spots, and we can assume the Holy Spirit wants you to know about them too (as the one who convicts us of Truth[293]), why should we think that information will be withheld? In fact, even those who aren't seeking God's correction hear him really loudly when he wants: look at Balaam. Look at Jonah.[294] If there's an issue God really wants to bring up in your life, he knows how to get your attention. And usually his voice will surprise you by being a lot gentler than you expect.

It's worth taking a moment also to understand the Greek word translated "repent," which means "to turn around." It doesn't mean you've suddenly got your act together; it means you change your mind about how you've been acting. Often we fear we have to totally resolve the problem—to "fix"

291. Jer 17:9 TNIV.

292. Matt 7:7 TNIV; see also verse 8 and Luke 11:9–10.

293. See John 16:13–14.

294. I am indebted to Brad Jersak's book *Can You Hear Me?* for this point about God getting through to people who aren't listening for his voice. Jonah, whose story is told in the biblical book of the same name, was a prophet of God who ran from God's call on his life; God got his attention by having a gigantic fish swallow him. Balaam, whose story is told in Numbers 22–24, practiced divination and wasn't even part of the community of God's people; God got his attention by making his donkey talk (since Balaam was the one being an ass).

ourselves—first, and then bring the fixed self to Jesus. For many of us, that's our working definition of repentance. But it's not an accurate one. Jesus is the one who fixes us. When the prodigal son repented,[295] he didn't bring back everything he'd taken and suddenly have a perfect work ethic and no selfish habits. His repentance was when he turned around and headed for home, a complete mess. His father accepted him, a complete mess, and his father is the one who got him fed and clothed. There's no point trying to improve ourselves *outside of* God's love, as if we first need to make ourselves presentable. In fact, it's impossible—first, because only the Savior Jesus can tackle the disease of sin in us, and second because shame is a really poor motivator. You'll always be wondering when you've done "enough," and the weight on your heart will tire you out long before you reach your goal. Love doesn't need to ask when it's enough: love starts at enough and joyously wants more. Love is the only motivator that doesn't get tired. We need to come to Jesus a complete mess, and let his love make our growth a joyous adventure.

So it's rarely as complicated as we make it out to be. If you've repented, you've repented. If you sin again, repent again. It doesn't mean you didn't repent the first time; it means that even those who have had a full bath still regularly need their feet washed.[296] Jesus said we should forgive "seventy times seven."[297] Do we really think that he who called us to this really wouldn't be willing to do the same himself—and even more?

If I still feel regret, does this mean I didn't have "Godly Sorrow"?

A friend once asked me about the verse that reads, "Godly sorrow brings repentance that leads to salvation and leaves no regret, but worldly sorrow brings death."[298] Her concern was that there were sins in her past that still caused her deep regret and shame, and it seemed like this verse was saying that regret meant her pain was not "Godly Sorrow." If it wasn't the right kind of sorrow, didn't that mean her repentance wasn't true repentance either? And if she'd tried for so long to repent and it still wasn't authentic Repentance, what hope was left for her?

First of all, when we start capitalizing things, it's usually a sign that we're making them a lot more complicated and mysterious than they really

295. See Luke 15:11–24.

296. See John 13:6–10.

297. See Matt 18:21–22.

298. 2 Cor 7:10 TNIV.

are. What God is giving us in this verse about "godly sorrow" is not a technical theological term whose standard we've got to live up to. It's a litmus test for distinguishing between the voices we hear. This verse isn't saying "you're bad and wrong if you feel shame;" it's saying "the voice that's tearing you down with shame *isn't God*."

Nor is it saying "if it still hurts, then you didn't do it right." It is appropriate to feel sorry about sin. That is a result of love: you feel genuine sorrow and remorse over the pain another person has experienced.[299] And it may hurt for a long time: I doubt that any of the times Paul looked back on the people he'd helped murder, he felt peppy and cheerful about it, or even felt nothing about it.[300] It probably made him sad each time it came to mind. That doesn't mean he hadn't repented; it means he *had*. Worldly sorrow is "I'm sorry I got caught." Godly sorrow is "it pains me that I hurt someone, but I don't 'mourn without hope'[301] because I know God redeems even the worst evils."

In this world that is still waiting for redemption to be consummated, many of our griefs don't fully go away—and that includes the ones that we ourselves have caused. What Paul is saying is that God doesn't leave us in the depths of despair. He's saying our sins and failures don't have the final word, because Jesus conquered all evil in his resurrection. He's saying that the sorrow that comes from God is redemptive, because it draws us closer to Jesus. You can be sad about the past. You can wish it hadn't happened the way it did. But you don't have to mourn without hope, because Jesus does not leave us condemned. And there will come a day when he will wipe every tear from our eyes.[302]

Am I too privileged to receive God's grace?

Whether material, societal, or spiritual, privilege has often felt to me like a barrier to God. After all, Jesus came to preach the good news to the poor and broken; I'm not poor and I was saved before I had a chance to break much . . . so does grace still work the same for me? Don't I deserve it less? Haven't I "received my good things" on this earth?[303]

299. I am indebted to Cloud and Townsend's book *How People Grow* for this description of appropriate sorrow for sin.

300. See 1 Cor 15:9–10; Eph 3:8.

301. See 1 Thess 4:13; see also 1 Tim 1:12–16.

302. See Rev 7:17; 21:4.

303. See Luke 16:25.

The first problem with this is that it implies that God has an algorithm rather like the welfare office does: that there's a numeric cutoff for income (or other types of privilege) that decides what level of God's mercy you'll get, if you get anything at all. And this simply isn't borne out in how God actually works. Among Jesus' twelve apostles were blue-collar fishermen like Peter and Andrew, as well as financially powerful tax collectors like Matthew. His female followers mentioned in Luke 8 were at least well-off enough that they were able to support the Twelve out of their own pockets—one of them, in fact, was married to the governor's chief of staff.[304] Although early Christianity attracted slaves in droves, it also attracted people like Joseph of Arimathea—a member of the Sanhedrin who was also wealthy enough to possess a new stone-cut tomb[305]—as well as Lydia, a dealer in the immensely expensive commodity of purple fabric.[306]

Of course, encountering Jesus changed their relationship to their wealth dramatically. Knowing Jesus *should* change our relationship to our privilege. It goes from being a "right" we use to our own benefit—or, more often, something we ignore as so expected and "deserved" that it's hardly worth mentioning—to being an opportunity to lovingly imitate his generosity. Whether material, spiritual, or any other type of advantage, we have a responsibility to "use whatever gift you have received to serve others, as faithful stewards of God's grace in its various forms."[307]

304. Chuza, Joanna's husband, is called "the manager of Herod [Antipas]'s household" in Luke 8:3.

305. The Sanhedrin was the elite 70-member religious ruling council in Jerusalem. John 19:38 tells us that Joseph had been a secret disciple of Jesus for a while (for fear of the political issues he would run into with that council) before he finally made his loyalties public by asking Pilate for Jesus' body. Matthew 27:57 explicitly refers to him as "a rich man," and the fact that his tomb was stone-cut and new (Matt 27:60; Mark 15:46; Luke 23:53; John 19:41) underscores this. Cutting a tomb out of the rock was a difficult and expensive process, and a new tomb would be even rarer and more expensive: burial space was limited in a city that had been inhabited for centuries, so the custom was to let a body decompose in the tomb for a year, and then gather the bones into a stone box, place it in a niche in the tomb wall, and continue reusing the tomb. I know, it's gross. The point is, he was rich and still a Christian.

306. Acts 16:14. Purple dye was rare and expensive in the ancient world, as it was made from the crushed shells of tiny crustaceans. This, incidentally, is how purple clothing became an ancient status symbol of wealth and royalty (no wonder it was Prince's favorite color!).

307. 1 Pet 4:10 TNIV. In context, Peter is talking about spiritual gifts, but the broader context of the Bible applies this mindset also to worldly advantages such as wealth and societal power. Our attitude is to be one of serving and building each other up—and where there is inequality, we are to use any unfair advantage we've been given in service of our disadvantaged neighbors, even to the undermining of our own privilege. Paul reminds us in Philippians 2:1–11 that this attitude was the practice and attitude

But even then, we can run into trouble if we think that God can only love us if we give *enough*. The thinking goes something like this: "I've been born into a first world country and given so many advantages, (including knowing Jesus), so I should do all I can to share with and serve others . . . *therefore* any time I spend focusing on God's love for *me* is selfish, since I already have so many blessings." The problem is that by acting like we don't personally matter to God—or being hesitant to admit how much we matter—we end up practicing the belief that we don't. (And then we wonder why we can't feel God's love!)

Another problem is that this greatly elevates the value of worldly privilege and minimizes the value of Jesus. To say "I don't deserve Jesus *because* I have all of these material blessings" is to say "these material blessings are a fair trade for Jesus"—as if God, in dividing up some vast estate, gave some of the kids money and some of the kids Jesus, and considered it equitable. It would be like saying "don't complain that you don't get to live in the house with Dad; he *did* give you his Mardi Gras beads, after all." Yes, money can distract from our relationship with Jesus. Yes, many of us can be "spoiled" by our societal advantages without even realizing it. But to jump from there to the idea that Jesus would withhold his grace from us is a non sequitur that cheapens his work on the cross.

It's also illogical to think God's special concern for the poor and oppressed means that those of us who are not poor aren't "interesting" or "deserving" enough for him to really care about us. In fact, the main implication of grace is that it's given to those who *don't* deserve it—and that includes those who wouldn't qualify for a "hand up" from any human agency. Think for a moment about this assumption that "God so loved the world *except me*": do we really think that Jesus includes rich and poor, prostitutes and Pharisees, Jews and Greeks, people of "every nation, tribe, people, and language"[308]—and doesn't include *you*? That level of unimportance would make you very special indeed!

What if I'm too judgmental to receive God's grace?

Just as often and far more painfully, I frequently fear that I won't receive grace if I still have any vestige of being judgmental. But that puts the onus on me to work up to a point where I "deserve" grace. It's a false assumption. It's saying basically that in no other area of my life do I need to be perfect, but I must be perfect in humility and non-judgment before Jesus can accept me.

modeled for us by Jesus.

308. Rev 7:9.

This notion that "the rules of grace work differently for me"—this idea that somehow, because of my privilege or my self-righteousness or my failure to have "interesting" sins or sorrows, I'm tolerated but not *really* included in God's family—well, it simply doesn't hold up in light of the cross. The cross is too big for that. The wonder of the cross is that it is sufficient for *everyone*, and we *all* get to be included. If it is for anyone, it is for you. It is sufficient for the poor and oppressed; it is sufficient for murderers and oppressors; it is sufficient for those who are imperfect in any and all ways *including* struggling with being judgmental; and it is sufficient for those of us who are too boring for anyone but Jesus to notice. The cross is inarguable proof that Jesus notices you, and you matter. You can say "I'm not all that important" to anyone around you; *you cannot say it to the cross.*

No matter what your questions and hangups are, this book will not answer all of them. In fact, no book will answer all of them, because only the living Word of God knows our hearts and knows each word we need. But Jesus does not fault us for having questions and hangups. So keep asking. Keep seeking. It is no accident that the people of God were known as "Isra'el"—"those who wrestle with God"—because in this broken world, it is a struggle to know the truth in the midst of all of the bent and twisted things we hear, and *God is pleased* when we are willing to undertake that struggle.

But the deepest beauty in the passage we've been examining is this: Jesus did not actually say no to the Pharisees.

Although he won't give them a sign that would sidetrack them further, he doesn't actually say "no sign will be given": he says "none will be given *except* the sign of the prophet Jonah."[309] This sign, he makes clear in Matthew 12, is his death, burial, and resurrection. This is not only the greatest possible sign of his divine anointing—the sign they asked for—but also the greatest possible sign-they-weren't-looking-for-at-all: the sign of his passionate, sacrificial, relentless love for them. And this is the sign he gives to his *enemies!* This is what keeps me returning to this passage again and again for encouragement.

The Pharisees *should* have known better. They shouldn't have needed any additional evidence of who Jesus was or what he was about, and with their attitudes they certainly didn't *deserve* additional evidence. *But he gave it anyway.* He gave *himself.*

This story of Jesus' interaction with the Pharisees and disciples isn't a story of God's grace and patience running out. It's a story of Jesus' relentless patience, of "grace anyway": of One who miraculously gives himself, and is

309. Matt 12:39 NIRV, emphasis mine; see also Matt 16:4.

misunderstood and rejected, and still gives even more of himself. It is the story of One who refuses to be stymied by our unbelief in his pursuit of us. It's a story that defines grace itself—that we shouldn't need more help, but we do, and he gives it without restraint—and it's a reminder of the ultimate proof he has given us in the cross.

And when *you* should know better—when you doubt, seventy times seven times, his love and forgiveness—he will not condemn you, or say it proves you never really believed, or tap his toe until you learn to capitalize "repentance." He will give you the sign of Jonah. May we have ears to hear, again and again.

"Food for Thought" Questions

Questions for Reflection/Journaling

- What are some of the signs I've been given of God's love and acceptance? (These can be from the Bible or from personal experiences or both.) Lord, are there ways I can take these signs more to heart?
- Have I judged myself for my doubts or my difficulty feeling God's mercy? What is God's attitude towards me on this?
- Do I have burning questions that need to be explored rather than tucked away? Do I have questions Jesus has already answered that I need help putting to rest? Lord, will you please be my anchor and my wisdom in these questions?

Questions for Group Study

- Which ideas in this chapter surprised or impacted you the most?
- Which of the above questions (about true repentance, godly sorrow, being too privileged to matter to God, or being too judgmental to receive mercy) resonates the most with you? How have you dealt with it?
- Have you experienced a time when it was better that you *didn't* get your question directly answered? How did Jesus give you himself instead?

17

You're Going to Get Hurt

(Do the failures of the church mean that Christianity doesn't "work"?)

As we've looked at some of the misunderstandings we pick up along the way, you may have found some anger coming up toward the people who have spoken into your life over the years. Whether they just didn't understand you, and so gave "answers" that didn't answer the deep questions of your heart, or whether they presented the gospel in skewed ways, the fact of the matter is that many times our brothers and sisters have just made our suffering worse.

For years I chalked everything up to my *own* misinterpretations and weaknesses, and denied that there was anything wrong with what I'd been taught. After all, I certainly didn't want to imply that there's anything wrong with the word of God—and anyway, there wasn't anything glaringly inaccurate with the things I'd read or the sermons I heard. But it's still true that how people said some things or emphasized other things, and the poor timing they chose, did real damage.

Finally I was honest with myself about this: about how people parrot theology without considering if that particular truth is helpful (or even applicable) right then. About how fearful protection of one principle (such as "no one is righteous"[310]) can make people unwilling to explore an equally important, complementary principle (such as God's delight in us.[311]) About the frankly stupid, ill-timed, insensitive things people say—and I found myself not only angry, but suddenly very "done" with these sorts of messages.

But that, of course, leads to some uncomfortable questions. What do we do with the fact that God's people—the very people to whom Jesus has

310. Rom 3:10 NLT.

311. See Ps 149:4; Zeph 3:17.

entrusted the truth—get it wrong so often? And so *badly?* Should we just give up on the church: just not bother with all of these people who are likely to say stupid things and hurt us? And most troubling of all, if the truth can get so skewed by the very people who are supposed to live it out . . . is the message Christians bear even true?

Among the many things that can shake our faith, this is probably the biggest and most destructive: the damage done by the church. Whether it's through abuse getting covered up, sisters being condemning, brothers saying thoughtless things that worsen our struggles, or people just being disagreeable and obnoxious, we can get hurt—badly—and be left wondering if this whole Christianity thing actually works. If this is supposed to be God's family, if we're the ones who are supposed to be transformed by the love of Jesus, if we're supposed to show the love of God to the world through our example . . . then why do we see such ugliness in the very community that should be a haven of kindness and compassion? What went wrong?

These are important questions that deserve to be asked. I do not want to minimize them in any way, and I believe that wrestling through them with brutal honesty can lead to a deeper, more Christlike faith than ever before. However, we can't let them keep us from asking some equally important questions.

If we're going to ask why the church is so full of "people like them," we might as well pause to ask why God also allows so many "people like me." If I'm wondering whether it's worth staying or better to just go it alone, I might also wonder if I *truly* believe I'm the only true, uncorrupted Christian, with nothing to learn from them. If we're going to ask how God could possibly be at work in such a mess, we might also ask where else *but* a mess God would want to work; and if we're going to ask why it's possible to get hurt in the church, we should also be asking "what did we expect?"

The fact is, Jesus hung out with sinners. We're kind of OK with that when "sinners" are the kind that don't affect us—ancient tax collectors long dead, or prostitutes whose profession mostly makes their lives, not ours, miserable. It's a lot less easy to say "Jesus is a friend to sinners" when those sinners have done real damage to us or to our families. Or when those sinners have acted completely contrary to everything Jesus taught, while touting his name. Or when they've made us embarrassed to be associated with them or anything they espouse. Or when they use God's word in inaccurate, unhelpful ways. But that doesn't change the fact that God's word is still true. And it doesn't change the fact that Jesus really meant it when he said "It is not the healthy who need a doctor, but those who are ill. I have not come to call the righteous, but sinners to repentance."[312] It doesn't change the fact that the whole reason Jesus came was to save people who can't save themselves.

Now, it is a beautiful thing to see how Jesus changes an individual life. How gentle he is with those who have messed up. How he doesn't erase their personality or history but transforms them organically. How much he grows a person from a "sinner" to a child of God. I know I've grown a lot over the years, and I'm so grateful for his patience with me.

But now imagine that you've got a bunch of those individual lives together in one group. Not one of them is completed; all of them are works in progress. Some are overcoming addiction. Some are overcoming a lifetime of learning to be hypercritical. Some are overcoming racist leanings, or misogynistic assumptions they picked up in childhood; some haven't learned a ton about God's word yet and say really stupid, inaccurate, even dangerous things.

Of course you're going to get hurt in the church!

Don't mistake me: I am not saying "suck it up and deal with it." Some of the things "God's people" have done and still do are truly reprehensible. If you have been traumatized in the church, please know that God will not leave your suffering unanswered. Jesus tells us that "on judgment day people will have to give an account of every careless word they say,"[313] and even says that people who were only Christians in name and not in life will be sent away with the words "I never knew you."[314] God has heard every word that has wounded you and seen every evil act *and will deal with each one.* Not that we should be glad at the prospect of people potentially "getting in trouble," (I myself say and do stupid things all the time, so I'm very much banking on the blood of Jesus here), but it is important to realize that God takes evil and sin very seriously and will eradicate all of it. So I'm not saying that it's not a problem when people get hurt in the church: it is. I'm not saying we shouldn't try to remedy it when people get hurt or call people to account for the damage they do; we must. I'm not saying we shouldn't be grieved; God is grieved too.

But we should not let our faith be shaken by things that are completely in line with our beliefs.

Very often we feel blindsided by things that are directly taught or logically implied in the Bible. The evil in this world frequently takes my breath away; the things that people do to each other mystify me, and I cannot wrap

312. Luke 5:31–32 TNIV; see also Matt 9:12–13 and Mark 2:17.

313. Matt 12:36 GW.

314. See Matt 7:23; see also Matt 25:12.

my head around most of it. But again and again I find I must ask, "Why does this surprise me?" After all, one of the basic assumptions of Christianity is that human nature is terribly corrupted; this is why Jesus needed to come and die to redeem us. Suffering challenges our faith, and yet the Bible talks extensively about suffering and reveals a Savior who does not "miracle" suffering away but rather suffers with us. When we find out about the level of persecution some Christians face in other countries,[315] it can shock and confuse us—and yet one of the things Jesus told us over and over was that we'd be persecuted if we follow him.[316] And the failures of the church can throw us, even though the entire New Testament heavily implies that salvation is the beginning, not the end, of our journey from sinner to saint, and even though every bit of logic we possess would tell us that people on that journey are going to mess up.

We can grieve these things. We can work to alleviate these things. We can even wrestle with them and ask God our questions about them. But we should not be shaken by them.

The fact that Jesus warned us about these things means that he is not surprised by them. If God already knows about this brokenness and is the one who told *us* about it, then it stands to reason that it hasn't been overlooked in God's plan: that it doesn't threaten that plan or cancel out the goodness Jesus came to create. It's not something Jesus is trying to shove under the rug, hoping we don't notice, as if it would invalidate his message of redemption. Indeed, if it's *part of* the message of the Bible, then it ought to be clear that our reality, as frustrating and world-shaking as it is, can't possibly *contradict* the message of the Bible—and that means it's not a reason to doubt or to lose hope. God is still God, and if he runs the world a little differently than we would . . . well, that too is to be expected from a Being capable of creating and sustaining an entire universe.

I feel it needs to be said here that these sober expectations need to be applied all across the church, not just where we might expect mistakes and failures. In our minds, it's one thing when someone new to the faith messes up; it's another when it's someone we see as "strong"—a trusted leader or someone whose life seemed to really exhibit God's power. What do we do with *that?*

I was personally devastated when news of Ravi Zacharias's terrible abuses came out. He had been an incredibly gifted apologist (someone who

315. The statistics and details are always changing as situations develop, but current information can be found on the websites for Open Doors (www.opendoors.org) and The Voice of the Martyrs (www.persecution.com).

316. See Matt 5:11–12 and 10:16–39; Luke 12:11–12 and 21:12–19; John 15:18–21 and 16:1–3.

gives the logical case for Christianity and helps people think through their intellectual questions about it). To all appearances, his ministry not only honored God, but had the hand of God upon it, with countless people coming to faith or being strengthened in their faith through it. I myself had benefitted greatly from his organization's work and from his teaching. When it turned out his personal life grossly contradicted that teaching, I found myself with uncomfortable questions. Had it actually been God's power we'd been seeing at work? If he was a fake, was everything connected with him fake as well?

It's of course important to acknowledge that we are in a spiritual battle where Satan would like nothing more than to discredit God's people (as visibly as possible). However, it's also important to realize *this*: giftedness does not equal emotional maturity or even godly character. My natural assumption would be that someone supernaturally gifted would also be trustworthy, both to live out God's word and to know what they're talking about with it (after all, it's *God's* power that's on them). But that's not actually what the Bible indicates.

Paul's letters to the Corinthians reveal that Corinth was home to a very spiritually gifted church. God was at work there, often miraculously.[317] And yet these letters also reveal that it was a terribly immature church, plagued by pride, competitiveness, sexual perversion, and general spiritual messiness. It was to this church that Paul wrote his most famous passage on love. It begins, "If I speak in human or angelic tongues, but do not have love, I am only a resounding gong or a clanging cymbal."[318] Paul goes on to say that some there had gifts of prophecy, but no love. Others had miraculous knowledge and insight; others had incredible faith—but still no love. So apparently, it's possible to exhibit a measure of God's power but none of God's heart. In fact, Jesus indicated that there would be some who perform miracles in his name but don't know him at all.[319]

This means several things for us. First, it means be careful. Not necessarily "be careful *whom* you trust"—because *everyone*, even the kindest, most godly, most gifted people will sometimes get it wrong—but "be careful *how* you trust." Be careful what you expect of people. Dedicated, caring

317. I may as well say here that I do believe God still gives the more obviously supernatural gifts, such as prophecy or healing—although I myself may not be gifted that way—but if that's not what you believe, that's OK. The discussion applies either way: Paul talks to the Corinthians not just about supernatural gifts, but also about more "mundane" gifts like generosity and self-sacrifice. If my mentions of the "weirder" gifts make your skin crawl, skim over those and focus on the ones that make sense to you.

318. 1 Cor 13:1 TNIV.

319. See Matt 7:21–23.

leaders can still screw up; people with gifts of prophecy or "tongues" can still be controlling or insensitive; gifted preachers are sometimes wrong about things, or give terrible advice to counselees, or ignore their families at home. Even the Apostle Peter, even *after* he received the gift of the Holy Spirit, needed input and correction.[320] If you're expecting someone to be 100 percent reliable, you're going to be disappointed at best, if not deceived.

I don't mean "never trust anyone"—far from it; we need each other! What I do mean is "remember who the real Jesus is." Jesus is the only perfect human: let Jesus be Jesus, and let imperfect humans be imperfect humans, without burdening them or yourself with expectations that will inevitably be dashed. What the Corinthian church forgot, and what we frequently forget, is that signs and wonders (or powerful preaching, or effective church work) aren't a sign for us to believe in a person—or even all of their ideas—but to believe in Jesus.

So as Paul instructed the Corinthians, "weigh carefully what is said."[321] No matter how gifted a speaker is, we still test their words against the Bible and reason and the witness of the Holy Spirit—and, I might add, we still follow child safety policies no matter how trustworthy somebody seems, and no matter how dynamically someone leads we still build in the breaks and the support that help keep them from burning out or blowing up. What's beautiful here is that Paul is assuming a community setting for this careful weighing: far from saying "don't trust anyone," he's actually asking imperfect people to *work together* to keep an eye out for their fellow gifted-yet-imperfect people. We avoid blind trust *by* putting some measure of trust in each other—because let's face it, I'm not infallible either and blindly trusting my *own* mind will get me into just as much trouble.

Another practical upshot that's worth mentioning is this: you aren't obligated to share your deepest struggles with everyone. You do need to trust *someone* with these, (ideally a few people), but common sense dictates that with some situations and people, it's better not to expose the hardest, most confusing parts of our lives for comment. That's not dishonesty; that's wisdom. It's alright (and often necessary) to save those vulnerable things for people we know we can trust—although even then, we need to take their words with "a grain of salt."

But the struggles of the Corinthian church teach us another lesson that is both beautiful and sometimes hard to swallow: God is still at work in

320. See Gal 2:11–14.

321. 1 Cor 14:29 TNIV; see also 1 Thess 5:19–21; 1 John 4:1; Acts 17:11. It is significant that in this passage, Paul is talking about weighing the words of people who clearly have supernatural gifts from God, again highlighting the fact that *gifted* people are not *infallible* people.

and through the lives of people who royally mess up. Paul doesn't say that it *wasn't* God's power that gave loveless people the ability to speak in other languages or move mountains with their faith. He doesn't say that prophets and preachers who sometimes got things wrong weren't actually hearing from God at other times. Their gifts were *gifts*, not a reward for godliness or wisdom—and unfortunately, the godliness and wisdom were slow in coming. This doesn't mean God was causing, championing, or giving permission for any of the mistakes they were making. It means that God loves people so much that sometimes it's frankly annoying.

God's power was present, but it hadn't "zapped" their souls into perfection when it first touched their lives. I would have probably done things differently, but thank God I'm not God. God loves us too much to take away our personhood. God would rather train us like a beloved child than fix us like a disgusting problem—and many of us, all the way back to the prophet Jonah, have found this quality of God's unbearably frustrating.[322] Why be so darn patient? Why allow people to represent you when their behavior says they have no right to do so?

The truth is, God loves you too much to stop working just because people aren't perfect yet. Nothing can stop God from reaching out to redeem people. God is too big to be stopped by human weakness, and has both a right and a habit of using unexpected means: God reached Balaam through a donkey, and Jonah through a whale. For that matter, God used the hate-filled Jonah and the pagan Balaam themselves, people I might have said were disqualified. And that's the other thing that's important here: God loves you too much not to let you participate. God wants to be around you and do meaningful things with you, imperfect as you are. God has always chosen—scandalously, annoyingly—to include the "least of these," and I think that *must* include "the least mature of these."

What we need to guard against is something else Jesus warned us about: our hearts becoming "cold."[323] God does not give up on the church, but it's very tempting for *us* to do so. Repeated disappointments lead very easily to disillusionment; repeated hurts easily lead us to withdraw and isolate ourselves. This is human. It's sensible and understandable, but it doesn't change the fact that when we joined the Savior of sinners, this life of being disappointed and hurt and yet forgiving and loving and bearing with people anyway is exactly what we signed up for.

322. See Jonah 4:1–3. I have to say, I love the audacity and irony of Jonah's tantrum here, as he accuses the God who spared him from drowning of being exactly as merciful as advertised.

323. Matt 24:12.

The truth is, God is at work in his messy, broken, often-ugly church. (And I use that word "ugly" with some sober trepidation; the Bible talks of the church as Jesus' bride,[324] and it is *never* a good idea to insult someone's fiancée in his hearing, especially not One so holy, who has worked so hard to redeem his beloved.) The Bible calls us to bear with and forgive each other, not just because our failures are to be expected as God transforms us, but because God is working *through* those failures to transform us. We are not called to forgive and love each other so that the institution of the church can save face; we're not even called to it merely for each other's sake; we're called to it for our *own* sake. When we forgive, we are becoming more like Christ; when we love even when it is difficult, we are living the miracle of his power in our hearts.

The church is a lab, and in a lab there are spills and explosions; the church is a playground of orphans learning to socialize, and in such places there are skinned knees and pulled hair and hurt feelings; the church is a kitchen full of children making pizza for the first time, and you'd better believe there's going to be flour all over the floor. We are learning to be like Jesus, and like it or not, Jesus was someone who suffered at the hands of the people around him and loved them anyway. In fact, Jesus didn't see that suffering as a hindrance to his mission but as the very reason he came. Without the lab provided by our very real brothers and sisters, we would not learn what it truly is to be like Jesus. And if we're going to receive God's grace and patience towards our own learning process, we need to be willing to extend that same graciousness to our siblings' learning process—and not consider it an exorbitant, unusual thing for when we're feeling particularly magnanimous, but a normal part of the Christian life. It's even, if we can swallow this, a privilege: it's how the Lord teaches us to be humble and gentle, and a way in which we can share in his sufferings.

You're *going to* get hurt in the church. You're there with people who have been rescued from all sorts of broken backgrounds, and still have habits from those backgrounds left over. You're going to hear some things that aren't true, because "the human heart is the most deceitful of all things"[325] and even well-meaning people can misinterpret the Bible or be influenced by false teaching. You're going to be annoyed by people who haven't yet matured much, or whom you just don't understand yet. If you're lucky, you're going to have your heart broken, because Jesus got close enough to have *his* heart broken, and having yours broken means that you care.

324. Eph 5:25–30; see also Matt 9:15; John 3:29; Rev 19:7–9; 22:17.

325. Jer 17:9 NLT.

This is not a disaster or a surprise or a sign that the Holy Spirit's work in our lives doesn't work. It's just the reality of living with people in whom the work is not yet finished.

Jesus did not promise us a perfect church this side of heaven. He just promised he'd take in sinners like you and me. If we're going to let anything surprise us, let it be that. And if we're going to let any of our beliefs be shaken by the reality of the church, let it be the pernicious belief that God can only work with perfect people.

"Food for Thought" Questions

Questions for Reflection/Journaling

- Where has the church done damage to my understanding of God? Jesus, what do you want to do with this?
- Lord, where are my opportunities to love, celebrate, and show grace to the people who make church hard for me? Will you please give me an overflowing of your love so I can do that?
- Lord, who has shown me patience and kindness in my growing process? How can I thank and appreciate them?

Questions for Group Study

- Which ideas in this chapter surprised or impacted you the most?
- What is the difference between acknowledging that Christians have committed some serious sins, and believing that "Christianity doesn't work"? Where have you seen God bring healing in the midst of Christians' sins?
- How can the brokenness of the church be good news? How would you encourage a fellow believer who is struggling over this subject? How would you share your hope in Jesus with a nonbeliever when the failings of the church come up?

18

Enough (or "Sometimes Even My Fishes are Small")

(What if I'm just not good enough?)

"SARDINES?!"

The boy felt his face burning.

"When you said *fish*, I thought you meant you had something *worthwhile*, like a mackerel or a tuna—what on earth do you expect us to do with *sardines?*"

"I—I don't know," the boy stammered. "I mean I wasn't planning on making a *banquet* out of it, my mom just said, 'make sure you bring a snack.'"

Peter sighed, sounding exasperated.

"They're good on crackers," the boy explained, as if it was helpful information.

"Hold up—*crackers?*" John burst out. There was a reason the rabbi called him and his brother Boanerges—"sons of thunder."

"I thought you said you had five *loaves.*"

"Well, yyyeah—" said the boy, "—big crackers, little loaves—I mean what do you call matzah anyway? It's like halfway in between."

"I don't believe this." Peter slapped a heavy hand against his own eyebrows.

Philip and the rabbi were nearing.

"Don't tell him!" hissed John urgently.

"Right," Peter agreed instantly. "It's just embarrassing."

"'Mountain-moving faith' we were going to feed them with," muttered John. "And here we are with *sardines.*"

Peter gave the boy a hasty little shove to shunt him back the way he'd come before the rabbi could see.

"Thanks anyway, kid; you can go sit down."

The rabbi and Philip were within earshot now.

"I mean, it would take a *lot* of money, like a *LOT* of money; I don't know where we'd get that and even then—" Philip's voice always strained to that near-whine when he was trying hard to get the right answer and was sure he was going to get it wrong.

"We've got a kid here with five 'loaves' and two fish," piped up Andrew with a smirk, before being pummeled from either side.

"Shhh!!!"

"Thanks a *lot*, Andrew," muttered Peter, glowering at his brother.

But Jesus reached out to the boy's uncertainly outstretched hands with a smile.

"Thank you," he said earnestly, holding the boy's hands in his for just a moment as he took the gift.

And then he looked heavenward, thanked God heartily for the meager rations, and handed pieces to his red-faced disciples to distribute. The boy sat down with all the others as instructed, and was startled when Peter handed him a stack of matzah and twelve sardines. The boy moved to pass some to the person next to him, but Peter stopped him.

"No, no, it's for you."

The boy looked up, bewildered, to see Peter looking just as confused, and handing just as much food to the next person.

"Apparently, there's enough for everyone," said Peter with a rather helpless shrug. "And you look like you're growing."

"Yes," said Jesus from behind him with a mischievous smile, startling them both. "So do you."[326]

One of the verses I find myself coming back to again and again for comfort is "he remembers that we are dust."[327]

I frequently wish that I had a stronger prayer life. On average, I probably pray quite a lot, all things considered, but still I wish I did it more. I wish I was more loving; I wish I was less selfish; I wish I was more fervent. Compared to the love of Jesus and the magnitude of God's goodness, it's really easy to see how I fall short. Compared to the needs in the world, the little I can do feels like "spitting in the ocean," as my Dad would say, and compared to all of the ways I *could* be deepening my spiritual life, what I'm already doing often feels lame.

326. If you're looking for this story in the Bible, it's recounted in Matt 14:13–21, Mark 6:30–44, Luke 9:10–17, and John 6:1–13. John is the one includes the details about the boy's contribution and about who said what.

327. Ps 103:14 NRSV.

The truth is that there are so many different and beautiful spiritual disciplines that one *can't* practice them all faithfully in the same period of time. It's not possible. (For those not super familiar with churchy lingo, "spiritual discipline" just means an activity that you commit to for a time in order to grow your relationship with God: just like someone wanting to get in shape might commit to exercising regularly—i.e., in a "disciplined" fashion—or how a married couple might commit to a regular "date night" to make sure that they get quality time together.) There are scores of possible spiritual disciplines, from fasting to journaling to worship to silence to service. It's probably not even possible to practice all of the different styles of *prayer* in the same season: praying the Scriptures, prayer walking, intercessory prayer, praise, listening prayer, praying the Jesus Prayer, prayers of thanksgiving, and scores of other styles and emphases.[328]

There's *always* a fresh way to seek God; you'll never come to the end of connecting with and knowing this fathomless person. It's like being in an endless mansion in which there are always more rooms to explore. If you're able to think positively, this is great news. But if you're obsessive like me, or insecure like many of us, or broken like all of us, the possibilities opened

328. If you're interested in some of these types of prayer, or just wondering what they are, there are tons of good resources out there, and some brief descriptions here.

Praying the Scriptures is exactly what it sounds like: taking a passage of Scripture, often a Psalm, and instead of just reading it, praying it as if it were your words, or incorporating some of the words into your own prayers and worship.

There are a number of forms of prayer walking, but in short, it's also pretty much exactly what it sounds like: praying while you walk. For many of us, it's easier to concentrate while we're moving, and many people use certain landmarks along their walk as reminders to pray for certain people or subjects; many will prayer walk around their neighborhoods and pray for their neighbors as they pass their homes. Pretty amazing transformations have happened in communities that have Christians doing this.

Intercessory prayer, very simply put, is praying for other people: being a go-between to take their problems and needs to God. *Intercessory Prayer* by Dutch Sheets gives a great in-depth treatment of the subject.

Meditative Prayer by Richard Foster is a good place to start for listening prayer; it has the advantage of being very short and compact, although if you want to go farther, you might try *Can You Hear Me?* by Brad Jersak and *Rivers from Eden* by Eden and Brad Jersak. This is a style of prayer that acknowledges that prayer is a conversation, not a monologue or religious thing-you-have-to-say, and focuses on becoming more attuned to the many ways God speaks to us.

The Jesus Prayer is a short and very ancient prayer—"Jesus Christ, Son of God, have mercy on me, a sinner"—based on Mark 10:47 and Luke 18:13. Many people find it very helpful in their spiritual lives; a good place to start may be *Praying the Jesus Prayer* by Frederica Mathewes Green.

Praise and thanksgiving are, well, praise and thanksgiving. It's where you tell God what you like about him, and where you say thank you. It's active appreciation, and it's super helpful to your growth as a Christian.

up by these disciplines can instead just feel like you're never good enough, because you can never do it all.

And yet, extraordinarily, this is not the Bible's portrayal of how God sees us. We're quick to see ourselves in terms of lack: "I don't love Jesus as much as he deserves," "I don't have as much faith as my heroes did," "I don't read my Bible as much as I should." But the Bible doesn't portray God as constantly dissatisfied. What it actually says is "The gift is acceptable according to what one has, not according to what one does not have."[329] Now, Paul was talking in this verse about a specific donation drive that was going on—he was assuring the poorer members of the congregation that they did indeed matter and that God wasn't comparing their offerings with what the rich could give—but the principle applies more broadly.

Jesus does not look at what we bring him in terms of lack, comparing our offerings to those of the spiritually or materially rich, or even to the magnitude of the need. He does not demand that we bring what we don't have, or look down on us for not having it. He doesn't look at us in terms of the standards we could never fulfill and say, "Too bad; that's the standard and you can either meet it or get lost." He remembers that we are dust. He looks at the little we have, and smiles because we brought it. He remembers that we are dust, and in the fathomless gap between dust and righteousness, he puts not his disapproval but his very self, filling it to overflowing.

The miracle of the loaves and fishes bears this lesson out, and takes it farther. First, not only does Jesus make our tiny offerings enough in God's eyes, but he feeds others with them. He's not humoring us while secretly embarrassed, like a parent who coos over the gift of a macaroni-art necklace but would never wear it in public. (Yeah, you know who you are; and no, not one of us is judging you on that one.) He doesn't say, "Well, *I* accept you, but you're never going to be any good to anyone else": he uses our sardines and crackers to provide the world not with inadequacy stretched even farther but with a feast. Second, not only does Jesus *not blame us* for not having enough, not only does he overlook our inadequacies—he is pleased by what we *do* bring.

Which is the greater wonder: that the One who created the universe could create a few more fish to feed thousands, or that the One who created the universe would burst out in delighted praise to the Father over the piddling little offerings we bring? And yet that is what the Bible teaches: that the eternal God, the living Standard of all good who has every right to be the first in line to criticize, delights in the little handfuls of dust we offer—and more, that he breathes life into dust and makes it far, far more than enough.

329. 2 Cor 8:12, TNIV.

Your life, in the hands of Jesus, is utterly amazing, and I can't wait to get the full view of it from the other side of heaven.

"Food for Thought" Questions

Questions for Reflection/Journaling

- Where do I feel inadequate? What does God have to say about that?
- Jesus, what do you praise the Father for in my life? Will you help me believe your answer to that question? (*This may be an answer you receive over several days; many of us are pretty nervous about asking things like this, which can create too much internal resistance and "noise" to hear, or believe we're hearing, anything at first. That is a time to exercise the belief that God *does* answer, and doesn't mind taking time with us to do so.)
- What "loaves and fishes" do I have that I can bring to Jesus? Can I trust him to use them well?

Questions for Group Study

- What in this chapter surprised or encouraged you the most?
- What does it mean to you that "the gift is acceptable according to what one has, not according to what one does not have"?
- There are a lot of ways to seek and serve God, and there's always more room to grow and more of God to know. Is that a sign of our inadequacy or of God's abundance? What makes the difference in how we see it?

Part 3:
Fairy Tale

Fairy Tale: A True, Unfinished Story

IF THIS WAS A FAIRY-TALE, it would pretty much have to start with "and they lived happily ever after," because I met the Prince quite close to the beginning—which would make for a terrible fairy tale, and worse, wouldn't really be true.

When I was a weensy-tiny thing, my Mom had a little booklet that explained the gospel to kids: that God is good and made everything there is, including us; that people decided to turn away from God and do hurtful, wrong things instead of love him back; and that God loves people so much that he sent his own Son to take our punishment in our place. It went on to say that Jesus came back to life after dying for us, and anyone who wants to can accept his forgiveness, follow him now, and live with him forever. At the end, it had a prayer that you could pray to accept Jesus and ask him to live in your heart. Apparently, I wanted her to read this booklet to me all the time, and when I was three, I told her I wanted to pray the prayer in the booklet.

It was so long ago that I don't remember it, but I do know that I was the one who initiated it, and that God has been the foundation of my reality since then. You may laugh and wonder what sins a three-year-old had a chance to actually commit, but I don't think individual acts have ever really been the point with God: God looks at the heart where sins get manufactured, and even at that young age it was easy to recognize that mine wasn't the way it ought to be. It was full of rebellion, stubbornness, and rage—par for the course for that age, perhaps, but I was both precocious and extraordinarily intense. No joke, my parents worried that I'd be in jail by the age of 14.

Instead, I became every teacher and Sunday School teacher's favorite student. Of course I enjoyed the positive feedback, but it wasn't a conscious attempt to be a "goody-two-shoes;" it was a sincere (and characteristically intense) love for God. I was hooked, and hooked deep. The first written record of my desire to be a missionary of some sort and to adopt children is in a notebook from third or fourth grade. I was baptized at my own request at age eight, because I'd been reading the Bible for myself for a while and was distressed when I realized no one had told me about the command to be baptized. Being obsessed with God has been the core of my identity for as long as I can remember.

I went to a Christian grade-school, but even though the other kids were all from Christian families, the obsession with God was not shared. I didn't know it at the time, but it wasn't shared with all adults either. At the time, all I really knew was that I was the best behaved in the class, the teachers all liked me, and it bothered me when kids did things that I knew were contrary to what God would want.

As I got into my teenage years, a couple of things coincided: I began to question my own seeming-righteousness, and my mental health struggles (almost certainly obsessive-compulsive disorder, though a milder case than some) began to blossom. As mentioned earlier in the book, OCD causes the distressing "something is wrong" feeling that was designed to help us detect mistakes, along with the burning need to correct it, to occur all the time without a triggering incident. But I was young and had no idea this was going on and so of course tried to find reasons for this burdening feeling that felt so much like guilt.

In addition to this neurologically-based, rather nameless guilt, there was also a more emotional, cognitive guilt as I started to realize I might not be quite as virtuous as I'd always appeared and felt. I noticed, with some distress, that I was excellent at obeying the rules, but not always great at loving other people. (Now, some of this was probably legitimately due to sin, and some of it was probably due to the fact that I was an introvert who never fit in with my own age group; small wonder that I didn't feel deep attachment to many people outside my own family.) I'd also started to suspect and fear that I might be guilty of pride: I'd always done well in school, had sung solos in church since I was eight years old, and gotten great feedback on my behavior and performance from adults, all of which had made me a pretty confident person, and I was starting to worry that this was a false confidence rooted in qualities about myself that were ultimately of no worth in heaven's eyes. Worse, I began to more consciously admit to myself the sense I'd long had: that God seemed to matter more to me than to a lot of other people. It was perhaps this, more than anything, that made me begin to worry that I was "a Pharisee": self-righteous, judgmental, prideful, and not right with God, one of the people Jesus was always addressing harshly in the Gospels, the elder brother or homebody sheep in all the parables that it seemed God didn't really like all that much.

When a wave of guilt would hit, people were confused as to why I felt guilty, and would point to how committed I was to God. This didn't really help (except for lifting my mood very temporarily), because deep down I knew that my own good actions weren't the basis of God's acceptance of me—and also because I was worried that these had become an occasion of the sin of pride, as they had for the Pharisees in Jesus' day. And then one day, I again expressed my guilty feelings, and someone talked me through the gospel instead of talking about how good I was. They reminded me that it doesn't matter how good or bad we are, and that God saves us because of what Jesus did on the cross, not because of anything we do.

This rang a lot truer than people's defenses of my goodness. And yet I was ashamed: ashamed that I had enjoyed it when people told me how well they thought of me, and ashamed that this—not the gospel—was the response I'd come to expect. I started to wonder rather horrifying things: had I always just been confident in my own virtue, and not the cross? And if so, didn't that mean I'd never *really* accepted what Jesus had done for me? And didn't *that* mean I still wasn't really saved? Yet my entire life had always been centered around Jesus; how was I ever going to "get it" or accept his sacrifice "enough" if I hadn't already?

After that I worked terribly hard at feeling my sinfulness: after all, it seemed my pride in myself was getting in the way of my truly, fully accepting the gospel. The challenge here was that I'd only had my toddlerhood in which to really be a full-fledged sinner; by age three my heart and life had been given over to the Holy Spirit. It seemed I had to either feel bad about the years since (which seemed to downplay and disrespect the Spirit's work in my life), or to feel *especially* bad about sins committed in my toddlerhood. This last point raised problems on a number of levels, the least of them being that I couldn't actually remember much about my sins from that far back. More challenging was the attempt to believe, deep in my heart, that whatever I'd done in that short period at that young age was on par with murder—after all, if I'm just as sinful as everyone else, it seemed to logically follow that this was what I was obligated to believe. Perhaps most troubling, although I didn't think about it very consciously at the time, was the concomitant implication that God would have sent a two-year-old to hell.[330] I

330. Although it is a tangent, I feel the need to address this issue because of the very troubling misunderstandings it can bring up about the nature and character of God. Although I do believe I was saved at that young age, it doesn't necessarily follow that I would have been sent to hell had I not responded to the gospel right then (and, obviously, had I also then died, which is generally a prerequisite for any post-death destination).

First of all, as Betsie ten Boom put it, "there are no 'ifs' in God's world" (ten Boom, *Hiding Place*, 67). We not only tread on the edge of absurdity when we speculate about

tried to make sure I *really* believed that I was worthy of hell and *fully* felt my need for Jesus, but I never felt like I completely, wholeheartedly got there. I was always afraid that there was still pride left in the way, and I despaired of ever being able to "truly" accept the gospel.

Consider for a moment the cleverness of this deception. I was steeped in biblical knowledge and theology; I knew all the right answers and arguments. I knew there was no sin that could keep a person from Jesus . . . except for a refusal to accept his sacrifice. The devil and my own mind had managed to convince me that I was guilty of the only unforgivable sin—and worse, (since I'd never felt completely successful in my efforts to dismantle the pride that was apparently blocking my way to Jesus), that I was incapable of turning away from the one sin in the universe that could prevent me from truly being a Christian.

---

what God "would do" or "would have done" when he has already in his sovereignty done something else, but we also get into dangerous theological waters when we speculate about matters on which God has not given us full explanations, especially when our theoretical speculations cause us to doubt or cast aspersions on the goodness of God. There is no reason to doubt in the dark what we've seen in the light, and when everything we *have* seen of God is good, it's illogical to assume that the parts of his plan that we *haven't* seen will be evil.

Second, Christians and Jews alike have long spoken of an "age of accountability" at which time a child becomes a morally responsible agent. This belief is based on verses like Isaiah 7:16, which says in part "before the boy knows enough to reject the wrong and choose the right," (TNIV) implying pretty clearly that there is an earlier age at which children do not know the difference between right and wrong and thus cannot be held accountable for moral choices, or indeed even *make* moral choices. Certainly, we are all infected from birth with the moral disease (usually called "original sin") that inevitably blossoms into all kinds of sinful attitudes, desires, and behaviors— this is why everyone ends up needing Jesus' redemption, regardless of their relative moral success or failure compared to others— but we should perhaps be careful about mistaking this inborn moral *disease* (which leads inexorably to moral infractions) for an inborn moral *debt* (like karma) that is somehow already counted against a person before that person has had a chance to incur it. I have always thought it was rather arbitrary to designate a specific numeric age as the "age of accountability," especially considering the differences from child to child in the rate of cognitive development, but in any case the Bible is clear that God is just (far more so than we), and that God's judgment comes in response to actual sin upon those who have in their free will chosen to commit it, not willy-nilly upon those who don't even have the capacity to choose. Add to that the overwhelmingly positive terms in which Jesus spoke of children, and we can be secure in the fact that God loves children (far more than we realize or fathom) and that he will not treat them unreasonably or cruelly in this matter.

Thirdly, the very fact that God started a relationship with me at such a young age shows that it was his express intention to mark me for heaven, not send me to hell. It would be pretty strange to assume that someone who picks up and cares for a stray kitten intends for that kitten to remain lost and abandoned, just because it "would have" remained lost if he hadn't adopted it. Taking a voluntary action *cannot* logically imply that the person intended the opposite; the action proves the intention.

Now, the Holy Spirit hadn't left during this time. There was always a tiny voice of hope, of defense, in the far regions of my mind and heart. At the time I interpreted this as an unwillingness to fully accept my sinfulness, but now I suspect it was the Holy Spirit whispering against the lies. I still knew the goodness of God. I still loved God with all my being, and my life still revolved around wanting to follow him. But there was a pain that came with me everywhere.

Words of grace became poisoned to me. Reminders of God's mercy were, to me, just reminders of how much I'd failed to properly accept it. Even as I clung to the ubiquitous phrase "it's not by works," that very phrase also tore me down inside—because the fact that people were reminding me of it implied they thought I still didn't get it. And if I still didn't get it, I still wasn't *really* a Christian. Compliments, especially compliments about my "virtue," were terrifying because they seemed like nothing but temptations to give in to the pride I so feared—and because they pointed out what I felt obligated, with such ashamed haste, to deny: that I seemed different from the people around me. But people kept pointing out the difference, whether it was teasing about being "by the book" and "teacher's pet" or the half-admiring, half-envious comments from peers; whether it was the praise of adults or the annoyance of my family at my strictness. I was isolated by something that everybody noticed about me but I myself wasn't "allowed" (I felt) to admit.

On the other hand, I had no defense at all against criticism. I was so scared of being "a Pharisee"—of being self-satisfied and thinking that the Lord's correction didn't apply to me—that I had no ability to assess whether or not a criticism was true, even if it was just in a sermon and not (perhaps) directed to me personally. If there was an opportunity for guilt, I accepted it; I didn't just accept it, but practically jumped at it and made sure I internalized it as deeply as possible. Running through all of it was the self-doubt I'd so assiduously taught myself and the deep, frequently half-buried worry about "never having really known him."

This might be why faith questions were able to rock me so much as a teenager. I wasn't questioning whether Christianity was true; I was asking questions about things like "the baptism of the Holy Spirit" and prayers for miracles—questions that, at root, were really about whether my faith was "good enough." A lot of charismatic teaching is very good, but people can frequently imply that unless you have certain gifts or do things a certain way, you don't have God's power in your life and thus you're barely even a Christian. In fact, a lot of well-meaning people accidentally imply that about whatever they particularly care about, and I fell prey to all of it. The fear that I wasn't a real Christian struck deep, and latched on to anything that stoked it.

And yet somehow, God was still there. Somehow, his love was still real to me, and still the center of my existence. When I was fifteen years old, I had a powerful experience where I really felt commissioned by God to pursue ministry in a form I had already been considering for some time: writing and theatre. Shortly after this time (a "coincidence" I now suspect may have had a spiritual warfare aspect), the struggle with the aforementioned questions began in earnest.

When I was seventeen, my mental health and spiritual struggles worsened until I became convinced I'd lost my salvation, and became very nearly insane. I would take things like the clock changing at a certain moment to be "confirmation" of whatever I'd been praying about at the moment. This had certain complexities as well; if it changed to twenty-five minutes past the hour I felt encouraged, while if it was ten minutes before the hour, God was probably upset with me. The clock was what had "confirmed" the loss of my salvation, and even though so many things told me I was still saved, no matter how often my blessedly patient parents talked me through it, I was in such a bad mental state that I couldn't let go of that obligation to believe what had been "confirmed" by these "signs." (Yeah, so . . . don't trust clocks. I'd like to claim that this principle is why I'm always late, but we all know *that's* not true.) I couldn't let go of my terror that I was somehow outside of God's grace. I would fast. I would pray. I would treat myself awfully; once I stood out in the cold for several hours praying, (this was December, in Massachusetts, in short sleeves) and I wouldn't stop until the "sign" came to stop: the flag next door had to stop waving completely.

One day, in the lowest point of this depression, I walked into my kitchen at home. I had lost my salvation, I thought, and I believed I couldn't get it back. But I still believed that everything the Bible said was true. If this was so—if the story of Christianity was true—and if I was left out, then there was no point in going on with a life that would be meaningless. Hell might be more painful, but there was no point waiting for it. So I took a knife out of the knife block in our kitchen and I prayed that if God didn't want me to do it, then the stove clock would change right then.

It didn't.

And yet I didn't cut my wrist. I knew somehow, somewhere deeper than what I felt or even what I thought, that it wasn't what God wanted. I just knew. The Holy Spirit had broken the spell, in his own way, by speaking Truth deeper than the lies. Had he changed the clock at that moment, I would have still been trapped—obligated to keep listening to this false and enslaving "sign." But somehow, Jesus' indwelling voice was deeper.

Somehow I healed, helped along by my amazing mom and by *actual* communication from God: well-timed Scripture, true words spoken and written by his people. That part of the journey—that acute period of illness and danger—is well in the past, but the larger journey—the struggle against the devil's lies, the quest to believe who I am in Christ, the changing of my perspective towards God's perspective—took much longer and in fact is still going on. Gradually, over years and only through a good deal of repetition and grace, I began to believe that I *had* actually been a Christian all this time, that my faith *had* been sincere since childhood, that the fear that God disapproved of me *was* false, and that even where I did legitimately sin, he forgave me. My journey has included therapy, good friends, good conversations, medications that didn't help, medications that did help, lots of thinking and journaling, patient pastors and mentors, and a *lot* of tears.

And the freedom of being a real Christian . . . is amazing. I still get into dark places sometimes—surprisingly easily and annoyingly often, in fact. Old wounds still get woken up and the devil still tries to steal my freedom. I still have baggage from spending such a long time thinking ill of myself, from seeing myself as unloving and offensive and unable to say anything useful to non-Christians. To be perfectly honest, sometimes I still get very mad and sad when I look at how deeply some of these things hurt me at such a young age.

But the realization, when I have the grace to realize it, that the gospel *is* for me, that I'm *not* excluded from it, that I've been redeemed by a holy God whose love surpasses all reason, whose salvation spans time and space, and from whose hand nothing can snatch me—I'm not sure if I have anything to call it but *life*. It makes me feel like nothing can stop me or hurt me: I am with the all-powerful God who made everything, and I'll spend eternity with him. I keep getting glimpses at deeper and deeper levels all the time, how much more exquisitely beautiful and loving God is than I ever imagined, how much deeper grace is than I thought, how much more secure and passionate and persistent and real and huge is Jesus' redemption than I ever knew or even know now.

So perhaps my life is a *backwards* fairy-tale. I started my journey with committing myself forever to the Prince of Peace, then went through hardships and mortal peril—and now am learning to be a child again. Once upon a time . . .

Afterword

"'My dear Frodo!' exclaimed Gandalf. 'Hobbits really are amazing creatures, as I have said before. You can learn all that there is to know about their ways in a month, and yet after a hundred years they can still surprise you.'"

—J.R.R. TOLKIEN, *THE FELLOWSHIP OF THE RING*

THANK YOU FOR JOINING me in the journey that was this book.

I completely acknowledge that you may have questions that I haven't addressed here, or that you may not be fully satisfied with some of the answers I have attempted. This is a good thing.

There will always be more of God to discover, more questions to ask, more glory to glimpse when we investigate. I have already used far more footnotes than should be used in polite company, because there is simply so much to be said about these things—and because, when we're talking about a real relationship with a real Living Being, no subject is ever in a vacuum: each one is connected to a thousand other subjects and questions. And the Word of God is so deep, so true, so multifaceted, that you can spend a lifetime reading it and still discover layers you never saw before. You can always fall in love more deeply with the One who is Unlimited Love.

I am sorry I have not been able to address all of your questions . . . and I guess I should also say "you're welcome" for the very same thing. The greatest disservice I could do you is to give you an excuse to stop here. Keep exploring. Talk to pastors; converse with commentaries; find reputable scholars who are talking about questions like yours; ask God directly.

Keep asking. Keep seeking. Keep knocking. Because there is a God there who is passionately seeking you.

Bibliography

Chambers, Oswald. "August 17: Are You Discouraged in Devotion?" In *My Utmost for His Highest.* 20th printing. New York: Dodd & Mead, 1946.

Cloud, Dr. Henry and Dr. John Townsend. *How People Grow: What the Bible Reveals About Personal Growth.* Grand Rapids: Zondervan, 2001.

Doidge, Norman. "Acquiring Tastes and Loves." In *The Brain That Changes Itself: Stories of Personal Triumph From the Frontiers of Brain Science,* 93–131. New York: Penguin, 2007.

Eberstadt, Mary, and Mary Anne Layden. "The Social Costs of Pornography: A Statement of Findings and Recommendations." Princeton: Witherspoon Institute, 2010. https://www.afaofpa.org/wp-content/uploads/Social-Costs-of-Porn-Report.pdf

Frankl, Viktor. *The Doctor and the Soul: Introduction to Logotherapy.* New York: Knopf, 1982.

Henry, Matthew. *Matthew Henry's Commentary on the Whole Bible, Volume 5: Matthew to John.* New York: Revell.

Jersak, Brad. *Can You Hear Me?* Oxford: Monarch, 2006.

Ratey, John J., and Catherine Johnson. *Shadow Syndromes.* New York: Pantheon, 1997.

Spangler, Ann, and Lois Tverberg, *Sitting at the Feet of Rabbi Jesus.* Grand Rapids: Zondervan, 2009.

Spencer, Aída Besançon. *Beyond the Curse: Women Called to Ministry.* Peabody: Hendrickson, 1989.

St. Teresa of Ávila. *The Way of Perfection.* Edited and translated by E. Allison Peers. Mineola: Dover, 2012.

Ten Boom, Corrie. *The Hiding Place.* New York: Bantam, 1974.

Tracy, Steven R. *Mending the Soul: Understanding and Healing Abuse.* Grand Rapids: Zondervan, 2005.

Villodas, Rich. *The Deeply Formed Life.* Colorado Springs: WaterBrook, 2020.

www.ingramcontent.com/pod-product-compliance
Lightning Source LLC
LaVergne TN
LVHW050627100826
845148LV00011B/1762